The Peace I Know

The Peace I Know

Udochukwu Vincent Ogbuji

To order additional copies of this book, contact:
Xlibris Corporation
1-888-795-4274
www.Xlibris.com
Orders@Xlibris.com
122226

CONTENTS

I dedicate this book to Lucy and Joseph, my parents, who gave me the name Udochukwu (God's peace). I also dedicate it to all makers and seekers of peace.

The road to peace can be cold, but the quest to find it has a way of warming our hearts.

—Father Udo Ogbuji

ACKNOWLEDGMENT

After my car accident, typing on the computer was close to impossible, and writing with a pen, pure torture. So, when I decided to attempt writing this book, mainly to fulfill the wish of my friends who wouldn't stop asking me to write a book, what I dreaded was the prospect of typing it on the computer or writing it with a pen. I, however, had a third option on how to accomplish this ambitious project, and that became my choice. That choice was writing the entire book with my BlackBerry cell phone. It was quite a chore to write a whole book using the small keyboard of the phone and mostly with my frail left thumb. Since you are now privy to part of what it took to complete this daunting task over a period of two and a half years, I believe you will agree to the fact that I had a lot of help.

I therefore owe a debt of gratitude for its success to God, whose peace I seek, and to my superiors: Bishop Anthony Nwedo, Bishop Lucius Ugorji, Bishop Andrew McDonald, Archbishop Peter Sartain, and Bishop Anthony Taylor, who trusted me to learn, work, and share the peace of Christ under their guidance. I am thankful for the support and prayer of family and friends who encouraged me to keep writing, especially at my dry moments when it appeared I would give up. I have to admit though, that at one point, I stopped calling my sister Sister Helena on the phone because she has the tenacity of a bill collector and the persuasion of a confessor. She wouldn't quit questioning me on when I would start writing this book, and after I started, she wouldn't stop asking me when I will finish it.

Many of my friends and family either read my punishing work or endured the pain of letting me read it to them; some expressed faith in me while others showed interest in my endeavor, and for their patience and faith in me, which paid off, I say to them "Thank you for believing in me." The corrections, suggestions, and encouragement of Sister Lillian Anne, Chief Mrs. T. E. Okekpe, Austin and Ifeh, Mel, Ijeoma (who took the picture on the front cover of this book, many years ago, when I taught at Spiritual Year Seminary, Ozu Abam), Ely, Father Martin, May, Father Ben, Pat, Father Okey, Monica, Nene-Otuomasirim, Chi Nwerem, Bobo, Nwanyim, Belinda, Kasarachi, Ugo, Sabana, Dr. Mac, Dr. Kiser, and many others I did not mention here, were invaluable. I am no less indebted to my friends Thad and Jeanie, who not only read and tolerated the raw draft but also told me it was good and pledged their full moral, financial, and spiritual support. I have many reasons to thank all my teachers and benefactors, the least of which is their not giving up on me. My parents, Lucy and Joseph, come to mind as my first teachers. I owe much more than thanks to Msgr. Gaston Hebert, Msgr. Frank Malone, and the members of Christ the King Parish, Little Rock, who gave me a home and much more after my accident and hospitalization. I will say the same for the Benedictine nuns in Jonesboro who accepted me as their chaplain and took on the burden of nursing me back to health. I particularly thank Mother Lilliann Marie who cares for us with grace and love, and Sr. Miriam Burns who went to work and artfully changed the cloud on the cover of this book to appear like a rainbow and face of Jesus. Adaeze, my friend, probably got dizzy from reading and editing the manuscript so many times. I truly cherish her enduring kindness and patience, and the help of Sr. Mary John who corrected the final draft. When in the hospital and after I was discharged, many people from around the Diocese of Little Rock, especially from the parishes where I had ministered, came to visit; they prayed, wrote letters, and lent their support in many ways, and I want them to know that I still call to mind their kindness and remain ever grateful.

As I grow older, I am reminded each day of how much more difficult it is to remember things; I am, therefore, reserving a big chunk of my thanks for all those I did not mention here but whose names, kindness, and love are carved in my heart for always.

INTRODUCTION

As a teenager, I constantly helped my mom with her gardening and small-scale farming. The section of the village where the farm work took place was infested with the tiniest bees you could ever see. We called those bees *Fri-fri Nta* (little bees). They were about the size of a fruit fly or smaller and did not sting. Although they could not sting, their aggravation was so persistent that, sometimes, you wished you were stung and left alone. The good thing about those bees was that they only bothered those who were idle, as if to say, "There is plenty of work to be done, get busy!" When you refused to work, they would not only fly around you, making an irritating buzzing sound, but would attempt to fly into your eyes, ears, or nose. They flew sluggishly and were easy to kill. However, it was a very bad idea to do so. Those bees had a strong smell that they gave off when killed, which, in turn, alerted the other bees; and soon after, you would have many more companions, and they would not be happy ones! They had a way of knowing that there was an attempt to scare them off, when swiped at, which also caused them to call for reinforcements. The only way those bees would quit giving you trouble was if you stopped being idle and started working. The small bees wanted human sweat and somehow knew that when a person worked, he or she would perspire. When you got busy and perspired, the small bees would quietly and gently harvest the sweat, and fly away without calling attention to themselves. Human sweat was part of the ingredients they used in order to make the purest and best honey you could find. Those clever bees blended the salty sweat from humans with the sweet nectar they collected from the flowers, and produced the most mouth-watering honey I ever tasted. I believe I can safely say that the resourcefulness of *Fri-fri Nta* (little bees) was ingenious!

Not all bees are honey bees, and those that are not often settled for food that was less strenuous to produce but, not as delicious as honey. Non-honey bees mostly lacked the number, agility, organization and defenses that honey bees have. Being ill-equipped, the non-honey bees have to be resourceful and work twice as hard in order to produce and enjoy some fine delicacy like honey. The tiny bees in my village were not really cut out to produce honey; they were very small, slow, and fragile, had no defenses except aggravation and could easily be killed off. Nevertheless, they worked against those dangerous odds and difficulties, endured the human sweat that sometimes could be smelly, to make their honey—but not just any honey, their honey was rare and pricey. If it is strange and miserable to have a bee world without honey, then it must be sad to imagine a human world and *life* without *peace*! We, therefore, search for peace all through life, just as the small bees searched for ways to make the best honey, and like them, we are frail, small, and feel defenseless some times, which can make our endeavor to find peace very difficult.

In this book, I will attempt to chronicle and evaluate my journey to find peace. My name, Udo, means "peace," and this makes my search for peace especially personal. There is also a measured degree of pressure for me to not only find peace but to discover peace that endures and be able to share it. Just like the tiny bees, I have not spared anything during this quest and mission! Sometimes I have had to "aggravate" God with the hope that he would sweat his grace to help me find his peace. This book, in some way, offers you some help as you continue to search for peace. My hope is that in reading it, you will come across something you can learn from or, possibly, should avoid, which will aid you through a fruitful search for and discovery of the peace that remains.

I do not intend this book to be a historical account. However, I adapted a few things that happened in time to highlight some perspectives in order to drive home some points. When my narrative revealed the bright side of people, I used their real names, mainly first names; otherwise, I omitted their names entirely or made up names. In that way, I tried to give the book a personal touch and, at the same time ensured that I did not compromise the anonymity, privacy, recognition and respect of those I mentioned in my stories. I wrote this book in the spirit of love and peace and I pray that it will be seen and read in that context.

Chapter 1

The Day I Died

Show me a person who has an endless love like a mother does and I will show you the one whose love is deepest.
—Father Udo Ogbuji

"You died, Udo," my friend, Father Okey, said as he took a brief break from his narrative to enjoy a long, slow sip from his glass of wine. He meant what he was saying to be funny, to minimize the impact, but the words came out revealing much more than he would have liked. His attempt at humor not only fell flat but failed to camouflage his pain, pain he had borne for a friend he loved very dearly. Many things revealed his true feelings, like the agony in his eyes, his fidgety fingers as he held the glass of wine, and his body language that said he had no desire to relive the past events. His total composure seemed to say "Please don't make me tell this story. We have just finished a great dinner and I am not about to ruin it." From all indications, my friend needed something a lot stronger than wine for him to muster the strength to continue the painful story of my recent stay in the hospital. I was under no illusion; I knew my life-threatening car accident left me in a precarious situation in the hospital. I was also aware that my friend inherited the excruciating task of making life-and-death decisions on my behalf. That whole agonizing experience must have been physically exhausting and emotionally draining for him. Far from adding to his stress, my hope was that by telling me the story, my beloved friend would unburden himself from the crushing load he carried and, eventually, find some form of closure.

Earlier that day, during a routine therapy session, I had fainted. Fainting had become a new reality for me soon after I was discharged from the hospital. The therapists encouraged me to practice standing with their assistance. The looming problem was that whenever I stood up with their help, my blood pressure dropped so low that I would lose consciousness. To determine if I was alert and oriented, the therapists would frequently ask me a series of questions while I was standing. An example would be: "What is the color of the grass?" If I said red—which had happened before—or I just kept quiet, they would know it was time for me to sit down, that I was disoriented and about to faint. On that afternoon, Father Okey witnessed what had happened but was not completely sure what it meant.

When my therapy was over, he approached me and said, "As I was watching you during your therapy, your eyes seemed quite large, and you had a strange look about you."

I could read the concern on his face, and I replied, "Yes, you're probably right, my eyes may have been bigger." I jokingly added, "They tend to get larger before I die."

I meant it as a joke, but my friend did not laugh. He appeared rather disturbed at my comment, and I wondered what I had said that changed his whole demeanor from a smile to one of deep concern. I felt responsible for my friend's somber mood, and I attempted to make things right by explaining in a subdued voice, "I fainted." I then revealed how my blood pressure would fluctuate to a very low level whenever I would stand up, which resulted in my disorientation and sometimes a loss of consciousness. I could still tell that something was troubling him. Suddenly, he said with a visible sense of relief, "I have something to tell you later about an incident in the hospital." He chose his words carefully in order not to sound alarmed.

That evening Father Okey and I had enjoyed a scrumptious meal and relaxed with a very smooth bottle of merlot, which we generously poured for ourselves. During the time we ate dinner and as we drank the delicious wine, we talked about many things, but did not mention the incident from that morning. It appeared that we were deliberately and mentally selecting what we were talking about since we were apparently avoiding my fainting spell and the hospital episode he had promised to tell me. We appeared to be waiting for the right opportunity to broach the daunting subject. The opportunity finally presented itself later that evening, and I said, "Best, in the morning, you said you had something to tell me, how much longer will you have me wait?" I call him Best when I want to be really nice to him or need a favor.

"Yes, I did," he replied, and with a friendly dry humor added, "I was counting on you to forget about it. It is the story about my worst day in the hospital, when I was taking care of you."

Rev. Dr. Felix Okey Alaribe has always been a quiet, gentle, kind, and trustworthy friend. We first met in 1986 at Immaculate Conception Seminary, Ahiaeke, Umuahia. It is a minor seminary in my diocese where young men are prepared, as early as junior high and high school, for the priesthood in the Roman Catholic Church. Okey was a student and a product of Immaculate Conception Seminary while my alma mater is Government College, Umuahia. After high school, I was sent by my former bishop, Bishop Anthony Nwaedo, to teach at Immaculate Conception Seminary for one year before proceeding to the major seminary. Father Okey was teaching courses there when I arrived. Although we knew each other at that point, we were not close friends. The opportunity for us to bond came when we attended the major seminary together.

The authorities in the major seminary discouraged friendships that could result in cliquish behavior or those that might reflect the characteristics of exclusivity. It was not uncommon for the young men in the seminary to have grown up in the same neighborhood and to know each other. Oliverdom Oguadiuru was such a friend; we were from the same parish, grew up together, and protected and trusted each other. He and I hung out most of the time, and that was exactly what the priests in the seminary frowned upon. We were instructed that having close friends was not bad in itself, but if not checked, it could lead to a lack of charity and terrible social etiquette. The logic followed that if we decided not to look beyond our familiar friends and embrace others in friendship and love, we would be limiting our knowledge and thinking to that small and elite group. Those actions might lead to an error in our judgment, which would come from our limited social exposure and possible bias or favoritism. Our ability to be comfortable around others might be stifled, thus inhibiting our aptitude to minister to the faithful. We were taught that we were our brother's keeper, and by investing so much time, emotion, and social resources in one person, we could impede our own awareness of others and may not properly care for them. With that in mind, the seminary staff instructed us to choose different persons to visit with during our recreational periods. At the time, it seemed it was one more torturous and unnecessary decree carefully chosen by the staff to turn up the heat and make the seminary a little more miserable for us. I was one of the many that did not religiously uphold that regulation. However, the many things I learned about outreach and interest in others has come in handy throughout my adult and professional life. I have discovered that in order to become an effective priest, one must possess, among other things, good public relations, plentiful charity, and genuine interest in others, even when they seem insufferable.

One of the nights when I actually obeyed the visit-with-others commandment, I met Father Okey along the road leading to the main entrance of the seminary. After we exchanged greetings, we sat and talked and, before long, found we had a lot in common. That Saturday night, we bonded. The time of the night set aside for us to visit on Saturdays began after supper and lasted for three hours. There were some nights when we wished we were not held hostage for three hours by someone who would bore us to tears. Should that be the case, we prayed that God would give us the grace to accept it as our penance and the fortitude to endure till the end. On such nights, we might have seemed to be out of luck because we ended up with someone we presumed to be unexciting. The irony, however, was that at the end of the free time, we would marvel at the fact that we had a good time and learned a lot. It may have been a prayer answered or part of life's paradox that joy and comfort could be found in unexpected places. Through that experience, God may have communicated that we should always be wise and learn to be kind, to love and to endure. You might be the one to gain by eventually enjoying yourself in addition to being edified. Moreover, there was certainly an added benefit of being prepared to minister to all kinds of people as a priest, and if you chose not to become a priest, what you learned would pay off someday when you would care for your own family or others. In case you are wondering if I thought Father Okey would be a boring companion when I met him that night, my answer is, no, I did not. He was always nice and a gentleman. I had no expectation that our conversation would advance my concept of friendship in a more defined and profound way, but it did. During that visit, we talked far into the night and wished the bell for the end of recreation would not be rung. We were completely consumed by the beauty of the moment. The only regret was that our wish did not come true; time flew even as we wished we could slow it down. What made the time I spent with Father Okey memorable and unique was not merely the topics and substance of what we talked about. The subject matters of our discourse were simple things, like family, future dreams, fears—things of that sort that got deeper and more analytical through the course of the night's recreation. The most important aspect of the bonding process came from the fact that our discussion was genuine and from the heart. There was evidence of an unspoken mutual trust that made it easy for us to talk to each other and to open up uncharted terrains of our lives. On that night, a deep bond of love and friendship was forged. It was that same bond that eventually led him, eighteen years later, to partially relinquish his pastoral duties at Our Lady of Good Hope Parish in Hope, Arkansas, to do me a tremendous favor. He took a partial leave of absence, with the permission of the Diocesan Administrator Monsignor Gaston, to care for me in the hospital after my ghastly automobile accident. Father Okey made medical life-saving decisions and some personal-welfare choices on my behalf. He was God-sent, and he became the family and guardian I desperately needed.

On that evening, at the back of the rectory in Christ the King Parish, completely cornered, my very dear friend reluctantly narrated the tale of his worst day in the hospital when he cared for me. "Udo, the decision was made to place you in a medically induced coma to enable your broken bones and bruised spinal cord to heal well after your two successful surgeries. You had a feeding tube for nourishment, and you were placed on a ventilator to breathe for you and assist in your healing process. After about three weeks in the Surgical Intensive Care Unit, the medical team decided it was time for you to be weaned from the ventilator. This had to be done to get you ready for the rehabilitation hospital."

At that point in his story, I noticed Father Okey's wine glass was almost empty. He looked at his glass as if to say, "I really need a refill—the rest of the story is horrifying." I pointed toward the bottle of wine, which, thankfully, still had a little portion remaining in it. After he poured the wine in his glass, he took his time to gather his thoughts while he firmly hugged the glass with the palms of his hands and examined the contents as if they had hidden power. I will not doubt that, at that moment, he prayed for fortitude and courage to continue his story as he wondered how to proceed.

After he took a big sip from his glass, he said, "I would have loved to share the remaining wine with you, but I'll need more before the story is over."

What he said was funny, and we laughed. As I laughed, I said, "I am almost drunk anyway. I don't think I need more."

He ignored me, lifted the bottle of wine that was almost empty, and poured what was left into my glass. The act of pouring the dregs into my glass may have been a gesture of kindness since he likes to share, but it may also have been due to an inherent cultural demand. In Nigeria, among the Igbo tribe to which I belong, we have a cultural practice that predetermines who should drink the dregs. The last part of wine must be poured into the glass of, or left for, the owner of the house, or with his permission, it may be given to the oldest person in the room. In my culture, that is a sign of respect for the host, but also a way to practice temperance and to guard against greed. As a child, I observed how that ritual was followed to the letter and with underlying seriousness. I thought the dregs may have tasted better or were different from the rest of the wine. Maybe it did, but that night, I cared more about the concluding part of the story than the wine and ritual combined. I, however, was patient with my friend because I knew the responsibility of caring for me in the hospital had entailed enormous physical pain, emotional drain, and mental exhaustion. I knew relating those events would bring back sad and frightening memories, so the least I could do was to be very considerate and patient with him.

"Well," he continued, "the ventilator tube was removed, and you were not able to breathe on your own. Your heart also failed to pump blood. You died, Udo! You crashed, and the medical team tried for a few minutes to revive you. It was like raising Lazarus from the dead." He tried very hard to be funny, to make light of it as I said at the beginning of this chapter, but did not succeed very well. He then proceeded to finish the painful tale. "Your ventilator tube was reinserted, and it once again successfully facilitated your breathing. All that happened in a short period, but it certainly felt like forever to me. I peed in my pants when I thought you had died! I was completely helpless and confused. I wondered how I would break the sad news of your passing to your Mom. Udo, I've never been so scared in my whole life. The Cardiologist had to be called in to perform an angiogram on your heart to determine if it was functioning well. When he confirmed your heart was stable, the doctors and nurses tried three more times on different dates to remove you from the ventilator. On the third attempt, your heart pumped blood, and your lungs showed positive signs that you were breathing on your own. I would say you died at least for a couple of minutes. And that was very unsettling."

It was almost unbearable to witness the agony and anxiety on the face of my friend as he spoke about my ordeal in the hospital. His apparent pain shed some light on the grief I had caused him during those horrifying moments. That he was in distress also revealed the anguish my many friends, family, and parishioners had also endured by extension. That whole revelation made me even more appreciative of the invaluable support and prayers I received during those edgy and uncertain times. I will admit, though, I almost laughed out loud when he said he peed in his pants. I thought it was funny even as I felt his pain and was delighted in his love for me, which was evident.

When he mentioned the difficulty of breaking the news to my mom, I had goose bumps because I knew it would be a tough act to accomplish. No matter how he delivered the message, she would be crushed like any mom would, especially since I am her favorite child.

Though it was presumptuous and lame on my part, I wanted to believe I was her favorite as a young boy. I might not be the favorite, but I believed (and there may be some truth to it) that the bond between mothers and their firstborn sons is powerful, strong, and undeniable. Many times I had joked with my mom, either privately or before my siblings, and I tried to get her to admit she loved me more than my brother and three sisters, but I was never successful. The truth was that she had only very little or no reason to like me, as you would find out later in this book.

When I was younger, an opportunity came when I thought the timing was perfect to get my mom to admit that she favored me the most. I was fifteen years old, and we were alone in the kitchen. My mom was cooking while I was helping her prepare the ingredients for the meal. As we worked, I turned to her and asked, "Mom, why am I the only one in here helping you?" I paused to make sure I had her attention and added, "How can you possibly not love me more than the rest of us?"

She was not rattled; she only smiled. That smile seemed to be saying "I have been down this road with you before. The only difference is the flowery way you put it." There was a possibility her smile meant an affirmation of my assumption—that I am indeed her favorite. The latter I would have liked to be the reality, but her answer shattered my dream. "My answer hasn't changed since the last time you asked." As she continued to smile, she added, "I have equal love for all of you."

"You have equal love for each of us?" I asked, and laughed. I did not believe she had equal love for each of us, so I pleaded amid my laughter, "Mom, you can confide in me, I won't tell the others."

She ignored me and offered her own diversion, "Let us hurry and get the food ready. Everyone is hungry."

I decided to let the matter go and did not ask again. Even though she claimed she did not love me more than my siblings, I knew she loved me enough to be utterly crushed by news of my passing. My friend was right.

As Okey chronicled his heartbreaking experience, I was lost in my own thoughts. I began to remember I had hallucinations while I was in the hospital. Those hallucinations and loss of memory were the side effects of the drugs I was given to keep me in a comatose state. Some of the hallucinations were bizarre and horrifying while some were soothing and encouraging. You will read more about them in the course of the book, but at this point, I would like to touch on a particular one. I am convinced that this one hallucination occurred at the same time Father Okey said he believed I died. The reason for my certitude that Father Okey's story and this peculiar hallucination were concurrent is the common threads with which they are woven. In both cases, there were parallel facts of me being taken off the feeding tube and ventilator so I could be transferred to another hospital (rehabilitation hospital). Moreover, in each situation, I was passing beyond this physical life. Here is my account of that one hallucination that, like the others, was so very real.

On that day in the Surgical Intensive Care Unit, as many other days, I was surrounded by many friends. I was able to hear people talking, and as I listened to their discussion, I came away with the impression that the decision had been made to move me to another hospital. The nurses appeared offended and concerned at the same time. Offended because they believed the decision to take me to another hospital meant that their services were not appreciated, and concerned because I might be in grave danger if my feeding tube and ventilator were removed. But since my friend, Father Okey, thought that the transfer to another hospital would be good for me and the decision was not negotiable, the nurses removed the feeding tube and ventilator from me and discharged me. I first had difficulty breathing and, after a few more minutes, became very weak. I was alarmed when I looked down toward my abdominal area, and the bandage that held my surgical wounds together began tearing apart. My whole body started splitting in half, and I was able to see my intestines as they pushed out of the open wound. My friend Mel, who is a nurse, was among those present. She suddenly bent over and tried to push my intestines back into my abdomen. She was crying and pleading with me not to give up. The commotion was very dramatic and intense. It was painful to watch my friends scramble to help me, and I knew they were terribly worried about my condition. Even in the midst of all the turmoil and confusion, the feeling of passing to the horizon of unconsciousness felt so peaceful. Each time I closed my eyes, Mel earnestly implored me to stay awake and remain with them. "Father Udo, Father Udo, please keep your eyes open. Please stay with us and don't die, please!" After a while, it was becoming too difficult to physically keep my eyes open, so I began to mentally utilize the power and influence of my mind. My mind kept me awake as it took me on a journey throughout my life. The day I died became the day I recaptured, in a special way, the beauty of my humble beginnings, the complexity of the man I have become, and my unwavering search for peace.

Father Okey and me, during his first visit to the U.S.

CHAPTER 2

Unusual Birth at an Uncertain Time

Being born is like a flower bud, just as the sun and oxygen assure a beautiful blossom, so does love and care insure a fine life.

—Father Udo Ogbuji

When I said "The beauty of my humble beginnings," I used the word *beauty* in a context that reflects my perception of beauty and in retrospect. When the portrait of the circumstances of my birth is painted, it will be anything but beautiful or rosy. When the story of my birth is told today, it would sound like an intense fiction or a thriller in which the heroes not only survived but also succeeded in saving the weak and vulnerable they had to protect. In that life's drama, the helpless and defenseless one that needed protection was me, and the heroes were my parents. Simply put, the beauty of my life's beginnings is encapsulated in the fact that my parents, whom I love and adore, faced horrendous situations with grace; and I am lucky to be alive to tell the story as told to me by my mom.

I remember the day I asked my mom to tell me about my birth; she was happy to tell me and so asked, "Which part do you want to hear?"

"All of it—everything." I entreated.

She then proceeded to tell me, "I was pregnant with you for almost a year—eleven months to be exact."

"So why didn't you do something after nine months?" I interrupted with a question.

"I didn't have any choice. You were hiding in my womb because you did not want to fight in the civil war," she said with a full smile and warm laughter.

I laughed too because she was hilarious. My mom has a dry sense of humor. She is mostly quiet and more formal than playful. Whenever she is in the mood to play, and you catch her blunt jokes, she will make you laugh very hard.

I believe you may want to know about the civil war that was being fought in my country when I was born—the civil war my mom joked about. I was born on the fourth of December 1968, as that Nigeria-Biafra civil war was raging. That unfortunate war started May 30, 1967, and ended January 15, 1970. I belong to the Igbo tribe, which made up the greater percentage of the population of those in the Biafran Republic. Nigeria gained her independence from the British on October 1, 1960. The Hausa and Fulani tribes lived mainly in the north, the Yoruba tribe in the southwest, and Igbo tribe in the southeast. The British amalgamated the different ethnic groups and may have patted themselves on the back for a successful scheme that was well executed.

After a few years of the ethnic groups pretending to live together, the British design was revealed as being contentious and showed signs of imminent implosion. The British created a superficial union that left the people with an internal bleeding caused partly by tribal rivalry. The initial reason the union cracked and bled was because it was too cosmetic and was forced upon unsuspecting citizens who trusted their leaders and the British Empire to know better. The inherent differences and uniqueness embedded in each ethnic group's culture, religion, and language should have been addressed. Those strong diversities were taken for granted and left to resolve themselves. The only attempt to hold that makeshift union in place was the introduction of a foreign language, English, by the British to help the tribes communicate with one another. The adoption of English as an official language was minimally helpful. Take, for instance, if a citizen did not have a formal education, he or she had, and still has, a high probability of being incapable of communicating with those from other tribes. That is unfair because one should not be officially educated in order to communicate with fellow citizens. The hot lava of confusion, misunderstanding, and animosity that brewed within the ethnic groups waited for the perfect opportunity for a deadly and violent rupture. Sadly, that destructive volcanic eruption of ethnic animosity began in January 1966, when a group of primarily Igbo military officers from the southeast led a coup to overthrow the civil government. That bloody coup left thirty political leaders dead. The Nigerian prime minister, Sir Abubakar Tafawa Balewa, and the northern premier, Sir Ahmadu Bello, were both killed. In July 1966, northern officers in the army retaliated. They carried out a more successful and much bloodier countercoup in which the head of state General J. T. U. Aguiyi-Ironsi, who was of Igbo origin, was brutally executed. Those northern Muslim military officers appointed Lieutenant Colonel Yakubu "Jack" Gowon as the head of the Federal Military Government. The coup and countercoup gave rise to the uprising and war that seriously threatened and tested the unnatural union forced upon the ethnic groups by the British. In September 1966, about thirty thousand Igbos were slaughtered in the north. In the southeast, my tribe, the Igbos, avenged the deaths of those killed by taking the lives of some of the northerners who lived in our midst.

On May 26, 1967, after negotiations and an attempt at reconciliation failed, the southeastern region voted to secede from Nigeria. On May 30, Chukwuemeka Odumegwu Ojukwu, the southeastern region's military governor, announced the independence of the Republic of Biafra from Nigeria. The grounds for secession were the killing of the Igbos in the north during the post-coup violence. His thought was that if the Igbo ethnic tribe, who lived mainly in the southeast, could not freely and peacefully live in the north without fear for their lives, then there was no reason to assume we were one or a united country. The northerners declared war on us after we announced our independence. The speculation was that the Hausa and Fulani tribes had no incentive to go to war with us except for the large deposit of petroleum that was discovered in the southeast. If you consider the fact that they have relatively no substantial natural resources in the north and may find it difficult to survive economically on their own, you could understand why they were willing to go to war. Another possible reason—perhaps unknown at the time, but very disturbing—was that most of the northerners were Muslims, and they may have relished the additional pious benefits of converting us, the infidels, to Allah. The Nigerian army had an entire arsenal at their disposal, but we, the Biafra, had ample determination but insufficient and ineffective weapons. It was often joked that while the Nigerian army fought with machine guns, Biafran soldiers waited to be slaughtered as they brandished their machetes and waved their big, long sticks. This could have been funny except that many lives were lost. After suffering so many casualties, the Biafran army got creative; they recruited scientists and engineers who manufactured explosives. One of the places that was utilized as a weapon factory, was the science and research development institute (National Root Crops Research Institute, Umudike) close to my home. They made deadly mines called *Ogbunigwe* (destruction of many). *Ogbunigwe* was comprised of a metal bucket filled with gunpowder and mixed with all kinds of pieces of lethal objects. The metal bucket was then buried with detonators. Many of those land mines were set off by unsuspecting Nigerian soldiers, who were killed or maimed by shrapnel.

Many young men who were not drafted into the Biafran army, like my dad, hid in the forest, for fear of the Nigerian soldiers who randomly shot and killed the men and raped the women. The enemy's army took for themselves some of our beautiful women as part of their trophy or souvenir. Since the women were also in danger, they joined the men in the forest. The Nigerian military made sure the roads, seaports, and airports were blockaded. Starvation of the Biafra citizens became an effective weapon of choice. After three years of war, with no farming or supply of food, the limited stored food eventually ran out. Those who took refuge in the forest around my village had no choice but to eat all kinds of different things for nourishment, including rats, lizards, and some big larva that lived in palm trees. Clean drinking water was a rare commodity; people were satisfied if they were lucky to find even rusty-looking water from the swamps. Salt for seasoning the food became a luxury no one could find or afford. Owning salt was more valuable than acquiring gold—you only have to eat some food without salt to know why.

It was under these frightening and miserable circumstances that I was born. When my mom told me that I remained in her womb longer than normal because I did not want to fight in the war, I thought she was funny and agreed with her in part. "Yes, Mom, you're right. I knew my little world, your womb, was far more peaceful. I was planning to stay there as long as was possible, but only because I was offering you protection. I believed the Nigerian soldiers had no regard for any Biafran, but they would have been nice to you if they saw you were pregnant." I would not let her get away with calling me a coward, so I joked, "I had to be there for you since your husband, Dee Joe, took to his heels and left you at the mercy of those depraved Nigerian soldiers. I thought it would be honorable to hang around a little longer to protect you." She smiled as if to say thank you.

My mom had a sad secret reason why she let me inhabit her womb for two extra months; she had a miscarriage during her first pregnancy. I would think that after a woman has had such an experience, she would be willing to go the extra mile to make sure the next one was safe and protected.

When my mom told me she was pregnant for eleven months with me, I believed her. But I did not want it to sound incredible whenever I decided to tell the story. I wanted to be able to tell it with conviction. So, I asked my mom again if she was sure that she was pregnant for that long with me, and she remained resolute and certain. She told me she knew when she became pregnant and started counting down the months. But not only that, she jokingly said, "You were a grown man when you were born, with a full beard." She must have known how fantastic that picture was and added, "Seriously, you didn't look like a newborn baby. You were so tall, strong, and grown that my sister was able to carry you on her back all the way home while your dad carried me on his bicycle. It is a six-mile journey to go from Oboro Maternity Home, where you were born, to Umuariaga, our village. Carrying a newborn baby on your back to make such a trip is almost impossible to pull off, except in your case."

In my country during those days, women carried children on their back by securing them to their body with a cloth wrap. My mom was right when she opined that it would be "almost impossible" to carry a baby in such a way as I was. New born babies, since they are too fragile would have to be at least six to eight months old before they could be carried on the back.

"Mom," I called out with such an endearing voice, "I can only imagine the burden you endured accommodating me two months longer in your womb, especially when I was as big a boy as you described."

She first was graceful in her reply. "You were a good boy and didn't give me any trouble." And then, she rubbed it in, "But after I gave birth to you, you turned into a little monster."

We both laughed very hard.

The name I was given at my birth was Udochukwu. In my tribe, names are chosen for newborn babies to express prayers answered or those yet to be answered. Names are also given to highlight the circumstances surrounding a child's birth. Some names denote thanksgiving to God or an invocation of his blessings. Names could depict a search to find meaning in life or sufferings a family had been through or still going through. They could express the wonders of God, life, creation, or things of that sort. The first part of my name, *Udo*, means "peace," and *chukwu* means "God," thus my full name means "God's peace" or "the peace of God." When I asked my mom how they came up with such a beautiful name, she proudly said, "It was my mother's idea."

There was no need to ask why my grandmother chose this name for me; the answer was obvious. My grandma was praying for God's peace in a country torn apart by war. There was also a chance she was looking beyond the war, to pray for her grandson who would need God's peace someday or whom she hoped to be a symbol of peace to others.

As I grew older, and maybe a little wiser, I began to adopt my name as a mission statement and also a mission, as was conceivably intended by my grandma and endorsed by my parents. I believed this pursuit would make me a happier and better person. My thought was that the awareness of peace and the mission it invoked would be beneficial whether or not I become a priest. In either case, I would have to try giving peace to others, and no one gives what he does not have. I, therefore, have to know and have peace. After many years of working on this peace project, I have come to accept the fact that this mission is not simple and would last a lifetime. In the course of this book, you will read how much I have progressed amid seeming failures to find peace. I used the word *seeming* because, as a matter of personal principle and pragmatism, even when I have not succeeded in my search for peace, I did not give up looking for it. That is because when my attempt at attaining peace is not very successful, that experience teaches me the lesson of what peace is not, which is unpleasant. Knowing what peace is not, arms me with a practical knowledge that makes me refuse to live my life drowned in a pile of turmoil, and it also points out the direction I should avoid when on this quest. This perspective that I espouse and the steady pursuit of peace I engage in bring me fulfillment and reinforce my resolve to continue the mission of finding peace. I will elaborate much more on this concept of progressive search for peace later. At the moment I will focus my attention on completing my mom's narrative about my birth.

"Udo, there was nothing to eat in the forest where we were taking refuge for fear of the Nigerian soldiers," my mom continued. "Breastfeeding you while I, myself, was hungry was the most torturous experience of my life. You were hungry all the time, and you ate like a starving big man. There was a day I thought I had taken all I could take. It was a normal day with no food to eat. Dee Joe had gone to hunt for rabbits with some of the other men in the camp. My big sister, Desi, had been gone for a week, after a month of caring for you and me. The forest was infested with sand-fly (*mkpum*). Because of the sand-fly bites and the lack of decent hygiene, you had a rash all over your body. The rash irritated your skin, and you would not stop crying. I suspected you were hungry too, since you kept quiet when I breastfed you. I was famished myself, and the only reason I kept breastfeeding you was so you would quit crying. Your cries and screams were uncomfortable and dangerous because they could give away our location. If the Nigerian soldiers heard you, we would have been in danger. I was so exhausted and I believed I would faint if I kept feeding you. I remember feeling and thinking, *If I tried one more time to feed you, you would grow up without a mother, if you survived at all.* There were two impossible choices: to keep feeding you or to let you cry. I chose to stop breastfeeding you, and you screamed uncontrollably all the louder. I knew sooner or later you were going to upset someone who thought, and rightly so, that you would compromise our hiding place and jeopardize our safety. My concerns were proven true when one of the old men who couldn't go hunting with the rest of the men approached me. He was visibly enraged and said, 'Have you considered the possibility of throwing away this saboteur you call your son?' I was stunned. For a minute, I couldn't believe what I heard, so I asked him to clarify his comment. He did not flinch, but heightened his harsh rhetoric. 'If this Bush-baby continues his screaming, soon we will not only have to accommodate him but also the sound of the blazing guns of our enemies. Or, do you suppose his life is worth the death of everyone here?'"

At this stage in her story, my mom started sobbing uncontrollably. That was the first time I witnessed her cry since the death of my dad, which had been about seven years. I was overcome with emotion myself, and all I could do was cry with her. I thought that taking care of me in the middle of the war was already too much to handle; she did not need that abrasive old man to multiply her pain with his choice of words and sharp tongue. Honestly, his calling me a Bush-baby turned up the volume of my dislike for him although I did not know who he was. *Bush-baby* is a nickname given to a unique cat in my village that lives in the wild. It is similar in size to the house cat I see here in America. It cries almost all night, which is a sign of weakness. His calling me a Bush-baby was a derogatory way of saying that I was the weakest of all the humans—just like Bush-baby is the weakest of all the cats. He had referred to me as a weakling, an enemy (saboteur) that needed to be thrown away. It was one thing to call me names, but talking to my mom the way he did was too much to take. I knew it happened many years ago, but listening to the story made the wound fresh and resurrected the pain, and watching my mom cry was heartbreaking. When I felt we had cried enough, I wrapped my arms around my mom, whose own tears were beginning to fade. Leaning closer, I offered with a whisper that had the air of conspiracy, "Would you like me to go and punch him in the face?"

I intended it to be funny, and my mom caught on. "Yes," she responded. "But he's dead."

We laughed and laughed; we laughed harder than we had cried. My admiration for my mom grew immensely when I learned that was the first time she told the story to anyone. Not only had she kept the incident to herself those many years, she also refused to tell me who the man was even though he was dead.

I knew the kinder thing to do was not to go back to the sad story after we laughed, but I was not done. I was curious about a few more things. I gently asked, "Mom, how did you respond to that old man who beat you up?"

"I told him I would address his concerns. I went as far away as I could go with you, where no one would hear you cry. As we went away, I cried silently to myself. The old man was right about the consequences of your crying, but I wished he had conveyed the message in a more compassionate way. After having a good cry, I prayed for a while and felt at peace. As we journeyed, we came upon a stream where I stopped, gave you water to drink, and bathed you. Soon afterwards, you fell asleep."

As she mentioned the stream, I had goose bumps, and I asked her the location of the stream. Her answer was surprising and left me in awe. Unknown to her, two years earlier, I had discovered that stream and had gone there three times. It had become a kind of sanctuary of peace for me. In the subsequent years, during different periods in my life, especially when I had important decisions to make and needed a clear mind and a quiet place to think, I visited that place.

When my mom returned to the camp, what she witnessed was the manifestation of answered prayers. "As we got closer to the camp," my mom continued, "I smelled a delicious meal cooking. As I began to salivate and dream of how much I would like to have a hot and nicely cooked meal, I quickly told myself to come back to reality. As we came closer, I saw my sister Desi, and she appeared to be cooking. Then, I saw your dad, Dee Joe, bending over behind some brush. As I got closer, I smelled burning animal fur. Your dad was cleaning a rabbit he had caught. During the week, my sister had gone to visit her family, and she had gone to Saint Peter's Catholic Parish where Monsignor John Ogbonna was handing out food from Catholic Relief Services. She got some rice, yams, milk, canned beef, and most importantly, salt. Your dad and my sister were finishing up with cooking when we arrived. You were still asleep, so I laid you down on a little mattress and helped them with the cooking. After a long time of being hungry and deprived, that simple meal we had was like a feast to us. That night, there were numerous stars that lit up the sky, and a gentle cool breeze that soothed the moment. It was Harmattan season—another lovely gift because I was able to count the stars in the sky at night, a hobby I love."

Harmattan season lasts from late October to early February in the southeastern part of Nigeria. It is brought about by the Northeast Trade Winds from the Sahara Desert. The wind during that season is cold, dry, and dusty. It is often joked that this is the best season to choose your dream girl or guy and get married. This, of course, is not just a joke, but a proven fact. The cold weather does not give unmarried individuals any incentive to remain single; in realty, the opposite is the case. The season also offers a clear advantage for those searching to find spouses with particular, authentic physical beauty with regard to skin color and tone. During Harmattan season, no one is able to bleach their skin with cream or apply lotion or makeup to enhance their appearance. With the wind drying up everything in sight, including humans, the only liniments that do not leave your skin dry, scratchy, and cracked are Vaseline Petroleum Jelly and *Elu Aku,* some oil extract from palm-fruit kernel. Those helpful lubricants only maintain your skin's natural looks, and any attempt to apply something different to your skin would actually make you look worse. Since no cosmetic help comes from makeup, lotion, or bleaching cream, you would only have your unadulterated looks to present to any interested party. That eliminates any guesswork or difficulty in making a choice of a spouse who will look fine in and out of season. Apart from getting married—and to any person of your dreams—the other good thing about this season, as my mom alluded to, is enjoying the majestic shining stars at night.

My mom watched the stars that night, after she enjoyed a delicious meal with those who loved her. Meanwhile, my dad and aunt drank some Palm wine as they listened to the news on BBC from his small AM radio. Palm wine is some sweet wine tapped from a tropical palm tree or from a raffia palm. Tapping wine from those palm trees is very intricate and only a few well-skilled people are able to do it well. When the palm tree grows almost to the fruit-bearing stage, the tapper prepares a ladder that helps him climb up and down the palm tree. The ladder has rungs broad and sturdy enough for the tapper to stand on through the duration of his tedious work. He surgically cuts into the middle of the palm from where the fresh palm frond grows out. He then places a funnel-like platform to channel the wine into a clay pot secured to the tree. A clay pot is preferred because it keeps the wine cool and fresh. That wine is delicious and has its own natural yeast and is generally accepted as a good source of vitamin A. Its richness makes up for the hard and dirty labor involved in producing it. The wine's nourishing nature gives cover and good excuse to those who wish to get drunk.

"There was not much to make one happy from the news on the radio." My mom said as she resumed with her story. "Your dad was enjoying his palm wine, and I guess that insulated him from the bad news the reporter was broadcasting. Since I was not drinking with them, I found my joy and peace from counting the luminous stars. I knew that God was somewhere beyond those stars and was watching over us. The BBC newscaster spoke about the horror of the war, the blockade, and the starvation in the southeast. He also predicted the Nigerian army's victory and the expectation of Colonel Emeka Odumegwu Ojukwu, the head of Biafra Republic, and commander of the Biafra army to surrender. Dee Joe turned off the radio when he couldn't stand the depressing news anymore. The hardships we endured as the war progressed were pure misery. We feared for our lives and lacked everything. There was no need to add to it by listening to the gloomy events played out on the radio, which was a different kind of torture. We preferred to tell and retell the happy stories of our lives. Your dad had his best one he never failed to tell."

She then stopped talking, maybe to get my attention and, of course, with the intention to tease. I looked up, and she smiled. If it was her intention to tease me, she was very successful. I wanted to know more about my dad, Dee Joe, whom I adored. The smile on my mom's face was different. It was a smile of a woman enchanted by an event she was excited to talk about. Whatever it was, I would pay anything to hear it, so I earnestly pleaded, "Mommy, are you going to tell me?" I call her Mommy when I want or need something really bad.

"You don't have to call me Mommy." She caught me, smiled, and continued, "I will tell you." Then she proceeded to let me into her world of romance with my dad.

"My girlfriend in school had talked to Dee Joe about me, and she also told me to expect a visit from him. At the time, I laughed it off. I didn't think any man would be bold enough to come to my home to see me and certainly not one from another village. I am from a very large family with many intimidating and overprotective brothers. The fact that your dad showed up at my home made me believe he's quite a determined and courageous young man. I was impressed, but nonetheless, I went into hiding when I saw him approaching. I was shy and was not ready for the attention his presence would bring. He was well dressed, clean-cut, and was riding his coveted almost brand-new White Horse, a particular brand of bicycle that has a silver color. I thought he was very handsome, and my heart was beating faster than normal. I have never felt anything like that before, which all the more made me want to run away. Even as part of me wanted to flee, another part of me was craving to take another look at him, which I did. He visited with my big brothers, nephews, nieces, and other relatives. Everyone looked for me to come and say hello, but I was nowhere to be found. He had to pay a few more of those visits to my home before I agreed to see him. Our meeting finally took place partly because I was persuaded by my girlfriend to see him. He had also won over my whole family by his charm, and at that stage, all I was doing was playing a pretentious game. I had already fallen for him, and he knew it because my friend was a convenient informant. I didn't want to pretend anymore or be mean to him. He was a very good man. He was even more handsome when I saw him up close. During our visit, we talked for about fifteen minutes, and I announced I had to go because I had dinner to cook. The truth was, I wanted to be with him, and my heart pounded even more rapidly, especially when he smiled. When he was sure we were alone, he said, 'I wasn't sure I would get to see you.' 'Why?' I asked. To which he replied with a smile, 'Because you seem to have perfected the art and career of hiding from me.' Not waiting for an answer, he added, 'I wasn't going to quit coming until I saw you again.' 'You've seen me before?' I asked. 'Yes,' he answered, 'my first visit. That day, as I got closer to your home, you were walking away in a hurry and then stopped and looked toward me. You were so beautiful I wished you were the one I was looking for. I was hoping to see you again and again. When I couldn't spot you in the crowd, I had a feeling you were the one. My yearning to see you again was unbearable. I think I was, and still am, under your spell. I hope I'm not revealing too much on our first date?' I was happy to see his bright smile again as he concluded with that question. I was not sure what my answer was because my own mind was clogged by the same feelings he claimed to be having, the only difference was that he had the courage to speak his mind. So, I kept quiet and hoped he could read my mind, my deepest thoughts and feelings and hopefully come again. He broke the silence as if he knew what was going through my mind. 'I have a gift for you. I have been hauling it to your home since my second visit. I wanted to give it to you in person.' Dee Joe is a very kind person. However, I didn't treat him very nicely."

I did not know what was funny, but my mom started laughing in the middle of her story. She was having so much fun laughing I thought to myself that whatever she did to my dad could not have been that bad. Knowing my mom, I had a feeling she pulled a prank on my dad. My assumption was partially right; she tricked and tested him at the same time. She confessed to me what she had done. "The gift your dad brought to me was a box of Imperial Leather soap. The brand I liked to use was Lux, so I made him take the bath soap back with him."

I could not believe what I had just heard, and I interjected, "Mom, you made him go back with it?"

"Yes, I did," she affirmed and continued. "The soap he bought for me was better and more costly. I know you are wondering why I was taunting your dad. I needed to know I was dealing with a patient man and someone who would not want to run my whole life to the point of choosing the type of soap I used for my shower. I told him to exchange it for the Lux and bring it the next time he visited."

Her strategy was brilliant. I, however, felt for my poor dad who was in love and under the spell of a beautiful girl.

From what I know of my dad, he most likely did not mind; he wanted the best for my mom. That was just who he was. He probably smiled and enjoyed her playing hard-to-get and played along with steady patience. I can argue that since my dad tried to give the best to my mom and to others who knew him, he also deserved the best. God blessed him with one of the best: my mom. That means that his patience and loving heart paid off. His strategy also guaranteed that he got a beautiful woman whose fresh skin stood the test of Harmattan season. He did not rush into things, and they dated for one year. During that time, he got to know my mom well enough. He started visiting her home in October 1966, and they were married in November 1967. Going to her home in October, during the Harmattan season, may well have been a coincidence. But knowing my dad, a goldsmith who stopped at nothing but the finest, he may have taken the natural advantage Harmattan season offers to help him in a search for a woman whose beauty was flawless.

When the war was over, my mom and dad moved to the city of Umuahia, which was six miles away from my village. In that city, my dad practiced his trade as a goldsmith. When I was four years old, my mom and dad enrolled me into kindergarten, which we nicknamed *otakara* (which means, "doughnut-eating school"). In that school, we ate more doughnuts than we studied; it certainly lived up to its nickname. After the teacher taught us the song version of the alphabet or some dramatized story from the Bible, we would eat doughnuts or crackers and have soda. School was laid-back and fun, and we played a lot. Today, as I look at the group picture from my graduation, it brings me many joyful memories, and I am thankful to my parents, teachers, and friends. A closer look at the picture reveals a boy sitting in the middle row—just as I was, to his right and one pupil away—who was picking his nose when the picture was taken. I am glad I was not doing the same thing as we posed for the picture! Hopefully, I knew better than that and learned enough to help me survive first grade and cope with life at that level.

My kindergarten Graduation Picture

CHAPTER 3

I Know Not How to Speak

Wisdom is not just how much you know, how well you speak and the good deeds you do. Wisdom is knowing how to perfect all three and more, and striving to do so.
— Father Udo Ogbuji

It would be an understatement to say that kindergarten was so much fun, and the fun part was mainly why I looked forward to going to school each day. Simply put, kindergarten was for me a sweet adventure and it nearly ruined my early days of elementary school. At first elementary school and all that it represented appeared foreign; being unexciting, it was in total contrast to my concept of school. A notable difference between the two schools would be that my Kindergarten classes were held in a building still under construction, a very informal setting. There was a small playground where little kids like me loved to play, and play we did. On the other hand, my elementary school was located in the same property where my parish church building was and there was no place to play and nothing to play with. Going to school was like going to church especially since my classroom was part of the church building and we were constantly reminded that God was there. Our teacher and Headmaster did not have to remind us to be quiet or not to play around because God was present; the aura of the sacredness of that church whipped us into needed decorum and piety. I would rightly say that the discipline we exercised because of the environment made the work of the teacher easier, but led kids like me who wanted to play to find the wrong place and way to do so. That school was named after my parish church which owned and managed it. It was called Saint Michael Primary School and was located in Umuahia city. My alma mater was later taken over by the state government, together with many other schools managed by different churches in the state. The rumor at the time was that the teachers conspired with the state government against the churches, which led to the government taking over the schools without the permission of the churches. The teachers' union alleged and argued that the churches were running down the schools and that the government could do a better job. The management of the schools by the churches was very efficient, contrary to the false allegations. The church indeed demanded excellence, with proven results from teachers and students. The only area in which the churches fell short was the teachers' salary, which was meager. To be motivated, the teachers had to really love their job and hope for a greater reward in heaven. If better remuneration was their driving factor, there would not have been any teachers left to teach the children. Almost everyone believed the teachers turned against the church because they wanted to be paid more, which they deserved, but they used the allegation of mismanagement as a cover. The teachers believed that the government would pay them more, which was true, and they aligned with the government to strip the church of their ownership of the schools. A few years after the government took control of the schools, the name of my school was changed to Urban School III, Umuahia. On the day the school opened for the academic year, my dad went to the school with me to complete the registration process.

After I was officially registered as a pupil, we were given a tour of the school by a member on the staff. It was during that tour which ended in my assigned classroom that I realized my new school was too large, and that there were many unfamiliar faces. That was another reason to resent my new school even more. I was supposed to join my class and learn with the other pupils for the day. But, as my dad was leaving the school to go home, I followed behind him, crying and wishing not to go to the class because I dreaded doing so. But my dad implored me, "Ogboo, agu adigi amu nwa ujo! (Buddy, a lion does not father a cowardly cub.) You don't have to cry. Before long, you'll be having fun, like in kindergarten. You'll be learning so much and making new friends." His comforting words did not make sense to me, and I cried all the louder because I wanted to go home with him. He then made me an offer I could not resist. "If you go to class, I'll buy you Miki-Miki." My dad knew what to say or do to win me over. Miki-Miki was a chocolate bar I liked very much. I would prefer to eat it rather than eat my food. My dad finally stopped buying it so I would have no reason not to eat my food. When he decided to bribe me with that delicious chocolate bar, I thought the offer was very attractive, and I accepted it. I stopped crying and went to the class. As I was heading to class, my dad called me back to say a proper good-bye and for me to say thank you for the Miki-Miki I would receive later. I hugged his leg and thanked him. He squatted to look at my face, brought out his handkerchief, and wiped off the tears on my cheek while he joked, "Ogboo, wait a minute. You still have tears on your cheek—let me help you get rid of the evidence. You don't want those pretty girls in your class to see you've been crying." When he was done, I said thank you and ran off to class. Before I went into my classroom I looked toward my dad's direction, and he was still standing there. He waved a final good-bye, and I went into the classroom the happiest kid because I knew when I arrived home, I would have my chocolate bar waiting. My dad lived up to his promise, and I enjoyed my Miki-Miki. However, I did not live up to my dad's expectation. When he told me the proverb that a lion does not father a cowardly cub, he meant that I should imitate him in being brave, honorable, and hardworking; instead, I became a little wild cub.

After a few weeks in school, I made two friends. The three of us had the same common interests—we hated school and loved to play. One of my friends was older, streetwise, and knew every fun place for kids to play in Umuahia City and the suburban areas. The other friend was my age and, like me, had no clue on where to go, but we both had a clever and persuasive leader. The school offered a fifteen-minute recess and a thirty-minute recreation every day. The three of us always sneaked out of school during recess or recreation. Our most favorite place to go was a government reserved area called "Government Field", and it was a mile and a half away from Umuahia City. We went there for two reasons: to pluck some fruits, especially the cherries, and to play at the big park located in that area. I liked to play on the swing. Sometimes we got carried away while playing and never made it back to school on time. There was a day we played for several hours, and by the time we returned to school, everyone was gone and so were our slates and chalk holders. I cried as I went back home and felt remorseful for disappointing my parents, especially my dad. The next day, I went back to school with a brand-new slate and a set of chalk in a new chalk holder, ready to be a changed pupil. After about a month, I forgot my terrible deeds and the consequences of my bad choices. I failed to remember how my dad anxiously looked for me all over the city when I did not show up at home, and when he could not find me on the school premises. I could not resist the tempting cherries, the swing, and my friends' company, so I went out with my friends again. My dad, at that point, could not tolerate my misbehavior anymore and made a trip to the headmaster's office. After that visit to the headmaster's office, I never saw my two friends again. I was transferred to another class that had different recess and recreation times. Without the distraction of adventurous friends, even as much as I disliked being in class, I stayed and learned with the other students.

In the second grade, my dad enrolled me to become an altar boy. My pastor, Father Patrick, was a very good man. The first experience I had of him was the day he taught us how to serve at Mass. After the altar boys' practice, he took us to the rectory and served us dinner. I felt like a little prince. We had rice and chicken with a tomato sauce we call stew. Our drink was water and Ribena, which is a special brand of concentrated grape juice. I drank the Ribena to my fill. Ribena was only served on special occasions in my family, such as birthdays, Christmas, or when I was sick. Sometimes I had to pretend I was sick to trick my dad into buying some for me. The altar servers' practice went well, and the meal afterward was unexpected and sumptuous, but my first day to serve at Mass was filled with unwelcomed drama and needed grace. I was so excited and nervous to serve that I was awake almost the whole night. As I lay on my bed that night, I dozed off a few times and dreamt about serving at Mass, and I was so good that Father Patrick threw another party just for me to celebrate how well I did. My first performance as an altar boy was nothing like the dream I had—it was a colossal disaster! I was so nervous because I knew my parents were watching me from the congregation, and I did not want to disappoint them. Sitting in the midst of the congregation during Mass is a completely different experience from being close to the altar and the priest while serving at Mass. The difference for me on that day was like night and day. The awe and glorious aura I felt being close to those holy activities made me numb. My expectations of feeling special and privileged as a lucky boy serving the priest evaporated; what I felt was impossible to describe.

The drama started when I forgot to bring the wine and water in the cruets to Father Patrick. He tried to help by pointing at something on the credence table. I was visibly nervous and confused and picked up the bowl of water for hand washing and the towel. I brought those to him, but instead of washing his hands, he took them from me. He leaned forward and whispered gently, "Bring the wine and water in the cruets." It then became clear to me that I had messed up very badly. Nervousness turned into paranoia and partial loss of consciousness. As I tried to pick up the cruet with wine in it, the handle slipped from my trembling tiny fingers and shattered on the floor. I was very confused on what to do, but I knew enough not to look in the direction where my mom and dad were sitting. As I bent down to pick up the broken glass, I could feel their eyes on me, together with those of Father Patrick and everyone in the church. Those were too many eyes looking at one person, but the imaginary eyes were the least of my problems. It was certain my mom would skin me alive, and my pastor would suspend me as an altar boy. As I knelt there frozen, I felt a large hand touch my small shoulder, but it was surprisingly light. It weighed far less than my troubled heart and head, which was filled with thoughts of the broken cruet, spilled wine, my mistakes, and the possible punishment awaiting me. Nothing could have been heavier if you added the fear I felt. The hand of Father Patrick on my shoulder was not only reassuring but became soothing when he pleasantly asked me, "You know how many of those I've broken in my lifetime?" He did not wait for me to answer his question but offered, "I have lost count. Don't worry about it, Udo, I'll clean it up later. Get up. I don't want you to get hurt." He was smiling as he spoke. His gentleness, patience, and kindness made a deep impression on me.

I saw Father Patrick as a very powerful man since my parents, whom I adored, had great respect for him—almost feared him. His having enormous authority while, at the same time, being so humble and kindhearted was stunning. It completely redefined any previous notion I had about authority, the prevalent concept of authority, and the exercise of it at the time, which was characterized by dominion.

The military leaders were not shy about letting people know who was in charge. Most of the rich sought to retain their status by exploiting the poor. Being a patriarchal society, the men kept almost all aspects of authority for themselves and conceded only those they thought were unimportant to the women. An example of this would be the kitchen and the cooking of meals. It was bad enough that the men tried to usurp almost all areas of authority and leadership, but equally bad was their display of ignorance in the fact that they overlooked the importance of meals and the kitchen. Since the women ruled in the kitchen, they also determined who would eat, what was to be eaten, and the portions. Men, both young and old, were terrible cooks because they excluded themselves from the kitchen where they could learn. In fact, the women appreciated that voluntary exclusion since the men were more of a distraction than help. At that time, there were only a few restaurants, and mostly single men would go there to eat. Hunger was one of the factors that forced many single men to desperately want to get married. That was because nothing came close to a delicious home-cooked meal. Married men who go to restaurants to eat were considered irresponsible, so they mainly ate at home. To the extent the men were incapable of cooking and dependent on women to find nourishment; to that extent were they vulnerable. It was a common practice for the women to use hunger as a domestic weapon or food as leverage. I would have to admit at this point that men, and even the children, occasionally used hunger strikes to push their agenda too. For the men, it was the last resort and the most effective, especially when the women were in love. That was because their refusal to eat was a sign of abject rejection and the first signal that there may be someone on the side if things did not improve. For the kids, it was less effective—at least, I know it did not work on my mom. Besides, the first day I tried to use a hunger strike to make a point, I was too hungry to follow through with my threat. After about two hours of my mom not coming to plead with me to eat my food, my only prayer was that when I arrived at the pantry where my food was locked away, I would still have access to it. My wish was that I would have a little privacy to lick my young, fragile, and wounded pride. It was different though, when my mom used the threat of starvation to beat me into shape or surrender. She did it twice, and her first attempt was very effective, and I knew I deserved it. There will be some opportunities to tell the stories later, but at the moment, I will explore the idea that the areas of power men thought were insignificant turned out to be ones that would, time after time, bring them to their knees.

On a day my mom was sick and my dad had to cook, we learned the hard way how powerless, defeated, and dependent men were, even when they think or parade themselves as having all the power. My dad was going to prepare dinner and decided to cook rice with tomato sauce. It was a very simple meal to prepare as it was not complicated and required minimal time in the kitchen. He had used a stove that required kerosene as fuel, and he had difficulty getting it lit. He fought with the stove for several minutes before he discovered the kerosene tank was empty. He decided to fill it up, which was something he had never done before, so he ignored the marker that said F for full and poured the kerosene beyond the F mark, spilling some kerosene in the process. It so happened that when he lit the stove's burner, the whole stove caught on fire. The blaze was like a fireball. The tall fire rattled my dad, but since he was intent on proving he could take charge, he proceeded to cook despite the active inferno. Thank goodness he did not catch on fire because he smelled like burned fur, which was an indication he almost did. When he finished cooking, the food tasted and smelled like kerosene. My dad threw the food away because he could not take the risk of poisoning his whole family. When I realized his cooked meal had been rendered inedible by the kerosene flavor, I sympathized with him, especially as he seemed visibly humiliated and frustrated. He went across the street that night and bought some *suya* (seasoned grilled beef) and bread for us to snack on. The improvised supper was so delicious probably because we were so hungry, and it did not matter what we ate. I was grateful for all my dad's effort to cook, but secretly prayed for my mom to get well in order that things may be normal again.

When we returned home after the embarrassing incident at the church, I expected a discussion to follow, but my parents stayed away from the topic. Instead, they treated me with love and care. The only thing said about it was very positive. My dad told me he was proud of me for serving. When you served as an altar boy in those days, it was not uncommon for most people to expect you to become a priest and even treat you like one. Some people would go so far as to call you Little Priest. My pastor's kindness impressed me so much that I began to think I wanted to become a priest like him, as many people expected of me anyway. One problem with that thought was that I did not like school. I neither understood nor liked what the teachers taught; I disliked the homework, and nothing made sense to me. It did not help matters for me that other students seemed to like being in the class, raising their hands to answer questions and even giving the correct answers. I felt like a buffoon and a disappointment. Going to school each day was like going to the torture chamber, and I did not have the discipline or wisdom it took to see things in a different light or work my way to success. My homework was only done when my mom threatened to spank me or my dad made me do it. Sometimes, when my dad was not home, my mom's threats or spankings were ineffective. Whenever I arrived home after school and ate lunch, I would go and play with my friends, and I would not come back until dark.

One particular day, my mom told me to stay home to study and do my homework. I, on the other hand, planned a trip to the park with my friends. I got out my books and pretended to study. When I thought my mom was gone, I tried to escape through the back door to meet my friends, but instead, I ran straight into my mom. She, of course, had me in her grip and pulled me to where the paddle was. She gave me one stroke, and I guess her left hand was hurting so much, she let go to get a better grip. Realizing I was free and not wanting to be spanked, I ran away from her. My mom pursued but could not catch me. That day, I was wearing one of the nice shirts she had bought for me. I stood at a distance facing her and, in protest, grabbed the front pocket of my shirt as my tiny fingers shivered and said, "If you don't leave me alone, I will tear up this shirt." As I said that, I started tearing the shirt so she would know I was serious and was not making an empty threat.

My mom saw through my childish rant and said, "You little rascal. Those tiny trembling fingers of yours would hardly do any lasting damage to that shirt." She looked at me with a mocking smile and then added, "I have a pair of scissors, and they will do a better job."

My mom's calmness, wit, mockery, and sarcasm were very crushing. I have never felt so dislodged and had no choice but to abandon my threat.

Since I felt defeated in academics before I even passed through the school gates, I turned to God for divine help on one of the days I was serving at Mass. That week, our religion class was on Solomon and how he asked God for wisdom and it was granted to him. That message was reinforced during Sunday Mass when Father Patrick ended his homily with this simple sentence: "If you pray, God will give you wisdom." I thought that if anyone needed wisdom, it was me, because I was getting weary of being the dumbest boy in class. I wanted to answer questions like the other kids, but I did not know a thing. I felt like the prophet Jeremiah who lamented, "I know not how to speak" (Jeremiah 1:6). Whenever the teacher asked a question, I almost wanted to hide under my desk. I recoiled whenever the teacher looked in my direction, and I died many times before the day at school was over. On that Sunday, after Father Patrick spoke, I found myself talking to God in prayer. I told him I did not want to look lame again in class, and I pleaded for wisdom because, for me at the time, wisdom meant mastering everything I was taught in school and reproducing it when questions were asked in class. Since I hated school and did not want to be in class but at the same time wished to be knowledgeable, I ventured to bargain with God. I prayed, "God, if you make me instantly wise so I can skip going to school, I will become a priest." He did not instantaneously make me wise, and I was never allowed to skip school, but God helped me learn to enjoy school after several years. In the interim, since I did not have any choice but to go to school, I began taking it seriously, and I was able to learn a few things. I liked the stories told in English readings, like the story about the dog that was rewarded with a big bone, but as he was going home with his trophy, he passed through a river. Looking at the water, he saw another dog with a bigger bone and went after the new dog to deny him his lunch, and not knowing it was his shadow, he drowned. That story has stuck with me since the very day our teacher read the story to us and explained the moral: we should appreciate what we have and not envy what others possess. Stories like that, among other things, made going to school a lot more interesting.

I loved Papa Dee Joe and, of course, Mama Lucy, but it appeared that as a young boy, I enjoyed being a thorn in my mom's flesh. That was only because it was hard to believe she loved me as much as my dad loved me. It took some growing up on my part and more revelations from my mom over the years to realize she did love me. It was difficult as a boy to imagine that my mom loved me when it appeared her sole mission was to make sure I never got away with anything. I believed she relished torturing me by setting rules she knew I would flout and then turned around and punished me because I broke them. When my dad was not at home, I felt like I was in a military camp. I did not mind being reprimanded or punished by her; in fact, sometimes I would intentionally go against her will and gladly accept whatever form of penalty she chose for me. My mom had to get creative to stay one step ahead of me and to keep me disciplined because, after a few times of using the same corrective measure, I became immune to it. Once, when nothing else worked, including spankings, she used the threat of starvation, which turned out to work better than any other form of punishment.

During holidays, I never stayed around the house to help with anything. After breakfast, I would go out with my friends to the park to play and would not come back until dark. My mom did not approve of my friends and told me to keep away from them. My dad did not particularly like some of them but exercised restraint in declaring a non-association decree like my mom. One day, knowing my mom would disapprove, I escaped to the park with my friends where we played all day. That night, when I returned home, I was in need of a hot shower and a complimentary meal. My mom hit me where it hurt the most when she said, "We just got through eating supper. Since you were not here and did not make a special request for your meal to be kept in the oven to remain warm while you run around the whole city, I presumed you had enough to eat and drink wherever you were. All I am saying is that you may have to go to bed hungry tonight if you have not eaten already."

I had not eaten all afternoon, and I was starving. I wanted to cry but was too weak to do so. I also believed it was useless to cry since it would not change her mind, and that was perhaps what she wanted. As minutes went by, I thought death was imminent. My dad may have been reading my mind, and he said, "You should quit disobeying your mom. Go and tell her you are sorry and don't do it again."

"Yes, Dad," I replied and then went to my mom and apologized.

My mom told me she had accepted my apology but added, "You will still go hungry tonight because I'm not going back to that kitchen to cook and certainly not for you."

I had never seen that side of her, and I think I drove her nuts that night. My dad came to me later that night, making sure my mom was not watching us because he probably did not want her to get mad at him, too. I never saw or heard them argue about anything, but I believed she blamed him for my being rotten. He did, in fact, spoil me because anything I wanted was mine just for the asking. That night, I did not even ask for anything when he slipped some money into the palm of my hand and said in a suppressed voice, "She is serious! Go and buy something to eat, and remember, I didn't give you any money." He smiled but was obviously distressed as he looked around, hoping not to be caught.

That night, I turned over a momentary new leaf. I thanked my dad and promised my parents that, going forward, I would be a good boy. I spent the rest of my holiday helping my dad in his workshop, and he taught me how to be a renowned goldsmith. He had a rare talent—turning bars of gold into the most beautiful jewelry, and I was hoping to take over his trade when he retired. I hung around his workshop and helped him get the fire started for melting the gold in the furnace. I squeezed out the juice from the limes and soaked the already carefully molded gold in the lime juice. In the afternoon, we had lunch together. My dad liked avocado pears and always offered me some, but I did not like the taste. I would decline his offer, and he would urge me by saying, "It's good for you. Fruits and vegetables are good for you." I ate it out of love and respect for him, but it made me nauseated, and I almost wanted to vomit, but I tried very hard to hold it down. For three weeks, I was an obedient child. I did not see my friends; I helped my dad in his shop, and I was very nice to my mom. Then my good behavior took a terrible turn.

My dad had sent me on an errand to the workshop of one of his friends, who was also a goldsmith. He had special equipment that flattened the bar of gold into a sheet. The sheet was then cut into different shapes. My dad checked my pant pockets for holes and asked me to stick my hand into my pocket to feel and hold on to the gold bar so that I would not lose it. I then went on my way. I did so well until I met some of my friends who were getting ready to play a street soccer game with kids from another neighborhood. They expected me to join them, but I told them I could not because I was on an important errand. My friend Nonye, whom I liked very much, approached me and told me how they were short of players and needed me. I saw their desperation; they needed to win so badly. They had been humiliated many times by those kids, who defeated them time after time by huge margins. I was torn. I did not want to displease my dad, nor did I want to disappoint my friends, especially Nonye. I decided to play until halftime—just thirty minutes—and I would be on my way. I believed I would have enough time to run my dad's errand.

As we played, I had my hand in my pocket to make sure the gold was secure. We were winning, and the joy of victory and celebration that goes with winning made me continue with the rest of the soccer match. I was so carried away I could not remember how long my hands had been out of my pocket. It was a few minutes before the end of the soccer tournament when I realized that my hand was not in the right place. I was too afraid to put my hand in my pocket, fearing the worst. I felt the pocket area on the outside and felt nothing but my quivering thigh. The shaking of my thighs was not from the exhaustion of playing soccer but from fear that the only day my dad entrusted me with something very important, I would disappoint him. Even though my friends were still playing, I could not see or hear them because I was crying and searching for the lost gold. The place was sandy, and with little boys like me running around, there was a good chance I would never find it. When the game was over, everyone left except Nonye, my friend, who stayed, sympathized, and searched with me.

We all called him Nonye, which was an endearing nickname. His full name was Chinonyerem, meaning "God be with me." He lived with his mother in the house next to ours. His father left his mother after he was born, and she raised him on her own. In those days, single mothers who had never been married were very few, and the culture did not have that much respect for them. They were almost seen as prostitutes. Nonye and his mom loved each other a great deal. He was very caring, kind, and did not talk much, but he was very protective of me. He was strongly built, and I never saw any one beat him in a fight. He was a gentle boy and usually not the one that started the fight. He was my most favorite after-school friend.

For some reason, I began to do better in school and soon found myself in the company of some rich boys. Some of them were altar boys; some were not Catholic. Nonye was not a very bright student, and he dreaded academic work just like me before I started improving. He did poorly in school probably because his mom did not care whether or not he read his books or did his homework. But he was good with crafts and was very innovative. When we were not involved in dangerous and dirty stunts, we made small toy cars with Peak milk cans and fashioned their tires from plastic flashlight battery covers. We built small miniature houses with sand and mud. Nonye had low self-esteem and did not want to have anything to do with my rich friends in school. I did not blame him because those kids picked on him and his mom, and he was tired of fighting them. He had the skill of a street fighter and beat up many of those boys when he could not take any more from them. But even after he won the physical battles, he lost the emotional ones. He would always hide and cry, and I would look for him and try to comfort him. He never told me why he cried, but I believed it was because he did not know who his dad was. The rich kids were not as much fun as Nonye. They always talked about books, homework, trips they made with their parents, and what they owned. One reason I did not care much about them was that they made me lose a girl I had a crush on. The girl's name was Njide, and she lived opposite our house, and she knew I liked her. I think she liked me too; at least that was what I wanted to believe. But she did not want to have anything to do with me because those well-to-do kids picked on her and called her my wife. It did not hurt that she stayed away from me because, at that age, girls were not much fun. They were not like my guy friends; they were disciplined and well behaved, like little angels. Some of my friends, including myself, did not think girls did things like pee or passed gas because of the classy way they conducted themselves. On the contrary, my friends and I broke most of the rules and boundaries on many things. For instance, we peed together in a kind of a contest to see whose urine would make the tallest foam.

Being in the company of some of the wealthy boys was good for me mainly because they helped me follow my resolve not to perform poorly on my tests. The school academic year at the time had first, second, and third terms. If you failed first and second terms but passed the third term, you would move to the next class. If you passed first and second term but flunked the third term, you would not be promoted to the next class. It did not make sense to me, but that was how it was, and I was bent on passing third term, so I studied with my rich friends. When I wanted to have fun, I would go with Nonye. We did things like catch lizards and pretended we were doctors and cared for the poor sick creatures. With discarded syringes, we injected disposed medicine into them, put them in a cage, and monitored their recovery. Some died and some lived to tell their story. I was bitten by a lizard once, and I was concerned I was going to die of rabies. I did not tell my parents, and thankfully, I did not die either, but that was the very day I gave up curing the lizards of their diseases.

We also did things like rolling down the valley while inside big tires. We found some eighteen-wheeler tires and dragged them up the hill behind Saint Michael Primary School. One of us crawled inside the tire; it was kept in balance and then let go. I am surprised none of us were hurt. There were big trees scattered around the valley, and many times, the racing tires with us inside collided with them. I wonder how we ever survived, and I am very happy my parents were not privy to those adventures.

We were often dirty after playing all day, especially since it was dusty during the dry seasons and muddy during rainy seasons. The band of wealthy boys had a name they called me when they wanted to taunt me for preferring to be in Nonye's company instead of theirs. They called me Uretu, which meant "dirty little boy." My sister Helena has fed and kept that name alive till this day. Over the years, I had threatened her with everything except a plague, but she has not quit calling me by that nickname. However, as adults, I have enjoyed hearing her call me Uretu as an endearing name.

On the day I lost my dad's gold, my friend Nonye was by my side and searched along with me. When I raised my head after tiring from digging through the sand, I saw my dad coming to look for me. He was probably worried because I had been gone longer than expected. As my dad approached, I said to Nonye, "My dad is here. I don't want him to think you are partly responsible for the lost gold, you have to leave." He left in a hurry without saying a thing but was apparently grieved. I was still crying profusely, wishing it was a dream and, if not, let a sudden earthquake open the ground for me to fall into. It was not a dream, and the earthquake did not occur. I told my dad what happened, and we searched for the gold bar but did not find it. What happened next was something I was not prepared for. My dad called off the search. He did not think it could be found, and besides, he had work to do. Before we left, we had a small conference, and as you might imagine, it was a very painful one. I would have preferred to have been spanked, and I would have gladly accepted it because I deserved it. My dad, in his gentleness and unrivalled prudence, had a better way of handling things. I never saw him lose his temper, and he did not on that day. He addressed me, and I listened intently:

"I have watched you grow, and I have been extremely proud of you. I believe that if I'm no longer here, I'll be leaving your mom and your siblings in capable hands. What you did today is a discomforting dent on my belief that I could entrust you with something important. I put food on the table, you go to school, and we keep the family together because I work. The gold you lost is not mine, and if you keep losing gold bars at this rate, you will put me out of business very quickly. I will pray and hope that you continue to learn to be sensible and responsible. The goat that plays in the mud has only itself to blame for the dirt and its awful smell. You have a beautiful and promising life ahead of you—please don't throw it all away. You have to work to better your life, and you have to start now! It's much easier to look for a black sheep while there is still daylight."

Even though I was in deep sorrow, I could not cry. When he finished, I mumbled, "I'm sorry, Dad. I won't do it again."

He said, "Don't worry about it. I won't tell your mom."

He smiled at me, which was very comforting. Nevertheless, I was still hanging on to every word he spoke, and they were weighing heavily on my heart. What made it excruciating was the fact that my dad had been sick for about three years. He and my mom knew his days were numbered, and somehow, I knew it too. It hurt so deeply to think he would die not believing I could pick up from where he left off. I felt like a total disappointment, and I promised myself that I would make it up to him. I hoped he would once again find a reason to believe in me as he did before I lost the gold. The last part about not telling my mom was the only happy news.

That night I ate just a little bit of food, and I was very quiet—in fact, too quiet. The next day, I was at my dad's workshop and was still feeling down and guilty. After the day's work, he went to the kitchen where my mom was about to start dinner and announced, "Your prodigal son and I are going to take a walk." When I heard *prodigal*, my heart sank. But when he turned around, he was smiling, and I knew he did not give me away. He had a habit of saying I have more of my mom's blood when I would do something bad. But when I excelled, he claimed his blood was running through me. Thus, he referred to me as my mom's prodigal son. My mom gave permission and added with a smile, "Dinner will be ready in an hour, don't be late, or you will eat it cold."

On our way to the park, my dad said, "I kept my promise. I didn't tell your mom. I wanted you to know I left out some truth about the lost gold." He was smiling when he said it to keep me from worrying. "I told you the gold didn't belong to me and that I couldn't afford it. It technically doesn't belong to me because the new owner paid for it, and I can afford it if you let me have your allowance." He laughed harder at this point and I laughed with him.

I was willing to forfeit my allowance, but I knew he would not accept it even if I gladly gave it to him. In the middle of his laughter, he added, "Don't let the incident yesterday eat you up, and I want you to know that I still believe in you!"

That evening, the bond between us became deeper. During that profound occasion, my dad told me plainly that he was sick and did not know how much longer he would be around. Before he made that revelation, I knew he was very sick because he went to the hospital many more times than usual, but it was never discussed. That evening, he joked as he revealed that painful reality when he said, "I have outlasted two of my doctors who predicted my imminent death three years ago. Who knows? If I continue like this, I might live forever. In case anything happens to me, I want you to promise me you will take care of your mom and siblings."

"I will, Dad. I promise!" I replied.

We were home in time to eat a warm meal.

From that day on, I tried to do everything right since there was very little room for error. If my dad was dying, I wanted him to leave the earth confident that I would not disappoint him. Unfortunately, I caused him one more headache before he died. I did not lose any more gold even though I had been sent on several of those errands. I learned to go on important gold missions quickly and successfully. I did not fight with my mom, either and, I made sure I had permission whenever I went to play with my friends. However, there was a day I told my parents I was going to play with my friends at the park on the other side of the city. A railway divided Umuahia City into two parts; on the other side where we went to play was a soccer field, a small park, and a big Anglican church named Saint Stephen. The park and soccer field flooded whenever it rained. There was a big gutter that was supposed to channel the water to the river and ocean, but because of poor construction, whenever there was a heavy rain, that area of the town flooded. It did not help that my own part of the town was on a hill, so the flood from the rain found its way around where we went to play. We had played for a few hours before it started raining heavily. We thought the rain would stop, but it did not. After about forty-five minutes, everywhere was flooded while it kept raining like in the days of Noah. I had never been so afraid of anything or anyone, but with one exception—losing my dad's love and trust. I admit I was scared of the rain on that day. It flooded everywhere, including roads, the big gutter, and the soccer field. Noah's Ark would have come in handy that day in the face of so much rain and enormous flood.

One of the classrooms in Saint Stephen Primary School provided welcomed safety. Who would have thought that we could find refuge in that school since there was heightened rivalry between Saint Stephen Primary School and my school, Saint Michael Primary School. On that day, my friends and I were not afraid of the boys from the rival school but more of the flood. The reason we were so scared was that a few days earlier, it had rained, and a drunken man had fallen into that big gutter, and the flood waters carried him off. After a few days, his remains were found in a small town about ten miles away.

As we shivered from being wet, cold, and afraid, I stood on a desk and looked out through the half wall of the classroom, and I could not believe what I saw. A man with an umbrella was walking toward where we were nesting. The closer he got, the more I recognized him as my dad. The visibility was poor, and his face was covered by the umbrella, which I recognized as one of ours. The mere thought that it was my dad brought an indescribable feeling of peace and safety. I called out, but the rain drowned out my voice. I decided to run to him, and as I did, my friends followed. We were rescued and brought home safely because my dad cared very much and knew where we were. I did not get into trouble because I had permission to go and play with my friends. It was after that experience that I realized the importance of telling my parents when I am leaving home, where I was going, and with whom, and to make sure I had their blessing. Telling them, among other things, was the difference between being alive and possibly drowning in the flood.

My dad died five months after that flood episode. On the day he breathed his last, he asked to have his most favorite meal for lunch, which was rice, black-eyed peas, and vegetables cooked together with tomatoes, pepper, ground dry crawfish, vegetable oil, and other seasonings. My mom cooked it like it was the last meal for him. That evening, he asked me to eat from the same dish with him as he had done on different occasions. That symbolic meal, although normal at the time, remains the best gift I ever received. Rice and black-eyed peas have never been the same since, and I only eat those together when they are prepared by my mom or I cook them myself. After my dad had eaten, he announced he was going to take a nap. He lay down to sleep but never woke up. While my mom tidied up the kitchen, I had stepped out so I would not bother my dad as he napped. I played soccer with my friends in front of our house. About two hours later, I noticed there were people visiting my home. It was not unusual for my parents' friends to come over for a visit. One of my mom's friends, a spoiled rich girl who was younger than my mom and always spoke before she thought, stood at the entrance to the house and shouted to me as loudly as she could before my friends, "Your father is dead, and you are playing soccer!"

Even as young as I was, I was wise enough to know this young woman lacked prudence and common sense. Before that incident, I did not like her very much because she was very loud and would not stop talking whenever she visited. After that incident, my dislike for her attitude grew even more. If she were a little wiser and more thoughtful, she could have called my attention, took me into the house, and broke the news to me in a more caring and private way. Rather, she announced it to whoever would listen, like a radio announcer. I thought she was kidding when I first heard her words. It could not be; my dad was invincible and a survivor. I stopped playing, went inside the house, and I saw my mom was crying. I hugged her and tried to comfort her.

Since Christmas was within a few days, my dad was buried two days after he died. My mom was strong and did not cry very much. I was very proud of her. I did not cry but almost did when I put some soil in his grave and said my good-byes. Because the doctors had predicted his death many times, he got my mom acquainted with his job orders and clients. All the finished jobs were given to their owners, and my mom gave the unfinished ones to my dad's friend to work on. A mistake on my dad's part was to keep my mom within the confines of our home. His excuse for doing so was that he made enough money to sustain all of us. That fact cancelled the incentive for my mom to take a job outside my home, leaving her no choice but to stay home and take care of the whole family. I do not mean to question my dad's good intentions, and I know my mom staying home helped me be a lot more normal, but I think there may have been other hidden reasons for his decision. I believe he thought my mom was very beautiful, and it made him a little jealous to think of her working for another man. My mom, being very clever, handled the situation very well. She wanted to have a career, perhaps work part-time or full time if she needed to. She asked my dad for permission and support to go to culinary/sewing school. When she received her diploma, she made my dad understand that it was important for her to put into practice what she had learned, or she would risk losing it all. I am truly grateful to my mom for making provisions for the future. If she had listened to my dad and did not take up a career, after he died, life would have been tougher.

Papam Dee Joe

After my dad died, I had to grow up very fast. I was there for my mom, and we spent a lot of time together. She would ask my opinion about different family matters and decisions. I was surprised at some of the issues my mom discussed with me, which reflected her level of confidence in me. Realizing she actually took my advice in some instances was edifying, and it made me feel like a wise and grown man. One of my duties was to open up, sweep, and clean my mom's shop for business. She made wedding cakes and sewed wedding gowns and other clothing fashions prevalent at the time. After a few months of watching my mom sew, I started messing with her sewing machine, and I taught myself how to sew. There was a day I was patching up my torn pants and ended up running the needle through the button, and it broke in half. The part of the needle that broke off fell into the spinning motor and clogged it. It was repaired, but I never told my mom what I had done. Many years passed before I told her the true story behind the malfunctioning sewing machine.

Though I was growing up fast, I was still a child inside in so many ways. There were things I did not understand or understood in a sense only a child could. In my culture, it is customary to invite other people to share your meal. Sometimes your invitation would be accepted, especially if you were very close friends. But most of the time, the invited guests declined the invitation. Those times when invitees do not join in the meal, they acknowledged your kindness, thanked you, and continued on their way. It actually was more of a customary gesture of thoughtfulness than anything else, a way for you to indicate you care and not come off as selfish. I was eating on a certain day, and one of our neighbors was passing by, and I invited him to come and eat with me. He was an older gentleman, and to my surprise and disappointment, he came and started eating my lunch, which was not even big enough for me. Even as he sat down to eat with me, I believed he would be considerate, eat a little, and then leave. I could not believe it when I realized he was determined to keep eating until everything was gone. I could not understand why he was so inconsiderate and greedy, and I wanted to stop him. I did so by crying, to which he had the audacity to ask me why I was crying.

"I'm crying because you won't stop eating my lunch," I replied.

"But you were the one that invited me," he said as he tried to defend himself.

"Yes, I invited you, but I was counting on you to acknowledge my invitation, say thank you, and go on to attend to your duties. But not only did you come to eat my food, you have almost finished it."

One of my duties was to do the dishes and to clean the kitchen after my mom was through with cooking. I did it for almost three years. At first I was happy to do it. But when my younger sister, Helena, turned seven, I had hoped she would take over. I had the feeling my mom was shielding her. That was the first time since my dad had died that I was not happy with my mom. To make matters worse, my sister ate slower than everyone, and after I finished doing the dishes, she would place her dirty dish where I could see it so I would have to wash it also, and if I did not, my mom would threaten to punish me. I was so delighted when my mom's cousin Daa Meke, came to visit my family and told my mom that Helena was old enough to start doing the dishes, especially since she was a girl and had to learn the art of cleanliness—she would get married someday and have to keep her home neat. My mom actually listened to Daa Meke and accepted her wise suggestion, which, unknown to my mom, I believed but could not verbally express. It was a sweet vindication to be relieved of that particular duty my sister unintentionally made me dislike so much, thanks to Daa Meke. From that day forward I bonded with Daa Meke and loved her very, so much; she filled in as the lovely big sister I always dreamt of.

CHAPTER 4

Rebellious Youth

Gentleness and love permeate a willing heart faster, soothe its maladies, while leading it to ways of loving service.
                                        —Father Udo Ogbuji

Daa Meke was in transit to Lagos where she lived with her husband and son. She was kind to come to visit and spend two weeks with my family in Umuahia. At that time, Lagos was the capital of Nigeria, a very large city where most people go to seek opportunities and adventure. As a youngster, I dreamt many times of visiting that city and could not resist when Daa Meke invited me to spend my holiday with her and her family. Lagos is about a nine-hour bus ride west of my home. It would not have been such a long and cumbersome trip; however, the road was bad, and we had frequent stops.

I enjoyed my holiday very much, and my favorite distant relative was super nice to me. She treated me like a prince and an adult. The next day, after we arrived, Daa Meke took me shopping and showed me the city. She wanted me to have the best of everything and almost changed my entire wardrobe. I have never had so many fine clothes and shoes. She worked in the sales department of Bata, which was a shoe company. Shopping for clothes was fun, but shopping for shoes was even more exciting. We went to her department, and her fellow workers were helpful and playful.

One of the girls, Nneoma, helped me pick out the best shoes, but she also put me on the spot. As we looked for my size of a particular sandal I liked, she turned to me and asked, "Am I beautiful?" She was so beautiful even a blind man would be able to pick her out from a lineup of many pretty girls. With such dazzling beauty, the answer was obvious to anyone, including her, and I wondered why she asked me that question. I was so shy that I looked away and made a concerted effort to avoid her piercing eyes as I inaudibly mumbled the word *yes*. My feelings were conflicted; I wished she would quit questioning me, but at the same time, I thought she was stunningly fine-looking. I liked her and secretly wished she was my friend. She seemed to have read my mind, and made me an offer which was a little more than I could handle: "I'll let you marry me since you think I am beautiful," she said as she flashed me a bright smile. I mentally sought for a place to hide because I did not think I could take any more.

Daa Meke could see through my awkward feelings and gracefully intervened, and said, "Leave my boy alone! He serves the priest at Holy Mass, and I don't want you to corrupt him."

"Oh, that works out well, I like the good ones," Nneoma replied, not willing to give up without a fight.

After more shopping, we had lunch at the company's lounge where I met many more of the girls who worked with my mom's cousin. Each had a line like "I heard your handsome and favorite relative is in town, so I came to say hello."

Their comments about me made me feel a little uncomfortable and, each new girl that showed up made me want to crawl under the table and stay there. It appeared the men were not that interested in meeting me, maybe because they were very busy with their jobs. I had my hands so full with the girls that their not taking notice of me was a wonderful relief. However, one of the men was pleasant and friendly, and I could tell he liked my adopted big sister, a lot—and me by extension.

"Udo, I am glad I finally got to meet you. I am Johnson." That was the way Johnson introduced himself. He was very polished and handsome, and he had a gentle and funny nature. "Your 'big sister' won't quit talking about you. She made me think you were a toddler, but you're a young man and handsome, if I might add. Don't feel bad about the attention you are getting from these pretty girls. Enjoy it, they are not that generous to the guys around here although they make us do their work," he joked and smiled.

Since Johnson told me to enjoy the attention I was getting from the girls, I wanted to see Nneoma one more time before I left, but I was out of luck; she had already gone back to work, and I did not dare ask my "big sister" about her.

I had just completed the fifth grade and took a special exam. If I passed, I would be eligible for secondary school (junior high and high school). Some teachers recommended to the parents of children that excelled in fifth grade to take this entrance exam even though it was meant for those in sixth grade. My mom let me sit for the exam although I did not believe I could pass. Before my holiday was over, I received the news from my mom that I had passed. I had the option to stay with Daa Meke and her family to attend secondary school or go back to Umuahia City where my mom and siblings currently lived, for the same purpose. My "big sister" did not have to convince me to stay with her and her family because I cherished and entertained the possibility even before she asked me if I wanted to. Being on holiday was an adventure and so was going to school. I had a monthly allowance, which was enough money for my needs, and I was able to save a little bit. Although I was a studious student, I also worked hard to be a good boy, but something went amiss with the passage of time. I suspected my mom may have written to "my big sister's" husband and told him that if he felt the need, he should not hesitate to discipline me. In other words, he should not let me run loose and wild.

During the era that I grew up, it was a standard practice in my village for kids who committed grave offenses to be spanked by adults who are not their parents. It was not considered as child abuse. The adults who carried out that corrective measure usually did so with a sense of duty to the child as well as the society. That was because every child was believed to belong to the community, and the proper upbringing of a child was seen as a communal obligation and a means to not only individual but, a societal success.

Dee Eze, Daa Meke's husband, was a kind person, he was gentle and a good man, and I looked up to him as my big brother. I respected and loved him, just like I loved Daa Meke! I did not have the intention of disobeying him or disturbing the peace everyone enjoyed in the home. But he may have misread my mom's letter and took it too seriously. I also suspected his assessment of me was solely based on something other than my own actions or merits. For some unexplained factors or reason, there seemed to be a birth of a new Dee Eze. That new person was completely different from the man I knew and loved. He was, for the most part, no longer a very happy man and certainly not very nice or gentle. It was clear that whatever happened brought out the worst in him. The first time he spanked me, I was utterly distraught and in total disbelief, not only because he did it, but also because of the reason behind it.

That day, I had stayed late after school to use a library textbook for my homework, and I explained to him why I did not come back home at the expected time. I even apologized for the anxiety I had caused everyone although there was no way I could communicate that I had an assignment I had to write and submit the next day. Despite my explanation, apology, and the fact that it was my first transgression, I was spanked anyway. It was agonizing because I did not believe I deserved it, and I cried almost all night. After what happened that night, I had doubts about staying with "big sister" and her family. Even though I felt hurt, I was ready to forgive her husband, believing he may have just had a bad day. If having a bad day was the cause of his bizarre behavior, it was going to last for a while because he appeared to be having too many unhappy days. The next time he spanked me, he had a very flimsy reason as well, and I did not give him any satisfaction by showing fear or that I could be intimidated. I turned my back, stood straight and tall, and braced myself to receive all the strokes of the paddle he could deliver. It did not hurt at all, and I did not cry or utter a word of apology. He was grossly disappointed to say the least.

Believing he had no good reason to spank me, the rebel in me was unleashed. I did not care anymore about obeying rules or instructions I considered senseless. I did things I thought were right and wanted to do regardless of the possibility of being punished. I anticipated and gladly received any penalty without exhibiting any feelings of fear, regret, humiliation, or pain. For the first time in my life, severe pain and humiliation were present, yet unfelt. The first night it happened, I remember thinking aloud and asking myself, *Was it real?* If it was real, then it meant I just made a unique discovery I could use to my advantage when life throws nasty things at me. Surprisingly, I did not have any feelings of dislike or hatred for my "big brother". I still loved him and gave him the benefit of the doubt. I wished he would come to realize that I worked hard to succeed at all levels and meant no disrespect. The peace I felt in the midst of all the adversity helped me focus on my studies and perform my duties as best as I could. Later in this book, I will review how I managed to block the pain his misguided action could have caused. At this time, it suffices to say my strategy worked, and Dee Eze gave up trying to punish me. I believed he stopped because he thought his disciplinary method changed me for the worse. I was not scared of anything or anyone. He lost my complete regard for his corrective measures when I had the impression his judgment and sense of justice were not based on fact and fairness. He may have loved and respected me, but I could not see it through the fog of his rather rash retribution. I was glad he refrained from the murky mission of trying to make me more reasonable and responsible when it was completely unwarranted. As soon as I could, I wrote my mom a letter, and I told her I wanted to come back home. Unknown to me, our letters crossed in the mail because she had also written, asking that I return home, but for a different reason. I was not sure if she knew about my being spanked, and I never told her anything about it. My sweet "big sister" and her husband were not Catholics, and my mom was mainly concerned that I attended church services with them and never went to a Catholic church for Mass. Even though I was ready to return home to my family, I had to wait until I graduated from the seventh grade before I did so.

Before I left home to stay with Daa Meke and her family, my mom confided in me about her plan to complete our family house in the village. My dad and mom had bought three plots of land and started building the family house before my dad passed away. I remembered how happy my dad was when he showed me this purchased land for the first time. It was the third trip I made with him to the village to visit his brother and other friends. His brother's wives fed us like kings, and after the meal, my dad conversed with his brother while I played with my cousins. When we were ready to go my dad walked ahead of me through a small pathway paved by human feet. The brush and grass-blades on both sides of that trail were beginning to close in, making it almost impossible for me to see where I placed my feet. My dad suddenly stopped and pointed while saying. "That beacon over there is the first of five marking the plots." He took me to all five beacons and, to special vantage points as he opened a long folded house plan, and said with a delightful but measured sense of pride, "This is the plan of the family house your mom and I intend to build on this part of the land." The next time we visited the village, it was to supervise the job done by the builders. He died while the family house was still under construction.

When I arrived home from Lagos, my mom had a surprise waiting for me. She had completed the family house and had moved in with my siblings. There was also a registered parcel waiting for me from Dee Eze, which had arrived before I did. When I opened it, I thanked God that I neither hated nor harbored any grudges against him. During those difficult times when he tried to spank me, I had my suspicion that someone had given him malicious information about me that was not true. There was a girl who had been living with the family before I arrived who was Dee Eze's distant cousin. She would have been about seventeen years old and perhaps six years older than me. She was not as fortunate or as privileged as I was. She dropped out of school after the sixth grade and was trying to secure an alternative to a high school certificate. I was in a good school, received a moderate allowance, and I seemed to have it made, which may have provoked envy in her. Before I came to stay with the family, she had all the attention, and that privilege was partially pulled from under her with my arrival. I did not have any solid evidence that she bore any secret false witness against me. However, there were resentful comments she made, which were repeated by my "big brother". This made her look more like an accomplice and someone who was not completely innocent. When I opened the package from Dee Eze, I could not believe what I saw. He had bought for me a set of the math textbooks that I stayed in the library to use and thereafter got my first spanking from him. I would be able to use those books until ninth grade. He also sent a money order to cover the cost of my other textbooks and school fees. There was a short, sweet letter that came with my parcel, and it read something like this:

> Dear Udo, if you are reading this letter that means you arrived safely, and we thank God for your safe trip. We enjoyed the time you spent with us. At least, I know Obi, my son, did. If Daa Lucy will let us, we want to help with your school fees and books. I hope you like your textbook; I know you will need it. We already look forward to seeing you again, and soon.

The letter was written by Dee Eze and signed by him and Daa Meke. I could not have been happier. I replied to their letter the next day and thanked them from my heart. I expressed how much I enjoyed my visit and extended stay to attend secondary school. I also indicated my interest to see them soon. I never got to see my beloved Daa Meke again. She died during childbirth ten months after I left. Two months before she died, she sent me new clothes and shoes for Christmas. Dee Eze was devastated, and so was everyone who knew her. Daa Meke was first on the list among the sweetest, loveliest, most beautiful (women) relatives I knew and loved. I grieved for her and I am ashamed to admit more than I did for my dad. It did not help matters for the family when Dee Eze lost his job a few months after she died.

Even before I arrived home, my mom had already chosen the school I was to attend and made the arrangements. The name of the school was Government College, Umuahia. It was considered to be one of the best schools in the state. The school ranged from seventh to eleventh grade, and those made up the secondary school. There were also two classes for advanced diploma that were referred to as Lower Six and Upper Six. Only a few schools offered those programs. On my first day of school, I wore the school uniform from my former school, Trinity Secondary Technical School, Apapa, Lagos. That uniform consisted of a white shirt and a pair of white shorts.

My dad's nephew, Dee Lovet, a very influential man, somehow knew the principal, and after they met, I was called in to see him. When I entered the principal's office, I glanced around and saw for the first time in my life a large collection of gold and silver trophies. Some looked ancient, while some appeared modern; which suggests that some trophies were as old as the school. I always heard of how competitive that school was in academics, sports and debates, and there, before my very eyes, was visual evidence of a school that earned its bragging rights. The valued trophies, in the form of cups and plaques, were so prominently positioned in that office, that I had no doubt who ever put them there wanted them to be seen and perhaps relished the power they projected. The principal asked me a few question about my former school and looked at my seventh-grade examination scores. He seemed to have been impressed because he smiled and told me I had been admitted into that coveted school. Before we left his office, which spoke loudly of power and glory, the principal said with a very clear voice wrapped in authority, "Mr. Ogbuji, it is my pleasure to welcome you to the most prestigious school in the country." Even I thought he was stretching the school's good standing a little bit too far, but I was thankful and happy to become a student of that school nonetheless. As he addressed me, I had my hands together tucked at my back while I stood and listened as a sign of respect. I had something to tell the principal before I left his office and trembled at the thought of doing so, but I did anyway. "Thank you, sir." To which he replied, "Don't mention!" with a deep British accent.

Thus, my eighth grade was officially launched. The school's academic dean took me to the classroom and interrupted the religion class going on when we arrived. The students did not seem to mind as they were bored out of their minds but, rather, appreciated the diversion that made their day a little more interesting. The dean was quick with the introduction as he was a busy and no-nonsense man. The students stood up, clapped, cheered, and jeered as they welcomed me. In all the celebration and commotion, I overheard some pupils shouting, "White Shirt!" "White Shirt!" "White Shirt!" I thought they called me White Shirt because I was wearing a white shirt and a pair of white shorts. A boy named Victor, who sat beside me in class and later became my best friend, told me why some students called me White Shirt. Victor was pleasant to be around and, during recreation, clarified a few things about my new school with grace. He said, "The term *White Shirt* is a generic name for students who were not admitted into the school through the entrance exam set by the Secondary School Board." In other words, if your seventh grade was in another school—or your secondary school entrance-exam score was not high enough to be directly sent to Government College, Umuahia—you are called a White Shirt.

As terrible as that sounded, it was true at the time that a few selected schools determined what score qualified a student for admission, and for Government College, Umuahia, it was quite high. I was a White Shirt, which was more like a second-class student, and I had to live with it. I asked Victor if there were other names or phrases I needed to know. There were, and he was happy to go through them with me.

"You should know the school's motto, 'In Unum Luceant,' by heart and show it in your actions. This Latin phrase means 'May we shine as one.' From the day you are admitted into this school till the day you die," he said and stopped, looked at me like he was about to hand me a code to some secret divine knowledge, and continued in a most solemn tone, "You are an Umuahian!"

That is how students past and present refer to and introduced themselves since the school was founded in 1929 by Rev. Robert Fisher. I am not sure if the tradition started at the inception of the school, but that was what Victor told me.

There was a stranger I met in a shop in Umuahia City after my third year in the school. I was wearing my school uniform—a pair of khaki shorts and a pink shirt, which was probably how he identified me. He introduced himself and quickly added, "I am an Umuahian."

I smiled at him and asked, "What year, sir?"

To which he replied, "From 1970 to 1975. I am in a hurry but wanted to say hello to you. I am happy and proud whenever I have an opportunity to meet a fellow Umuahian."

The school had just resumed, and I had gone into the city to buy supplies. When I was ready to check out, the cashier told me my supplies had been paid for by the man who had just left. I could not believe it. That experience made me realize how strong the fraternity and brotherhood of Umuahianism was. When I asked the cashier if he knew the man who paid for my supplies, he said he did not. But he informed me he had overheard someone say the man I inquired about was a minister in the Nigerian federal government. I regretted the fact that I had no opportunity to thank him but vowed to be a true Umuahian, to be my brother's keeper with the hope that "we shine as one." Being our brother's keeper was one part of what the principal opined was the true Umuahian spirit since it helped us to realize our motto. He often advised, "Never shed the true Umuahian spirit. Always be kind to those you meet on your way up or your way down. Strive to leave this place, and wherever life takes you, better than you found it."

As the orientation progressed, Victor told me that the generic name for a freshman is Unyo and that the first Umuahian law was "Obey before you complain." He also let me in on the nickname the students called the principal. Victor was happy to announce, "His real last name is Nwaogu, which means 'warrior.' We shortened *warrior* to call him War. To keep the students from any rebellious activities, the principal got into the habit of including in almost every speech to the students 'Any disobedience from even the least among you is a declaration of war on this noble institution.' His frequent declaration-of-war allusions provided an added inspiration and choice of the name: War. We call him War secretly but also openly, depending on the occasion." Victor's explanation helped me understand many things about the school.

My third day in school was quite a drama. It had been raining for two days, and my mom insisted I go to school. I had wished for a day off, and it was not uncommon in my former school for the authorities to give us a day off when it rained. On that day, I grudgingly went to school despite the rain and later found out my mom had been right because I was spared of possible humiliation and punishment. I had spent my recess with Victor in the Assembly Hall because the rain would not quit. High on the walls of that huge and magnificent building hung many plaques. A closer look revealed that the names of previous Prefects and Captains of the school, and the years they were appointed were engraved on the plaques. Victor pointed at one of them and asked me, "Do you recognize that name?"

"Yes," I answered. The name was familiar; he was the state commissioner of Agriculture and Natural Resources.

"Most of those whose names are on these plaques are in public service and positions of authority in the government," Victor concluded.

I read each name with admiration and respect, and there were names of two renowned authors that caught my attention, Chinua Achebe and Elechi Amadi. Chinua Achebe was the author of the book *Things Fall Apart*, and Elechi Amadi wrote *The Concubine*. Both books were top on the list of books studied in English literature in secondary schools. I coveted those plaques and hoped that, someday, if I worked hard enough, a tablet with my name would hang on the wall of that Assembly Hall, too. That never happened because I did not rise to the level of academic excellence and great leadership that earned those students an indelible and honorable place in the annals of the school.

It was ironic that the Assembly Hall—a sacred space for prayer and a place that illustrates the past and possibly future glory of the school, as symbolized in the plaques—provided a platform the next day for spanking students who skipped school because it rained. The principal had a better strategy than punishing all the students who missed school on that rainy day; he set an example with just four students from Upper Six who were among those who stayed home. Perhaps he surmised that if he made scapegoats of those young men in the higher class, the rest of the students would learn from what they suffered. It also may have been that he expected them to show good judgment and leadership; to be models for us the younger students to emulate and, he punished them because they did not. Four of them were called up on the stage where the teachers and principal were. That summon was not one that marked the reception of an award for outstanding performance but one of humiliation and reprimand. It took place during morning assembly, which started with hymns and prayer and ended with announcements. The four culprits were called up to the stage after the announcements, prior to our proceeding to the classroom for studies. I felt for those young men as they stood before the students while the principal gave a ten-minute lecture on responsibility.

"Just assume the lives of people in the world depended on you or that the sustenance and excellence of this school were entrusted to your charge. How justified will you be, how will you grade yourself, if you never did your due diligence, or never carried out your duties and caused the destruction of many? How satisfied will you be if faced with the knowledge that your failure was as a result of you staying home because it rained? What you do at this moment as a student forms the foundation of what you will do when you go to live in the world and work to save it. I can only tolerate the best and responsible you. So, I give all of you a new commandment today: There is no provision for a rainy day!"

The entire student body had never been so quiet as the lone voice of the principal profoundly and clearly drove in the message. After his speech, the four students mounted a very long table one after the other and received twenty-four lashes each. Legend has it that they made a secret pact that they would not cry before the junior students. The last one among them could not bear the agonizing pain of *uta anu*, a special thin—but unbreakable—solid bamboo branch. That was the principal's choice of whip. He drove it mercilessly down the buttocks of the last young man. I counted twelve strokes before he started crying, and I was heartbroken for him. After the spanking, the principal walked toward the exit door, seemed to have forgotten something, stopped, turned around, and gazed intensely at us. We were still quiet and frightened. He had one last important message for us.

"And let me remind all of you," he warned in a calm voice of someone in control. "Don't you ever, ever break my new commandment!" He paused, stared at us some more, but this time, he was smiling and said, "You nonentities!" The principal spoke these two words very slowly and with authority that brought out the desired details he craved and maximized the effect he intended. At that point, all the students cheered with great excitement and chanted in unison, "War! War! War!" I chimed in with everyone else. We all went to our various classes happy, I guess, with the exception of those four students who had their buttocks bruised up. We were happy because, even though War punished us when we strayed and deserved it, he also knew how to make us laugh with his unmatched rhetorical skills and dry humor. We simply loved him and were afraid of him at the same time.

My academic performance was very poor that year, a little below average, and I could have been expelled but for the intervention of Dee Lovet, who had a few more effective cards he played on my behalf. Instead of being withdrawn, the academic dean recommended I be moved to ninth grade, on the condition that I improve on my academics. My grades did not get better by any standard. I flunked ninth grade. It was a bit of a surprise to me since I did put in many extra hours studying in the library. I did not have any strong distractions at that point in my life; at least, my interest in girls was not too great, nor was I interested in worldly things. I was still serving as an altar boy, and I hoped to become a priest. I did not have any friends whom I treasured more than my studies. I could not believe how poorly I had performed, nor could I make sense of it all because I had tried to do everything right. I later found out why I failed, and it was heartbreaking! A letter from the academic dean accompanying my deplorable result was even more devastating. The letter stated that due to the fact that I failed to meet the academic standard of the school, I was to be withdrawn. I did not want to bother Dee Lovet, who had saved the day before. For all I know, it would be unfair to ask him to pull more strings for me—if he had any left at all. I did not want to put my mom through the humiliation of facing the feared principal either since I was convinced he would not change his mind about my expulsion from the school. He believed students like me were muddying the scholarly waters and damaging the shining image of the school. I felt like a prodigal son when I had nothing to show for all the extra money my mom spent to keep me in that prestigious school. She could have spent far less money if I were in a local school. I had in mind the image of the lofty careers I would pursue after high school that ranged from being an aeronautic engineer, being an aircraft pilot, joining the Nigerian navy, or becoming a Catholic priest. I had put down those goals in my school's cumulative record, a chart that contained each student's information and statistics on different areas. I thought any one of them would be within reach, but with my removal from that fine school, I could no longer look forward to my dream career. If I could not make it there, then I could not make it in any other school.

With that new perception, I decided to scale down my ambition to a more realizable level, and on a particular night, I discussed my poor result and pending withdrawal from the school with my mom. I believed I could persuade her to let me quit school.

"Mom, I am planning to quit school altogether," I announced.

"And what do you intend to do?" she asked.

"I will learn a trade, which means you will spend less on me, and the money leftover can be spent on my siblings. It will also take me less time to learn a trade, and I can begin to make my own money and contribute to the financial well-being of the family."

I did not convince my mom. I had sought an easy way out and was somewhat happy with my proposal to skip school for good. Unknown to the school authorities, their recommendation of my expulsion would have favored or consolidated the old me who disliked school as I had indicated earlier (in Chapter Two).

Because my mom is a resilient woman and is able to read me like a book, she knew me well enough to know my intent and, therefore, was not ready to throw in the towel. She did as I feared and took the hard-line. "You are going back to school, back to that same school. I promised your dad I would do everything in my power to see you are educated." She was calm and confident. "Besides," she continued with a smile, "I don't want a bum beside my dying bed. That is certainly the worst way to die—my own failure, my son, staring me in the face with some small silly talks."

I laughed with her, and shortly before the discussion was over, my mom told me to be ready in the morning for a trip to the principal's office. That night, as I lay down in my bed, I reflected further on all we talked about. I secretly admired my mom for her toughness and the fact that she did not give up on me too quickly. In fact, part of me still wanted to go to school and believed I could still succeed, and my mom's encouragement appealed to that part of me. The reasoning that partly led to her continued belief in me was the fact that I had very good scores on some of my courses. She knew that things may not have been as hopeless as the school wanted her to think. There was nothing that should have kept me, she argued, from doing well on the other courses I failed unless there was something wrong. If anything was amiss, it could be made right if identified. Her resilience and surviving spirit, or what I call rare stubbornness, came in handy during times like that. I had heard stories told about her and witnessed that quality in her on many different occasions.

When my mom was about twelve years old, she visited a sick aunt in a small town named Umugbalo. The only source of water was a stream, which was at the bottom of a dangerous valley. There were sticks cut out from tree branches, about three inches in diameter and six feet long, staked to the ground on either side of the small trail that led to the stream. As the indigenes of that village went to fetch water, they held on to those wooden poles while they descended down the valley or climbed up the hill to avoid slipping and falling. The hill was not only very steep; it also had topsoil that was very muddy and slippery. There was not much room for error for anyone who went to that unsafe place. My mom learned that lesson the hard way on a particular day she had gone to the stream several times. Each time, she had an empty calabash with her as she ran down the valley and fetched fresh, clean water from a giant rock at the bottom of the valley. She then carried the whole weight of the water on her head and climbed up the hill on her way home. Things went well until her last trip, which ended tragically. Although going to that stream was a dangerous endeavor by all accounts, some kids, including my mom, who knew the trail well enough ran down so fast and climbed up so quickly, you would think it was an illusion. There were instances when villagers fell while descending or ascending the hill, but most of those falls were harmless. On that day, my mom was making her last trip when she fell down the valley, a fall which resulted in a life-threatening episode. Unfortunately, when she slipped, she fell on top of one of those wooden poles. That particular pole was shorter than the others; about two feet long, and had a sharp tip, which was hidden among the overgrown brush. It had been broken off and had never been replaced. The accident happened in the early afternoon when only a few people came to the stream, and there was not a soul around who could help. My mom pulled herself away from that sharp broken-off pole that pierced through her chest, and blood gushed out uncontrollably. She did what only a few people could do; she covered her open raw wound with the palm of her hand, which still bled and hurt, went down to the stream, fetched some water and went home. My mom thereby defied and overcame all the tall odds that she was faced with, even at that young age! To this day, she still has a large scar in the middle upper part of her chest as evidence of the horror she endured and survived.

I was thoroughly amused by my mom's joke about a son who became a disappointment staring her in the face as she breathes her last, but I also understood the painful message she wrapped in her humor and the cultural implications. The conventional wisdom at the time was that a boy raised by a single mom almost always turned out badly. That meant that if I turned out to be an abject failure, then that failure would be perceived as a reflection of my mom's incompetence in raising a boy. I would never agree with that assumption because, if anything, my mom worked very hard to make sure I turned out right. She put aside her own hopes and dreams in order to take care of me and my siblings. When my dad died, my mom was young and still very beautiful; she had many suitors but, refused to be married again because she wanted to devote the rest of her life to caring for us. Because of all she invested in our well-being, it would kill her to think she performed miserably in her responsibility or that she was unable to keep her promise to Dee Joe, her husband. She loved him so much that, even today, she still calls his name when she is overly excited about something good that happened to her or when she is in possible danger.

On a certain day, when I was about fifteen years old, I had gone with my mom to get rid of the weeds from her small farm. My mom was working on some tall grass at the time, trying to pull it out of the soil. She pulled it with more force than was required, lost her balance, and fell backward. My mom was sitting on the ground with some tall grass in her hand when I arrived at the scene. I knew she was in trouble when I overheard her shout "Dee Joe!" At the point, she probably lost control. When I was sure she was fine, I teased her with my mischievous jokes and comments.

"Mommy, when are you going to stop calling him, he's been dead for a hundred years. Besides, I've been taking care of you and cleaning the mess he left behind."

Finally, she could not take any more and broke out into a boisterous laughter. I laughed too as I stood close by. She laughed while trying to ask a question and choked in between each word, stifled by her uncontrollable laughter, but I made sense of it. She asked, "So he left me a mess, huh?"

To which I responded, "He did, indeed!"

We laughed louder and harder, and I had to sit down because I could not stand any more from being weary with laughter. I could sense my mom's chest was beginning to hurt as she sat and laughed because she rolled over and laid down on the dirty wet soil in order to breathe easier. She made another attempt to speak by asking, "And do you know you're the biggest mess he left behind?"

Saying I was the biggest mess my dad left behind was very true and funny. I laughed harder and louder and wished I could stop laughing but with no luck. When I could not keep myself from laughing—and it also became more painful to be in a sitting position—I lay down on the dirt with my mom. As our laughter began to fade a little bit, I responded, "Of course, I am." Then the laughter caught fire again, this time with the volume turned up. I pressed my chest with my two hands to put enough pressure so I could get more oxygen and not be smothered by my excessive laugher. I did not know how long we laughed, but I knew it had lasted long enough and that we should stop before someone got badly hurt. If I felt that much suffocation and helplessness, my mom, who was older, must have been feeling far worse. It was not easy to stop laughing, and the more I tried, the more daunting and close to impossible it became. I finally got it under control when I decided not to say another word, but I still laughed so as not to choke. As soon as I had enough energy, I stood up and moved away from my mom as far away as I could. Whenever she heard my laughter, she laughed even louder. As I got farther away from her, I listened for her laughter, and when I heard it, I continued to run away. When I could no longer hear her, I stopped running and, then sat down and rested. When I returned to her, she was still lying down on the dirty wet ground, with tears of joy rolling down her cheeks. She was very quiet and peaceful. I helped her up, and she said with recognizable sarcasm, "Don't ever do that again." This time, we only smiled.

As I was saying before I digressed, if I ended up a failure, my mom would have depleted her life savings on a venture that was not only disappointingly unrewarding but grievous for her as well. Unlike the Western world where there are nursing homes and assisted living homes, we do not have anything like that in my country. But we do have a system where the parents see their children through school from kindergarten to university. All costs are paid for by the parents, and often with their life savings. There would not be much left after they make that ultimate sacrifice, a sacrifice they make with the hope that their efforts will be credited with success. That success is rewarding not only because they did well in their duties as parents but also because their children would care for them in their old age. Parents who did not raise good kids often ended up vulnerable and miserable in their old age. That underscored part of the bitter message and reality hidden in my mom's humor about a prodigal son beside her deathbed, which would be the most agonizing thing for any parent to endure. Despite my mom's willingness and passion to help me be the best I could be, I wondered how she would handle things when we arrived in my school in the morning. It was bad enough that my school did not tolerate poor academic performance, add to it a principal who had no fear of man and worshipped absolute excellence like a religion. I therefore believed my case was beyond redemption and that even my tough mom would not have a chance. I could not help but think of how she was going to plead my cause before War and what his response would be. I reflected on those disheartening matters as I lay on my bed to sleep that night. I was suddenly scared for my mom because I did not wish for the humiliation that was all but certain to come. No student had ever been admitted back to the school after he failed. I was truly remorseful and sorry for the sustained suffering I put my mom, and everyone involved, through. Before I finally slept, I prayed for the visit to the principal's office and for a good outcome. I also promised God that I would work even harder as a student.

The ride to my school was fifteen minutes by public bus and, for the most part, was quiet. We arrived about nine in the morning. Though the school was not in session, the members on the staff congregated in the Administrative Building. The teachers all looked happy and without worries as they teased one another and laughed. Their laid-back attitude was a big contrast to the tension in the air when the school was in session. When the students were in school, the air was so dense with anxiety you could slice it with a knife. For a minute, my mind was taken off my troubles as I thought the teachers were doing just fine without the students in school and probably wished the holidays lasted a week or two longer. If in fact the teachers wanted extra days of holiday, then that may be something they shared in common with the students. As we approached the principal's office, I saw people already lined up in the waiting area. I saw some students with their parents, but none were from my class, which somewhat gave me a sense of privacy and relief. No one would know I was in trouble, and I was comforted by the thought that some of the students were there for the same purpose. I was not the only one that had performed badly.

When it was our turn to see the principal, my mom told me to wait while she spoke with the principal first. I did not know the reason behind my mom's decision to speak with him alone, neither did I ask. If anything, I was thankful I would not be the one before War or his line of fire. After about twenty minutes, my mom showed up with teary eyes, but something about that got me a little confused. She appeared slightly stressed but, at the same time, relieved. She motioned to me that it was time to go back home. I was afraid to ask her what happened. Nevertheless, I wanted to talk about anything she was interested in because the silence was torturous. She probably read my mind and volunteered to break the silence.

"When does school start?" she asked.

"School will resume in a week, Mom," I answered.

Then she hinted that in a few days, we would go and buy the supplies I needed for school. That was how I knew she had convinced the principal to reconsider the boldly written injunction on my report card, which read, "To be withdrawn." It took three years before my mom told me how she was able to change the mind of the principal to scrub my expulsion notice. She did not have to tell me; I knew meeting with fiery War for clemency on my behalf would be tough, and I vowed to justify my mom's thoughtfulness and sacrifice by making sure I had a quality education.

Keeping my pledge to justify my mom's efforts to have me educated did not come easy. It came through answered prayers; God sent a friend who helped to guide me to success. My mom enrolled me for extra tutoring with Lawrence Nwali, one of the lecturers at National Root Crop Research Institute, Umudike—an institution of higher learning close to my home. Brother Nwali, as we called him, held classes for junior and high school students like me who needed help with math and sciences. He was a very good man and deeply spiritual. He took me in from the very first day, and we became good friends. When he learned I was an altar boy, he encouraged me to switch over to his parish so I could serve at Mass and help him train the new boys he recruited. Other kids paid for him to tutor them, but because I helped him with the altar servers, he let me attend classes for free. He recommended the textbooks I needed for school. After a few months of attending classes, I found out that the physics and chemistry textbooks in the school library I used for my studies were obsolete, and the formulas that I got from them were no longer applicable. That, in fact, was the reason I had failed my exams in science subjects. From that point on, I enjoyed reading and excelled in my studies. The recognition I received from being one of the top students in class was an added bonus. Relishing the joy of success made me want to succeed more, and that led to more hard work.

That progress did not come without a few rough patches. During that time, I had lived almost like a prince. My mom sewed women's clothes, baked wedding cakes, and catered meals for her customers. She also took a course in house construction and obtained a license to build new houses and restore old ones as a contractor. Things were good, and I lacked nothing. My monthly allowance doubled, and all my school supplies were provided for me. I even got an upgrade on my school uniform. I no longer wore the basic dull-looking khaki shorts and cheap, overly pink shirt sold by the school. For shorts, I bought high-quality, custom-made, tight-fitting cream-colored Italian cotton. My choice of shirt was rich faded pink-colored cotton from India. There was a rule that students should only wear uniform supplied by the school, but the enforcement was weak.

Time was needed to enforce more important rules, and there were only a few boys who wore the custom-made clothes just to stretch the limits. I also discovered that when you excelled in academics, you got away with a few things in school. Fate, however, did not let me get away with my luxurious lifestyle for too long, perhaps for my own good. After the second term in tenth grade, my mom informed me that I would no longer stay in the dormitory, but go to school from home. She did not tell me the reason, and I did not mind. My home was three miles from school, and I did not like the food served in the cafeteria anyway. Besides, I would have a furnished room to myself, which was better than living in a large hall with many other students with absolutely no privacy. Furthermore, I was home twice a week to eat and to restock provisions. In fact, I realized my stay in the dormitory was a waste of money. Being a day student allowed me more freedom, which I would later abuse. Even as I went to school from home, I was not a poor student. Apart from my monthly allowance, my mom gave me money for riding the bus. Walking three miles under the hot sun was uncomfortable, and it left me hot and sweaty, to say the least. I rode the bus on those hot days, but when the weather was good and sometimes just for the fun of it, I walked all the way home with some of my friends who could not afford to pay for the bus. By doing that, I would make extra cash for the month, which partly explained the reason for my rebellious attitude when my mom made a unilateral decision to cut off my transportation allowance.

The next morning, I was still in bed when I should have been ready to leave for school. My mom accosted me and asked, "Are you taking a break from school today?"

I was so upset, I did not want to respond, but I did not want to appear disrespectful, so I said, "I have decided to quit school until my transportation allowance is restored in full. I am not walking all those miles to school."

My response touched a nerve in her, and she did not hold back her knockout punch, which came in the form of intense questioning and a blunt monologue. "Do you know you are a thoughtless blind bat?" She neither expected nor waited for any reply and proceeded with more questioning, like an experienced lawyer in a heated court cross-examination except, in this case, no answers were required or expected. "Do you assume I am unaware that some of your friends don't take the bus to school? Do you think that I do not have the audacity to ask you to walk to school like your friends do? How can you presume that I do not know the many times you skipped the bus and kept the money? The sweat on your shirt when you walked back home gave you away. The fact that I knew all that and still gave you money for transportation was my personal decision. I made a conscious pledge that if you improved on your tests, I would be a little more generous as long as I can afford it. If I gave to you willingly, wouldn't you have the common sense to know that I stopped because I could not afford it anymore? If that is how small your brain is, then I am not going to waste my money sending you to school, and you are very insightful to decide to stay home. I'm beginning to think that sending you to school is a waste of resources."

Her words felt like prickly jabs, and the atmosphere at home was very uncomfortable, so I knew I could not stay home. I was already late for school, but I got ready and went anyway.

That night after supper, my mom and I had a long, cordial, and revealing conversation, which enabled us to reconcile our differences. During our get-together, my mom frankly told me about the financial distress she was experiencing. Her sewing and bakery business were not doing so well because she was not getting enough new clients. Store-bought clothes were becoming more prevalent and were much cheaper, too. She had not taken any refresher courses on the current fashions or on the new styles in cake decoration for weddings. Also, during that time, fewer and fewer people were getting married because of the bad economy. All those things contributed to my mom having a sluggish business, dwindling income, and tighter budget. We did fine because her business of building new houses and restoring old ones flourished for a while. But all that changed when her contracts eventually dried up, too. She did not receive any new contract work because those who bid on the jobs with her would agree to give kickbacks of up to 30 percent and would inflate the cost, too. The misguided contractors and their corrupt counterparts who worked for the government agreed to those illegal practices even though it left some government facilities in shambles. Because of those scams, the projects were either abandoned or were poorly executed. My mom refused to engage in such fraudulent practices and stood by her work ethic of doing the best job possible with integrity and fair price. It was unfortunate and unfair that her honesty led to her losing the bids. My mom's financial means and options eventually shrank, which led to the declaration of a few more austerity measures. With that full revelation from my mom, I did not mind my transport allowance being among the other things that made it to the chopping block.

When I became aware of the ugly reality my family faced, I realized that I was in fact an ignorant "blind bat" to have failed to note my mom's financial difficulties and anguish. The most disheartening thing was not my lack of perception but the fact that I kept making my insensitive demands. I will never forget the pain and fear in mom's eyes as she related all the frustrations she was grappling with. She did not want to dwell on the negative, so she changed the topic. "I am very proud of you. You have exceeded all my expectations in school. I don't regret the humiliation of going to see your principal and all the drama that took place in his office."

Since we were in a lighter mood, and she wanted to talk about our visit to the principal's office, I pleaded, "Mom, when are you going to tell me what happened in the principal's office? I can see myself breaking one of his legs if he was ugly to you."

"On the contrary, he was very kind," my mom interjected.

I pressed her a little further. "If he was Mr. Nice, then why were your eyes teary when you came out of his office?"

"You!" she succinctly answered. We laughed harder at that point. When the laughter stopped, my mom told me what occurred: "I apologized for your poor academic performance and pleaded with Mr. Nwogu to give you a second chance. He accepted my apology but refused to let you come back. He told me he was not willing to go against the school's policy. I went close to his desk, knelt down, and told him that I am a widow who is wishing for a better future for my son and doing my best to fulfill a solemn promise I made to my husband before he died. I told him I promised my late husband I would see to it that his son got a quality education. I argued that if you could not do well in that renowned school, you could not make it anywhere else. I showed him your result. I pointed how well you did on the non-science subjects and pleaded with him to give you one more year while I put you through preparatory classes. I was crying hysterically at that point, and he asked me to quit crying before those waiting outside thought he was beating me up. I began to laugh because he had a great sense of humor. He said I should give him time to think about your case before he made a decision. I thanked him, but as I was leaving his office, he said, 'Mrs. Ogbuji, tell your son to come back to school, and he better not disappoint us again.' I could not believe what I heard. I walked back toward his desk and thanked him. When you refused to go to school this morning, all the humiliation I faced going to see your principal, the pain of the challenges I have battled with, and the frustrations I have encountered in my effort to keep the family in one piece burned inside of me. The fact that you eventually started doing well in school and the agony of watching you throw it all away was too much to bear. I am glad you changed your mind and went to school this morning. My dad died when I was a little girl. I never got to know him very well. My mom was so poor, she could not pay for my tuition, so my big brother paid it until I was in the fourth grade and could not afford it anymore. During those days, primary schools stopped at fifth grade, which was known as Standard Five. I told my teacher I would be quitting school after fourth grade. It was not my wish to quit because I wanted so much to finish primary school and take the certificate examination. My reason for telling her was to see if there was any way I could be helped, and what the teacher did surprised me. She asked the headmaster to let me take the final examination with the fifth graders. The headmaster agreed only after he saw my previous results. I did not give up on receiving an education despite our financial setbacks and other challenges. I took the examination and did better than some of the fifth graders. If I could do it, you could too. You know you have my support, so keep up the good work."

When my mom had finished speaking, I was even more remorseful of my conduct that morning but, at the same time, inspired by her story of overcoming impossible circumstances in her life.

I could not help but think, almost aloud, *She is good. She was able to hold her own even before War, the most feared man in the world.* I had even greater admiration for my mom. I was more determined not to be a disappointment to her, and I was resolute in my resolve to work harder and to excel in my endeavors. That night, a deeper bond was established between my mom and me. I also believed I was growing up too quickly in different ways, perhaps maturing much faster than kids my age.

CHAPTER 5

Coming of Age

Managing our energy and passion may be the best part and truest lesson of growing up.

—Father Udo Ogbuji

There are different signs that indicate a growing boy has come of age, and the most complex and prominent is that, for some unexplained reason, he begins to like girls more than he ever did before. He bears all the physiological and mental signs, the least of which is the urge to happily remove the sign on his door that reads "Girls not allowed except Mom!" The adults around him sense and see this transformation but often are reluctant to touch the subject, not even with a long pole. A young man going through those changes may have multiple questions and yearn for guidance but does not feel comfortable discussing them with adults sometimes. He occasionally may learn through his experiences, mistakes, and successes, in addition to some help from his peers who do not know any better but nonetheless are willing to share whatever small knowledge they have.

The above description summarizes my dilemma as a young man. My sentiments and reflection on the attitude of the adults on this matter evolved over time. Before I came of age, I was not very accommodating or compassionate toward adults, like my uncles, aunts, and cousins, who were not very discreet or who showed any form of human weakness in that area. At the early stage of my coming of age, it was disappointing to witness the lack of interest on the part of those who were older to give direction. As I progressed in my life's journey and grappled with the complexities of coming of age, my own struggles led me to a better understanding of the human condition in this regard. Humbled by my personal experience, which revealed to me a glimpse of part of what it means to be human, I began to treat the adults whom I thought were flawed and weak with greater respect, love, and compassion. It also occurred to me that since life was so complicated and the adults had their own issues to deal with, it was possible they did not have a clue on how to help me, which explained their seeming reluctance to lend a hand. Being in an all-boys school may have been rewarding in many ways, but it also presented certain challenges too. I will tell a story that is reflective of a typical all-boys school in this respect, and hopefully, that will help to clarify my point.

In the ninth grade, there were three blind students in my class, and one of them sat next to me. He was a very brilliant student, and we became close friends. I helped dictate lessons to him, which he put in Braille to enable him to study. He wrote his examination with a typewriter, and so did the other blind students. My friend had been blind from birth and did not even know what different colors were. There came a time when we had a new female English teacher. She was not physically attractive by my standard but was very nice and had a captivating voice. Her voice would make most men turn around to take a look. My blind friend could not see, but the pretty voice of that teacher got his attention. You could tell how overly excited he was; it was written all over his face and demeanor. As the class was going on and he could not bear it anymore, he leaned forward and asked me, "Is she beautiful?" I wanted to tell him the whole truth but did not; I thought it would be cruel to kill his joy because he really liked that teacher. I was happy that the new teacher was making his day, and it was delightful to see him so happy and engaged in class. So, I replied, "Yes, she can make heads turn." My friend understood my reply to imply the teacher was beautiful, which heightened his interest and he could not be held down. He continued to raise his hand, anxious to ask a question. When the teacher finally called on him to ask his question, he froze as he forgot what he was about to ask. This behavior was not just peculiar to my blind friend; it was widespread. There was perhaps a little bit of my blind friend in every one of us in the school; the majority of us got overly excited whenever a young girl who was not a teacher showed up in school. During those periods, some boys whistled and called out, perhaps to get the girl's attention or to pay her compliments. I guess the confinement and the fact of seeing boys most of the time turned every girl who showed up on our school property, even one that was not so fine, into a beauty queen.

Secondary school at the time ended in eleventh grade. If things worked to my advantage, I would have graduated at the age of seventeen, but I was not very lucky because I failed and had to repeat ninth grade. Repeating ninth grade was humiliating, but immensely rewarding nonetheless. I had neither the time nor the pleasure to get excited about the English teacher or any other girl. My books were the only treasures that captured my interest, especially after I met my older friend, Brother Nwali, who showed me how to study, what to study, and gave me extra tutoring. With my friend's help, my academic performance improved tremendously. Becoming one of the top students came with fame that was intoxicating. I was no longer ignored by the students or the teachers, which was redeeming. It also felt good to be among those chosen to go to science workshops and debates. The first time I was exposed to one of the seeming benefits associated with being famous in school was when I was among the five students from tenth grade chosen to go to a Geography debate. I had just turned seventeen, and the venue was in an all-girls school named Holy Rosary Girls Secondary School, Umuahia. After the debate—which we won, of course—I found out that there was something my school had in common with that school. We were treated like princes. The girls did not just stop at whistling and cheering like in my school, I actually received three suggestive notes with real names of girls who asked me to come back and visit. I believed the other boys did, too. I did not know what to do with the love notes nor did I want to know, because reading my books was addictive enough and was all that concerned me. Furthermore, it was not my wish to go back to those deplorable days in my academic life when I could not pass my exams and was almost nonexistent in the school. I destroyed those notes, but after a few months when my coming of age bloomed out of proportion, I regretted doing so. It is important to note that, although I paid no serious attention to the love notes, I believe they still created an awareness in me that crystallized in due time. When doing well in school was no longer a problem and I grew older, nature could not delay any more or exempt me from coming of age at different levels. I learned the lesson of the onslaught of human sexual attraction and its temperance the hard way.

As I improved on my studies, I made myself available to students who struggled and tried to help them out. My first cousin and her friend Ulumma, who were in tenth grade as I was, needed help in math and science. I helped them with their homework and had prep classes for them once a week. They were four years older than I was and should not have been in the same grade as me, but they started school late, had failed and repeated different grades, and were in one of the worst schools in the area. There were many basic things they did not know, which surprised me. They evidently needed lots of help, and my only intention was to help them. Two months into my new tutoring endeavor, my cousin's friend, Ulumma, began to ask me not just to teach her how to do her homework but to actually do it for her. She would also show up at my cousin's home and invite me over when no one was there. On such days, she would wear a miniskirt and blouse that modestly showed part of her chest. It could be that she never intended to start anything or that she invited me over for the sole purpose of the help she received. Furthermore, she may have been dressing the same way all the time but, I was only beginning to take notice. I would assume there was no plot on her part, if there were, I did not see it until I became part of it, in my naïveté and new found, overpowering feelings that rendered my brain inactive.

On a certain day, Ulumma had invited me over to help her with math, and after about an hour of tutoring, she announced she was thirsty and was going to get some soda to drink and asked me if I wanted some. I told her I did not want any. She got two bottles of Coke anyway and handed me one with a smile and the words, "The teacher can't teach this long without being thirsty." I thought that was really a lovely act, and I thanked her. I believed that on that day she was aware her skimpy skirt showed her pretty straight legs and all the fine curves from the back view, and she was not shy in showing them off. Ulumma probably knew that I may have been gazing at her as she went out of the room because she appeared to walk in a way that suggested that she was not about to tone anything down, but rather willing to milk every attention her sexy look elicited and was worth. I quietly and secretly admired her model-like walk, which I thought complemented her nicely shaped body. At that point, I was left with no choice but to like what I saw and want more! For a moment, and to my surprise, I enjoyed looking at her lustfully but was remorseful and embarrassed when she caught me in the act. I was even more baffled when Ulumma did not mind that I was coveting her sensual maneuver. In fact, she seemed to want me to and even seemed happy that I did so. When she turned, perhaps to make sure I was following her lead—and confirmed that I was—she smiled at me with sparkling eyes that seemed to flirtingly ask, "Do you like what you see?" I was glad we were done with teaching before those brief romantic fireworks because my brain felt nice and numb, like too much of a good feeling had flooded it too quickly. Of course, it did! I would not have been able to teach under such an overpowering circumstance. I was so shy and did not say a word about what had just happened or the tumultuous feeling inside of me. The fact was that I did not know what to say! My cousin returned and that, among other things, may have helped to save the day; briefly bringing me back to my senses.

I could not sleep that night, and the insomnia was not bad at all because my mind was too busy replaying the incident with Ulumma. I also thought about how clueless I was and how she seemed to just want me to say something, but I was tongue-tied and could not. She may have thought I was a timid nerd or, worse still, the most inexperienced young man she ever met, which may be true. As I lay in my bed, I thought of a plan on how to reassure and impress her. I would have to prove to her that I was up for the challenge, but how?

There was only one person who could help me solve that mystery fenced all around with exciting but puzzling bricks. His name was Eric, but I call him Erico. He was—and still is—one of my best friends. He had a way with girls; he knew everything about them, was not intimidated by them, and commanded their respect. Erico was far ahead of me and his own age when it came to relationships with girls, and somehow, I knew he was having romantic adventures. I never asked him because I was too busy with my studies, and he did not tell me, I guess, because it fits the profile of his being very protective of me. He wanted me to remain a good boy as did the girls in his circle. As an altar boy and a friend of Brother Nwali (who did nothing but pray all the time except when he was at work or teaching), I did not have, and was not exposed to, wild opportunities my friend probably had. When it was time for schoolwork and when my friends wanted to feel good, laugh, or needed advice on a plot or intellectual matters, they came to me. But when it was time to party, I was left out for obvious reasons. I am convinced I only reminded them of going to church and school and doing homework.

Erico protected me so much he would not even let me smoke a cigarette. There was a night I was tired of being a bookworm and believed I was watching my whole youth and life fly past me while buried in my boring books. I needed a little spice and fun out of life, so I asked my friend Erico to give me a cigarette, thinking that would bring me fulfillment. He intended to deny me the opportunity of having my first nicotine-high experience

and so said, "No, no, no, Udo!" And without waiting for me
to ask why, he offered the reason for saying no to me: "This
is a very bad habit, and once you start smoking, it is difficult
to stop. Please promise me you won't start smoking." I did not
promise him anything but, on the contrary, actually bought
a pack of cheap cigarettes named Target from the store as I
returned home and smoked half of the pack that night. I never
got rewarded with the compensating buzz I always heard of;
the only reward I received was clogged lungs and a very bad
headache. That night my head pounded like there were some
tiny creatures having a loud party in it. Perhaps the excessive
smoke I inhaled was the tiny creatures, and my agony that night
made me wonder why anyone would want to smoke a cigarette.
My mom was horrified the next morning to see the mountain
of cigarette ashes and butts outside my window. "Who smoked
these cigarettes?" she asked.

"My friend visited last night," I responded.

She said nothing else, which made me very uncomfortable.
She knew I was evading her question; she knew I was guilty. My
mom disliked the smell of cigarettes and never failed to show
her disapproval for men who smoked (although very few women
smoked those days, it was unheard of). Faced with the reality of
a son who just turned into a smoker, she was speechless. She was
probably taking a page from an Igbo proverb which says that
"A child should not be spanked on a day he spilled the palm
oil but the day he spilled the leftover dirty residue." Palm oil is
very costly and takes a lot of work to process. Spilling it is the
worst thing you can do. On the other hand, the leftover residue
is useless and is thrown away anyway. The moral of this wise
saying is that when a child does something terrible for which he
deserves to be punished, he may already feel bad and contrite
and, that would be somewhat enough chastisement. When a
child is disciplined for something far less grievous after a series
of serious offenses that were forgiven, he/she is usually aware
of the previous clemency and knows that the punishment was
appropriate and learns. It is also true that the awareness of those

moments of grace and mercy, should lead a child to a change of heart. If it does, that justifies the power of love and pardon received. But if not, it gives credence to the disciplinary measure that would be applied if he/she faltered again, even in very small things. Furthermore, it puts the burden of responsibility on the child who is to be blamed for misbehaving after many chances of reform were offered. On the part of the parents, it teaches them patience, temperance, fortitude, compassion, and love in dealing with a child. After I spilled the palm oil by smoking cigarettes, I was forgiven, but I did not learn my lesson and behave; I eventually spilled the leftover dirty residue, and my mom did not spare me.

I knew my friend Erico loved me and shielded me because he did not want me to run wild with him. However, I made it clear that I was old enough to make my own decisions on what to do and when to do it. After he understood I wanted to be a grown young man, he was moved to help and made a confession. His confession was that he had the impression that all I wanted to do was read my books and go to church. He then agreed to let me go to the next disco party with him. I had clothes I was going to wear to the party, but the two pairs of shoes I owned had holes in their soles. I had been so preoccupied with my studies that having good shoes were the least of my worries. Besides, when the wear and tear on the shoes started showing, I could not afford new ones because my mom had begun to face decline in her business ventures. To survive as a family during those inopportune times, each one of us had to sacrifice little luxuries so that we could afford the basic necessities while making provisions for the future. I was not going to miss the first opportunity to go to a disco party to dance, nor did I intend to wear shoes with holes in them, not when I was planning to impress the girls. I had never looked dull or shabby because my mom always bought me the best and durable outfits, and I was not planning to settle for something cheap. I believed Erico had a solution because he was a rich young man and always had many nice things and spare to share. He gave me one pair of his shoes and told me I could keep them. The shoes were fairly new but were hungry for some polish. Just one look at them told me they had never been polished and that they may have been scratched up from too much twisting on the dance floor. The color of shoe polish they needed was an off-brown color, which we could not find in the stores. If I wore those shoes in the condition they were, the disco hall bouncer would have mistaken me for a homeless young man and not let me in. And if Erico helped get me into the club despite my shoes, I would have been a joke for the boys and girls, and that would have killed me. My friend had other neat shoes he was willing to let me borrow, but they were not my size. Since the unkempt shoes were my only option, and I was bent on going to the party, I had to get to work. I became a little more creative and made my own shoe polish almost exactly the same color as the shoes. After I fed those hungry, scratchy-looking leathers with my rich blend, my friend could not believe his eyes. He gave me a bear hug, saying, "Udo, how did you do that?" Not waiting for an answer, he continued, "You've got some good talents, man!"

"No, I don't," I said, protesting and trying to be modest. "I only tried to make my Chemistry come alive." I misspoke, I meant to say, "I only tried to make the Chemistry I learned in class come alive."

Erico latched onto my gaffe and joked, "Do whatever you want but, don't make your chemistry come alive in the dance hall tonight, or you'll have all the girls following you home."

We were both laughing so hard and in the midst of our laughter, I said, "In case I do, and in the event of a resulting stampede, I will trust you to watch my back since you're the designated chic magnet."

Making shoe polish was one of the things I learned when we had gone on a two-day science show and workshop. I was lucky to be one of the fortunate chemistry students selected to go. I liked shiny well-polished shoes, so it was easy to have the shoe polish-making ingredients and procedure on the tip of my fingers as we learned during the chemistry exhibition. You only need to cook a certain proportion of candle wax in the pot until it melts, add kerosene—about one-seventh of the quantity of the candle wax—and then enough black ashes to change the color. You can add more ashes if you want a denser color. Stir and turn off the heat to let it cool, and you have your black shoe polish. The creativity on my part would be to find the dust or ashes with the exact color I needed or mix available colors to match the shoe color. I then went on a hunt for small colored stones in a wooded area of my village where there were plenty of them. I found ones that were orange and dark brown in color, and when I crushed them separately into dust and mixed a certain amount of each, I had almost the exact off-brown color I wanted for the borrowed shoes. The shoes looked so good my friend withdrew the offer of letting me have them.

The dance was good; I had fun, and no girl followed me home. Getting the shoes to look good was worth every drop of my sweat and effort. I was happy to give them back to Erico in addition to the unique polish I made because I knew that was the best pair of shoes he had before they got a terrible beating.

After my friend, Erico, began to understand me better and we bonded more, I felt at ease to approach him with the riddle about Ulumma. It was not difficult to tell him about my encounter with her because I knew he would be respectful of my secret feelings and keep it to himself. I also thought he was an expert on girls and knew so much about them, which meant that I would get the best advice. When I told him about Ulumma, he was not shocked, which surprised me. He also did not chastise or tell me I was a clueless nerd, which endeared him more to me. He only asked me, "Is she beautiful?" I wanted to say yes, but I refrained from doing so because, it was not my place to say who was beautiful or not. Moreover, I knew that he did not specify which aspect of beauty he meant. Beauty in humans can be put in three categories—namely, beauty of the body, soul, and spirit. Lastly, I did not want to appear to be bragging, so I did not tell him the truth that Ulumma was beautiful in every way. As I kept quiet, Erico probably realized that his question may be unnecessary or that I was not going to answer it, so he asked the next one. "Do you like her?"

"I think I do," I responded.

He then instructed, "The next time you see her, tell her you like her."

That evening, I saw Ulumma, but I did not tell her what I had in mind because my cousin was there. I was so nervous even before I left my home that evening, which made me doubt that I would have told her my inner feelings even if we were alone. Since my nerves were working against me, I decided to write her a letter. That became my very first love letter. A love letter I would later regret writing. The following week, I went to teach my cousin and Ulumma, and in one of my pants' pocket, safely tucked in, was a fancy pink envelope. In that envelope was a card that read, "You are very caring, and I like you." I also enclosed a short letter I had written to her. There was no private moment, so I asked to see Ulumma for something important. Another move I would regret making. She came with me outside, and I handed her an envelope. "That's for you," I said, and since it was night and dark, I could not read the expression on her face.

Two weeks went by without my seeing Ulumma or getting a reply from her. I became apprehensive after my sister informed me my cousin came to visit and asked to see my mom in private. The details of that visit remained a secret. On the first and second day I waited for Ulumma's response, I was optimistic. I was sure she liked me because I had seen it in her inviting and flirtatious eyes and also the way she moved whenever I was around. I told myself to be patient and wait, and that things would work to my advantage. By the third day, my hope for any reply, even an unfavorable one, had faded. It was utterly humiliating to accept that I may have been wrong in thinking that the feeling was mutual. I felt crushed when I wondered and realized that the hand of friendship I extended to Ulumma may have been rejected. Being turned down would have been a better gift than the events that unfolded.

I was awakened by a moderate knock on my door at three thirty in the morning. It was my mom. Instantly, I knew I was about to be summoned to explain a serious misbehavior of mine and to receive a corresponding reprimand. That kind of summit was set aside for the times when my blunder was severe or when my bad behaviors had accumulated to a dangerous degree. The last time I was dragged through such an uncomfortable and highest level of meeting was when I was named among those who punished a stubborn junior student in school. He was brought into the dormitory of the senior students for the offense of disobedience. Any noncompliant attitude to one of the senior students was considered an insult to all. About five senior students took turns in punishing that disobedient student before he became submissive. His dad, who was a wealthy and very influential man, threatened to take reprisals on behalf of his son. He probably told the principal he would withhold his financial contributions to the school until we were all brought to justice. Although disciplinary measures directed toward the junior students were part of the school's culture and accepted at the time, we got into trouble. I would admit, though, that our punishment of that junior student was more severe than normal because he would not give in, and we were not going to accept defeat. Defeat had consequences; the respect and fear that seniority commanded since the foundation of the school would die a miserable death on our watch. That was not a precedent we were ready to embrace. All of us in the dormitory were each given a letter for our parents. We were suspended until our parents met with the principal and the school disciplinary committee. The next morning, after that awkward meeting my mom had at my school, she woke me up in the early hours of the morning to have that dreaded conference with her. That early morning strategy was always effective. At each episode, I felt trapped, and after it was over, I was docile, sensible, cooperative, and on my best behavior.

That morning, when my mom woke me up, I was unaware of what I had done. I had forgotten my cousin's visit the day before and my love letter to Ulumma. My love letter was now in my mom's hand as she sat down to address me. I had been so sleepy at first to notice what she had in her hand. But as soon as my dull brain finally processed the situation, my heart sank, and I was wide awake. I suddenly became privy to what my cousin's private visit with my mom was all about. I began to ask myself questions: What really happened? Why did Ulumma not give the letter to my mom herself? What happened and, how the letter got to mom was not my biggest problem; facing and dealing with my mom on that matter was. It was a mammoth one, indeed! I could not look her in the eyes out of shame. All the humiliation I had faced in all my life until that moment put together paled in comparison. Although I was looking down, I could tell she was opening the envelope, because the living room was so quiet that I could hear the ruffling noise of the paper. I started a silent prayer and asked God to stop her from reading that love letter back to me. It was bad enough to see it in her hands, to hear her read it aloud would simply kill me. She seemed to know what I was thinking and was not in a hurry to stop the torture. It was her intention to use the moment to her advantage, to the very last minute. Finally, after an intended, prolonged, agonizing interval, she spoke up and asked, "You wrote this?" as she waved the letter in the air. The answer was obvious as she knew my handwriting, and I had signed my name. Even though the question may have been an attempt to mock me, I answered with a nod of my head and hoped my docility and cooperation would speed up the occasion so that the agony would not last a second longer. "You said in this letter that you will take care of her and give her whatever she wants. You can't even afford to buy your own underwear without my help." Her words were so painful, my brain felt heavy, but I was relieved to observe she already read the letter and possibly would not read it to me. Just when I thought there would be no more punches, she landed the last deadly blow; she went for the kill, and inflicted on me an imaginary concussion that would last for months. "I'm going to give this letter to my brother, Elijah, and

I believe he might have a few words of advice for you after he reads it." she said as she threateningly waved the letter again in the air. The weight of that threat was heavier and more lethal than the rest of what I already faced combined. My mom was certainly saving the worst for the last. Most of my holidays were spent at my uncle's. I called him Dee Elijah; he is my mom's little brother, and he loved me very much, like I was his own son. If he read my love letter to Ulumma, I had no doubt that his high regard for me would evaporate.

Following my mom's threat, I avoided going to my maternal home and never saw my uncle for months. I, however, ran into him after six months when I went to Mass. I was surprised he smiled at me and gave me a bear hug while saying, "Udo, my son, you haven't come to see your favorite uncle. I hope you come and see me soon. I'll have Fresh waiting." Fresh is a nickname for unadulterated palm wine, which is as pure and as best as you can get it. He had a faithful supplier and knew I liked it, so I promised him I would visit soon. Since he was so kind to me, I thought that either my mom did not give him the letter or that he had forgotten about it. He said he would have Fresh waiting. Was the promise of Fresh a ploy to lure me to his house? No, my uncle is without guile and much too laid-back. He probably read the letter and thought I was only being a boy.

My friends and I always enjoyed going to my uncle's house because he was so funny and taught us so much about life. That he had a constant flow of Fresh, I have to admit, was an added attraction for my friends and me. On one occasion we went to visit him, my friends and I had been drinking, talking, and laughing loudly. We could not help but notice that while we were drinking and having fun, there were some ants that had been working very hard. They were so disciplined; they picked their food and sent it to their nests. Sometimes, the food was six times bigger than the ant; in that case, there was a team effort of eight ants or more hauling it to its destination. I personally thought the discipline, dedication, and teamwork of the ants were brilliant and worthy of emulation. But under the stupor we were, my friends and I thought and did something silly. We determined that the ants had worked hard all day and deserved to have a little fun, like us. So we poured some of the sweet wine on their route. They happily accepted our kind offer, took some break, and started taking a sip. We noticed that before long, there was no more order among them; most of them were drunk. They ran all over the place and could not find their food or nest anymore, nor were they in the mood to work. The soldier precision with which they walked was replaced by a sluggish, staggering walk, and some of them seemed to be dancing. We laughed and laughed so hard and loud. We could not believe what we were witnessing: that the wine made the ants joyful too, but it also impaired and inhibited their productivity and work ethic—perhaps what it does to humans, too.

On the day I went to see Dee Elijah, I prayed and hoped my uncle would not bring up the issue about my famous letter to Ulumma. He first brought Fresh, which I was thankful for. The offering and drinking of that local wine was a ritual that started off our camaraderie whenever I visited his home. But on that day, I needed that opening rite much more than ever to help calm my nerves. As I approached his house, I was so nervous and jumpy, not knowing if I was walking into a trap or if I was going to get a slap on the wrist for my misbehavior. My uncle was very happy to see me and was as pleasant as could be. Despite his good cheer, I was still a little apprehensive, but as I started drinking Fresh, my misgivings disappeared. We talked about everything fun and it was a great joy to visit with him, for many good reasons among which included my peace of mind. When I was ready to head home, Dee Elijah hugged my neck and squeezed my shoulder, saying, "You've really grown into a handsome young man, my boy." That was a great compliment. He then asked, "You have a girlfriend now?"

My heart skipped because I thought almost aloud, *Here comes my moment of reckoning. He certainly knows of that letter. I'm about to be chastised.* When I looked up to confirm my assumption, my uncle was smiling at me, which was very reassuring. I tried to smile back, but I think I grinned while I answered, "No, Dee Elijah, I don't have any girlfriend."

"And when you do, make sure she is a good one," he advised.

"I'll bring her to show you for approval," I managed to joke, and we both laughed.

As I left my uncle's house, I had the impression he was unaware of my love letter, and even if he knew about it, he may have thought I was only being a boy who had come of age. I loved and respected him more for his understanding and felt I could confide in him in matters that were of concern to me.

Ulumma, as I later found out, read the letter I had written to her and liked it. It was not her idea or intention to give the letter to my mom. She learned about my mom being in possession of her letter after my cousin's conspiratorial visit. My self-righteous cousin found the letter in Ulumma's textbook she borrowed, read it, and decided my mom ought to read it, too. The resulting embarrassment of my first love letter being made public made me stay away from partying and from girls. Going to church and reading my books became my only hobby once again. I read all my textbooks from cover to cover, and when I became bored with textbooks, I read novels. I was content and found solace in my isolation, but my friends were worried about me, and my mom did not know what to make of my new behavior. By the end of first term in the eleventh and final grade before university education, I had completely read through all my textbooks. I, however, needed to read them through one more time to be ready for a major West African School Certificate Examination that would qualify me for higher learning.

Because my mom's business was still not going well, she relied on small-scale peasant farming to sustain the family. I helped as best as I could; at least, I cleared the brush on the farming area, tilled the soil, and made small mounds for planting the crops. The major crops we planted were cassava, yam, and corn. The planting of these crops and removal of weeds from the farm were done by the girls. I also helped in harvesting the ripe crops. It was much easier to team up with two of my friends to do the hard labor of clearing the brush and tilling the soil. We took turns working as a team for our different families until the work was done. Working was fun when I had my friends to pick on, when we told stories and sang songs as we worked. Whichever family we worked for fed us well. All those benefits were incentives my friends and I could have missed if we worked by ourselves for each of our families.

As secondary school was beginning to come to an end, the pressure of the final examination was building up faster, and I felt the need to read more. I knew I had to ferociously read my books to make the best grades. But that meant not helping more with house chores and farm work. I mentioned to my mom my concerns and suggested to be exonerated from chores and farm work until after the final examination, but my mom would not grant my request. At that time, we had a guardian and counselor for students in school whom we called Mrs. Anya. She was the students' advocate whenever a student had issues with the teachers, other students, or family members, and would advise the student on how best to proceed. When my mom failed to see my predicament, I approached Mrs. Anya to talk it over. She was impressed with my determination to have a good result and thought my concerns about not having enough time to study for my examination was legitimate. I pleaded with her to accompany me to my home and talk to my mom. She did not have any problem convincing my mom.

I had only about four months before my final examination, and I read fiercely. My mom was kind to let me study without interruption—that was what I thought until the morning she said, "Udo, I have changed my mind about you not helping with chores and farm work."

I could not believe my mom said those words to me, much less meant them. So I asked her, "Mom, what about my examination? What about your word to Mrs. Anya?" I could not comprehend what was going on in my mom's mind. Obviously she needed help, and I would gladly help but only on a case-to-case basis and not to the point where it would affect my studies. I hoped my mom did not think I was lazy or that I did not care for her or my siblings. I was not slothful. I worked hard by myself and with my friends when we teamed up to work for our families. Care for my mom and siblings had been my life's mission since my dad passed on. That mission was the reason I studied so hard in the first place. I knew that a good education was the best way to help keep my family afloat on the troubled waters we found ourselves. I loved my siblings and tried to be a father figure and even improvised sometimes to make sure they did not go hungry.

I remember a day when we got back from school and there was no lunch prepared. My mom normally had some food ready. But there was none either because she had to leave in a hurry to run errands or there was nothing to cook. I was lucky to get some special yams, *Adu*, from my mom's old garden area. That particular area of her garden was not cultivated that year and had brush and shrubs, which would make it fertile for the next planting season. The local yams were growing wild in that place, and I was lucky to spot them. It appeared to be a crop missed during harvest season that had grown back.

I picked the yams and spent two hours cooking them. Apart from cooking the yams, I separately cooked the sauce to go with it. To prepare the sauce, a half cup of olive oil is cooked in a pot until it is hot, chopped onions and a little salt are added and stirred for thirty seconds. Half a gallon of ground tomatoes and peppers, precooked meat or fish, and seasoning, like Maggi cubes, are added; and the whole cooking ingredients are stirred. After it boils for twenty minutes, you can add a spice, like basil, stir some more, and let it cook for thirty seconds; and it will be ready to be served with rice or yam.

At that time, meat or fish were luxuries we could not afford; however, the onions smelled so delicious after it cooked in the hot oil that we could not wait to eat. The local yam I intended to cook was edible and sweet, but there was a species of this yam that grew wild and had the same exact appearance. The one that grew wild could be safe to eat but it was as bitter as quinine. The only way you could tell the difference between the two kinds of yam was from the taste. I presumed what I was cooking was the good type because it was a perennial crop and was at the spot where my mom gardened a year before. The moment of revelation came when I took a big bite, and it was the wild and bitter kind. We went hungry until my mom came back, and we were lucky she had gone to get some groceries.

If my mom thought I was lazy or did not care, she still had a lot to learn about me. She believed she was justified in her insistence that I should help out with house chores and farm work. On the other hand, I was convinced my intention to devote my time to studying for my examination without interruption was the right thing to do. I decided we would have plenty of time in the future to determine who was right, but at the moment, I told myself, *I must do what I think is right.* I had been a good boy and had not disobeyed my mom since my father died. It weighed heavily on my heart that I was about to do so. I did not want to be obstinate to my mom, but obeying her would produce a devastating result. My future was somewhat in my hands and depended partly on my final examination. As my mom and I agreed to disagree, she gave her final word on the matter: "I hope you have enough books stored away because that will be your meal for as long as you refuse to do any chores in this house."

That was not an empty threat; I had been through that once as a little boy when my dad saved the day. Starvation was a rare corrective whip she used when there was repetition of a bad deed or I did something grave. Having experienced hunger for the first time, almost to the point of being famished, I knew there was no way I could study under that circumstance. If I let my mom follow through with her threat, my intention to read would be sabotaged. So I took the spare key to the pantry so I would have access to food. Just as I had anticipated, I was barred from eating and locked out from the pantry. But since I had kept the spare key, I had a secret free access to food. After a few days of living in that tense environment, with the air so stuffy it felt like every freshening element of love had been choked off, I could not study and decided to move away from home.

When I left home, I stayed with one of my friends, Steve, who was in one of the local schools around my home. He lived in a room he shared with a friend of his. They were very kind to invite me to move in with them. The problem was that that school was a good place to be only if you were a student refugee like I was. It was a mixed school with girls and boys, and most of the students did not care at all about studying. Unlike my school, which was located in the middle of nowhere and had no single dancing club within the vicinity; that school had many clubs camped around. The students patronized those clubs and had plenty of parties. While the dancing-club business boomed, the academic performance of the school declined. Their academic standard was so abysmal an average student in my school would be a genius in that school. Some students wanted me to help them with their examination, but not in the way you would think. I would have been willing to tutor those who wanted to learn, but they believed that since I was from a notable school with rich kids, I would somehow be in possession of leaked questions for the final examinations. I, however, made it clear to them that if I knew what the questions were, I would not be working so hard to read through my textbooks all over again.

It takes personal conviction and determination to be an industrious student. It is also true that the fine qualities of hard work sometimes slowly erode when the students surrounding you are so laid-back, partying most of the time and thinking you are a lunatic because you are studying all the time. I was tempted beyond what a student from a boring all-boys school—and one who was a nerd—could withstand. The feeling of being deprived and of wasting my youth set in again. I ditched my books and joined the fun partying crowd. It was in one of such dancing clubs that I met Ulumma for the first time since the love letter saga. I had forgotten that she was a student in that school. Tired of dancing, I sat down with my buddies and was drinking beer when I spotted Ulumma, whom I assumed had just arrived. She went to the dance floor and danced really well. She was provocatively dressed, as usual, and I suddenly had a surge of feeling that rushed through me, not one of attraction at that point, but to find out why she connived with my cousin to humiliate me. I had grown more mature since the incident and knew I had to play cool or risk being beaten down again. The DJ started playing a slow song, and Ulumma did not like it, so she went and sat down at a table forty feet away from me. I glanced in her direction and hoped not to give myself away. She was still very attractive, in fact, seductive. Her table was at a corner, but I could still see it from my sitting position. She sat beside a guy and two other girls I did not recognize. I could not help but think, *That guy could be me.* But I had to beat that out of myself; no need to fantasize about someone who toyed with my dignity. After a few futile glances toward her direction, I gave up. A dancing club around her school would be the last place she would have expected to see me, and it was not clear whether or not my presence would ruin her night. As much as I tried to convince myself to be calm and cautious, it felt like my thoughts were too loud inside of me. The Guinness beer did not taste good anymore. Even my friends noticed, and one of them asked me, "Udo, are you okay?"

"Yes, I am, why?" I retorted.

"You suddenly became awfully quiet," my friend noted, and he was right. While he inquired after my well being, the other friend was busy smoking St. Moritz, our favorite cigarette. Halfway blowing out some smoke, he joked, "I think the reading boy is lonely. I have to get him a cute girl to dance with." They both laughed. What my friend said was funny, but I was too confounded to find any humor in his mocking offer.

While it felt like nothing was of interest except what preoccupied my mind, I requested for a cigarette, which I hoped would help to clear my thought. When I finished smoking, I announced, "I'm going to the floor to dance, who wants to join? No girls."

As I went to dance, I avoided looking at Ulumma or the direction of her table. I danced like I was the only one there. I had so much fun I forgot the reason I went to dance. After we returned to the table to resume drinking, I switched seats with one of my friends and had my back to Ulumma's direction. As I drank my beer, I strongly felt someone was looking at me. I somewhat expected she would see me dancing, and the reason I changed my sitting position was to avoid making eye contact with her. I believed there was a chance she would approach my table, and she did. As I felt her eyes on me, I almost turned to confirm my assumption and feeling. I thanked heaven that I did not. After a few seconds, I looked up at my two friends, and their eyes had sparkles while their faces were transfixed toward her direction. They had the kind of look on their faces only a pretty girl can make possible—I had been in an all-boys school long enough to know. One of my friends, at that instant, suddenly swallowed something—perhaps his saliva—to soothe his dry throat. I knew it was not a sip of his beer because he had momentarily forgotten about it. As I looked at the other friend, his eyes seemed bigger, and his jaw dropped. I could tell my two friends were in a deep spell, and only Ulumma could do that to young men; I knew from my own experience. Right then, I knew she was coming to my table. I had to be mature and clever in my reaction. I felt a gentle tap on my shoulder, and a soft alluring voice I recognized sweetly asked, "Will you dance with me?"

Before I could answer, one of my friends came to my defense, maybe because he thought I was not thrilled with the offer, and said, "He doesn't like dancing with girls."

"I'll dance with her," I offered. I did not want Ulumma to feel embarrassed, not after she kindly requested to dance with me.

As we left to dance, I said in an attempt of self-deprecation or to lower the expectations, "You know I don't know how to dance."

"You're a liar, I just saw you dancing," she replied, smiling.

"I'm going to try to dance well, but don't tell my mom," I said, trying to be funny, but the look on her face told me she was not amused.

"There are things I have been hoping to tell you since you wrote me that letter."

"Why don't we talk first and then we dance?" I suggested.

We talked almost all night. She told me she quarreled with my cousin for giving that letter to my mom and thought the letter was a piece of delight. "I read your letter many times because I enjoyed it very much. You're the first person that ever wrote me a love note, and you won my heart over by that lovely act. I actually started writing you a reply that very night you gave me the letter. Did you know I carried your letter with me wherever I went and preferred to read it instead of my books? That was how it ended up in one of my textbooks your cousin borrowed. I forgot which textbook I had put the letter and looked for it for days before your cousin told me she saw it and gave it to your mom. I was crushed because I thought she was my friend, and she betrayed me and also sabotaged us."

It was a great relief to finally hear the true story of what happened and comforting to know things were not as bad as I thought. Under those circumstances, it was much easier to make a joke. "My mom didn't think that letter was a good one. She was jealous and, I can see why: you wanted to steal her boy from her."

She laughed, thinking it was very funny.

I then continued, "Did you think I could take care of you as I said in my letter?"

"You could in the future and, I felt flattered reading it."

I did not tell Ulumma how much trouble I got into for the sake of that letter and how many sleepless nights it caused me. I did not think there was any need for those details; they would upset her some more. However, she apologized for the way things turned out.

"Would you dance with me now?" I asked, and without waiting for an answer added, "I hate to have to apologize for not keeping my promise—to dance after we talked."

That was the last time I saw her because final examination started two days after that reunion.

I cannot conclude Ulumma's story without saying what happened to my first and only letter to her. It had been five years since the uncomfortable incident concerning the letter. I needed my original high school results to prove the authenticity of the photocopies I had submitted to the seminary. There were two days left before the seminary resumed after a long holiday and I had to get my things ready. My mom normally kept our documents in a safe place. When I asked my mom for my original high school certificate, she pointed to the file cabinet she kept the family records in. I had been looking for what looked like a scroll before my eyes caught a fancy pink envelope that looked familiar. That envelope was, in fact, the one that enclosed Ulumma's letter. The letter and card were still inside of it, and I called out and asked, "Mom, so you didn't give Dee Elijah this letter?"

She started laughing; my siblings and I joined in the laughter. I read the letter to everyone's hearing and retold the story of how much I was tortured for playing Romeo. We all laughed, laughed, and laughed. After a protracted amusement and laughter, my mom then filled in the missing part of the story.

"I did not give that letter to my brother as I had threatened," she said. "However, I told him that you wrote a letter to a girl and asked him to advise you."

I had even greater love and respect for my mom, who did her best to save me from further shame and humiliation. It is strange how laughable embarrassing things and events become after many years have passed and after we have grown up.

To say that I did not study my books when I moved to stay with my friends after I quarreled with my mom would be an understatement. The environment was anti-study at different levels. As I said before, many of the students did not care about being educated, and there were ample opportunities for partying. I quickly forgot about my examination and books and partied as hard as I could. After the examination was over,

I returned home. My relationship with my mom was strained before I left home, and for two and half months, I did not speak with her. I imagined that my relationship with her was going to be anything but cordial. If an angel came down from heaven and told me that my mom and I would be having tea and laughing soon, I would have been skeptical. I thought that I had a lot to forgive her for, and my guess was that she was thinking the same thing of me. Besides, I had come of age, and I just found out I could go away from home and still survive.

My prediction of a mother-versus-son feud was, unfortunately, true. As expected, I did not receive any hug when I got back home, and we tried too hard to be civil and kind. Being home felt like camping with an enemy, except that, in that case, it was my mom. It did not feel right; it was suffocating, so I left home after three days, and my destination was to a city called Owerri. I was going to stay with my great uncle. Everyone knew him as Odoboro. He repaired old and damaged car engines by regrinding the crankshafts to fit a new set of metal plates, and re-boring the engine block so as to accommodate new pistons. He was very good at what he did and was respected—or I should say feared—by his peers. My great uncle's trade seemed attractive to me, and I was going to settle for it while I waited for the outcome of my final examination. If my result was poor, learning a trade where dead car engines are brought back to life would be my first option. If my result was good, which I doubt because I partied much more than I read, I would go back to get a higher education.

It did not take a long time for me to find out that my stay with my uncle and his wife would be rocky; the indicators were all over the place. The first sign was that he was very erratic, and that concerned me. My uncle demanded excellence and accuracy, which was a good thing for the kind of work we did, but the way he went about it was not refined. He bullied his way through it even when there was no need to do so. Whenever he spoke softly it was because he was sick and weak, or high on a joint or joking. At those times, he was usually so much fun to be around.

There was an incident that took place after two weeks of my staying with him. There was a day he was craving so badly to smoke a cigarette, but he did not have any change on him. He sent me to buy a pack of cigarettes on credit from a store owner he regularly bought from. The woman who owned the store refused to sell anything to him on credit until he paid a substantial amount of money he still owed her. The amount he allegedly owed this woman had grown to an unbearable level over the years. Some of his debt was written off by this woman because she could no longer keep track of it. It was upsetting to carry water for such a careless uncle. After returning from the store, I told him the owner of the store no longer sold on credit. He was so infuriated I was glad I conveyed to him the least of what the woman who owned the store said to me. What he did next surprised me; he reached into his pant's right back pocket, pulled out two bills in the amount of two Naira and said, "A pack of Benson, and bring me back my change."

"Yes, sir," I replied and left.

Well, I bought the pack of Benson cigarettes but did not bring the remaining money. The woman told me she did not have the change but that I could return at a later time for it. I believed I had made the right decision to get him his cigarettes first, because I sensed he was upset for a different reason, and smoking usually calmed him down. But I almost got killed for that innocent initiative; I received a beating. He often shouted and threatened anyone when things did not work out his way, and behaved like he would follow through with his threat. Many times he did not, but on that occasion he did and I had to get away from him.

Later that day, he apologized to me for his bad behavior. He said the reason he had me beaten was because he thought I was dumb, since I got outfoxed by an old woman and let her keep his money. While I listened, I wanted so much to say out loud, "You won't let her keep your few pennies, but you're keeping her tens of Naira." But I did not. Nevertheless, he seemed to have known what I was thinking and said, "For your information and for anyone who is listening." I was alone with him, so when he said, "And for anyone who is listening," I thought he was high or had lost his mind. I therefore, paid closer attention, because I did not want to get hurt, he then continued, "I don't owe that jackass and her dumb husband a farthing."

I did not have all the facts and did not know who was speaking the truth. I just did not want to get in between them. No matter who was right or speaking the truth, my uncle's words and tone were very disrespectful and disturbing to me. I actually thought he was the jackass and that he was self-absorbed, although I did not say it. On that day, I wondered how much more I could take and for how long. And for the first time, I thought about returning home.

CHAPTER 6

The Call of the Lost

*Our paths are guided best when the sweet light of love shines
from the deepest layer of our hearts.*
                                        —Father Udo Ogbuji

The bizarre behaviors of my great uncle, Odoboro, went
from bad to worse, but I had made a conscious decision to stay
with him because it would take a few more months before the
final high school examination results were published. It was
clear to me that how well I performed on my scores would
determine my final plan for the future with regard to pursuing
higher education or doing something else. Another reason I
thought that staying with him was the right choice, in spite of his
ugly conduct, was that my preoccupation with learning how to
repair car engines was better than returning home and possibly
getting into fights with my mom.

In order to remain sane while I lived and dealt with someone
as eccentric as my great uncle, God led me to rediscover him.
I became deeply religious and regularly attended Mass. I was
truly bewildered that I enjoyed going to church activities and
Mass since, for the first time in my life, I attended Mass not
because I was expected to or wanted to avoid a big conflict
with my mom but because that was the only place I could find
peace. The spiritual food I received at Mass, in addition to the
complimentary soothing words of the priest's homilies, were
more than I could ask for. I had to talk to someone, but I did
not think anyone could understand my situation. I believed

God would listen to me, and I spoke to him from the depths of my heart. After I talked to him in my prayer, I would observe a few minutes of silence, hoping that God would say something to me, but he never did, at least not in the form of a vision.

My uncle was raised a Catholic but stopped going to church; however, his wife occasionally did. The church I attended was Saint Paul's Catholic Church, a very large church located in the middle of Owerri City. The sitting capacity of the church was about three thousand. In such a church with mainly affluent members and large crowds, it was very easy to be lost in the midst of the congregation. Fortunately, I was never invisible as the associate pastor, Father Paul, always found me in the church, figuratively speaking, even with many members of the faithful in attendance. Whenever he preached, it was like he singled me out from the gathered worshipping community and addressed me personally.

The first time I attended the Mass he celebrated, something inexplicable happened. During that Mass, I was awestricken by the richness of the entire celebration and how Father Paul's homily made Mass truly come alive. That was the first time in my teen years that I had an experience of that sort at Mass. After Father Paul's homily, during the offertory, I bent over the pew and wept. The reason I wept was clear to me, and I told God about it: "As I grew up, this was what I was searching for when I intended to be a priest, to touch people like Father Paul just touched me. I truly regret that the longing died because I became a bad boy." When I eventually looked up, there was no one in the church but me. The church was very quiet, and it occurred to me that I may have been in that state of mind for a very long time. I had a series of questions I asked during that experience: Is God here? Is he listening? What does he want of me? How will he communicate his will? Unknown to me, he was right there with me; he listened and answered my prayers.

The last time I felt the call to be a priest was at the priestly ordination of my mom's cousin, Father Benedict. However, the next day, when he celebrated his first Mass, I convinced myself that the vocation to the Catholic priesthood was beyond what I had in mind or what I should seek. On that occasion of his first Mass, I was among the altar boys chosen to serve. At the time, I was in tenth grade, and I believed that the choice of the much older altar boys with experience was made because of the seriousness of the celebration. I was happy to be at the sanctuary area where I could have a closer observation of the events of that magnificent day. I watched with keen interest and enjoyed the ceremony until the Introductory Rite, which included a blessing and the sprinkling of holy water. Father Ben, as we called him, said the prayer for blessing the water and appeared nervous as he sprinkled the people with holy water. As his fingers trembled and he waved the plastic holy water container, sprinkling the faithful, the container slipped out of his fingers and hit a woman in the face. It was a nerve-racking incident, and I felt sorry for him. I wanted to close my eyes and hope that when I opened them, things would be completely different. Unfortunately, they were not, and the reality of that incident was imprinted on my mind. When Mass was over, I went home thinking aloud, *If this is how nervous and fearful being a priest makes a person, I do not want to be one.*

My longing to be a priest one day and the decision to stay away from Catholic priesthood after twenty-four hours as I watched Father Ben supposedly struggle at his first Mass is something worth explaining. The ceremony of his priestly ordination was grand and spirit-filled, and so I felt I should be a priest too, perhaps because of the glory of the priesthood I witnessed and had coveted. My change of heart the next day was not difficult; it came easily after I thought that the glory I observed might be an illusion and paled in comparison to the demands. Fast-forward to my experience a few years later at the Mass celebrated by Father Paul, my yearning to become a priest was profound and born out of the longing to serve in love rather than a draw to glory. My weeping in the church was somewhat an earnest prayer to God to call me to his service where I hoped to seek nothing for myself but something that was beyond me—a quest and mission to be there for others in whatever way God wanted of me. While still in the church, I cried some more and prayed silently until people started arriving for the next Mass. I left the church but did not go home because I was not in the mood to go home to face my great uncle or his wife. Instead, I went to the home of Chuka, a new friend who had been kind to me and very supportive. He was in the same trade as my uncle and about three years older than me, but he was a very rich bachelor. He was no longer an apprentice and was paid very well by the company he worked for. He knew how crazy my uncle was and freely offered me material and moral support. He actually taught me more about the trade than my own uncle. Chuka once told me, "Udo, whatever you need, let me know. Apart from saving to start my own company someday, I don't know what else to do with the money I make."

"You're going to need every penny you make and then some more," I said, knowing how costly it was to buy a regrinding machine, and then I joked, "You may also have to sell both our limbs to be able to afford that machine."

We laughed heartily. I never asked him for any help, but he would anticipate my needs and voluntarily gave me some money. On that day, as I left the church, I was not in the mood for anything, and he was cooking when I arrived at his house. I hurried over the greetings we exchanged and went straight to his bedroom and laid down. After he was done with cooking, he came and woke me up, announcing that lunch was ready.

"How long have I been sleeping?" I asked.

He replied, "Forty days—I mean, forty minutes." He meant it to be funny, and we laughed, but I actually felt like I had been sleeping for forty days. Then he said, "I checked on you earlier, and you were sleeping soundly. You must not have slept last night."

I was still overwhelmed by my experience at Mass, and I wanted to talk to someone, but to whom? As we ate, Chuka asked me, "Are you all right?"

"Yes, I am. Why?" I replied.

"Something is different about you today, but I can't put my finger on exactly what it is. All I know is that you have not said much today," he opined while looking perplexed.

"Something happened at the church today," I finally admitted.

I told my friend, Chuka, the story of my life in an abridged version as I did not want to weigh him down with all the unnecessary details. I limited my emphasis on areas that would help him understand the event in the church earlier. The relevant things I thought he should know were—

How my dad went to church during a fundraising in our local church at home and, while making a donation, did something surprising. There was the custom and option of speaking before you made your offering. As my dad concluded his speech, he said, "If it pleases God to accept my gift, in addition to this donation, I will also pledge today, in this church, that if God gives me a child that survived and he is a boy, I will offer him to God as a priest." He was speaking from the heart and like a man whose wife just had a miscarriage. He began to fulfill his promise to God when he enrolled me to be an altar boy at the first opportunity he got. Chuka was not a Catholic, so I had to explain to him that as an altar boy, I was expected to behave like and perhaps become a priest. I also told him how I had entertained the idea of being a priest at one time or another and how I felt drawn to it after my experience in the church.

Chuka listened to me attentively, without saying a word. When I finished talking, there was about a three-minute period of silence. The pause could have been awkward, but was not for obvious reasons, namely, I could see he was deeply touched and may have been reflecting more on what he heard. I also believed he was seeking the best way to help or what to say. He finally broke the silence, "I can see you're really passionate about being a priest. If you're this fervent, it would be a disservice for me or anyone to discourage you. I guess I'll be the one to lose when you leave to go to the seminary."

I thought he was joking about the part he said he would lose if I left because he was smiling when he said it, but something made me think he was partly serious, so I asked, "How so?"

To which he replied, "I was hoping to talk you into working with me when I open my own business." Although he meant what he said, he did so in such a way that it was funny, so we laughed. Then he asked, "What will it take for you to become a priest?"

"First, my high school result has to be excellent, and I strongly doubt it will be that good," I answered. "If it is, I'll apply and then wait to see if the bishop will accept me into his diocese. After my application is accepted, I'll be sent to the seminary and, at the end of my study, will be ordained a priest, if I did well."

When I was done, Chuka said, "I'm sorry I can't help you, but if God wants you, he will make it possible. I believe your yearning is enough to persuade him—at least, I know you have me convinced."

I did not know if I should believe Chuka or not, because, he made my dilemma sound so easy to resolve. The question I had was: Did he speak out of conviction or out of a sense of what I needed to hear? Either way, his words were comforting, and the chance that God might still be interested in me was exhilarating.

I got home later that Sunday, and my uncle teased me, "Buddy, where have you been?"

"I have been at the church, big brother," I replied.

"You have been in the church? I know you said you were going to Mass before you left this morning, but after many hours passed, I thought you ran off with Ada." He laughed out loud and his laughter was endearing but at the same time a ploy to probe further.

Ada was a girl who lived close to the shop where we worked. Her mom ran a restaurant business down the street, and we went there to eat lunch. I had gone there several times to eat before something unusual started happening. Each time I went to the cashier to pay for my food, I was told it had been paid for. The first time it occurred, I did not think it was my uncle, but I went against my belief that it was not him and expressed my gratitude in case I was wrong. I was not wrong because I found out that Ada gave an instruction that my meal would be free until she told the workers to accept money from me. I thanked Ada for her kindness but nonetheless informed her that I wanted to pay for my meal. I had to stop going to eat at her mom's restaurant altogether because my payment was not accepted. It took two days before I realized Ada was not going to give up, not yet! When I did not show up to eat at the restaurant, she brought some food to me at my uncle's workshop.

"Why are you doing this? You know how I feel about what you are doing," I asked in mild protest, even though her persistent kindness warmed my heart.

"It's not from me. My mom asked me to bring some food to you," she interjected, correcting my assumption.

"Are you sure?" I quizzed her.

"Her exact words were, 'I don't want my son to die of hunger.' My mom was worried that you haven't come to eat at the restaurant. She even asked me to apologize to you if she made you uncomfortable by deciding to feed you free of charge. She also said it would be a great pleasure for her if you will let her send someone to bring you lunch each day," she reported.

I felt so bad when I learned it was Ada's mother who made the decision to feed me without charge; if I had known that from the outset, my response or reaction would have been different. I would have at least personally thanked her for her generosity. I have had some people take interest in me or show me kindness, but this was more than I had ever experienced. Her charitable acts would have been easier to accept if I had understood the reason behind them. Since Ada liked me very much, and I liked her too, it even entered my mind—although I fought it off—that Ada's mother may have been nice to me for many good reasons but also because she thought I could make a good son-in-law. A terrible wishful dream on my part! I did accept her charity, believing she simply wanted to be kind and for the right reasons. So for the remaining months I stayed in Owerri with my uncle, Ada came by during lunchtime and brought me some food to eat. She would also come in the evening to take the plates, and we visited whenever possible. It was at one of those evenings that Ada told me she had a brother who died, and her mother thought he looked like me. After she made that revelation, I felt very rotten to have fantasized that her mother may have liked me as a future son-in-law. However, I was glad Ada told me about her deceased brother and how her mother thought I looked like him, because that predisposed me to be on guard whenever she was present. The chemistry between us was mutual, fine and strong, and I would have liked to marry her if she would have let me. But the initial thing that kept me in check in that charged situation was my resolution to work on becoming a good boy by attending Mass and to try to faithfully obey God's commandments. I would have to admit, though, that Ada's beauty, care, grace, constant loving presence, and what I felt inside were beginning to slowly wear off my resolve. I could almost see and feel my being in a real romantic relationship with her. Those fantasies and intense feelings began to evaporate when I became aware of the fact that her mother thought I looked like her deceased son. I started thinking of her more like my own sister. It also helped me find the courage to say no even when I wanted to say yes. Although she exercised understanding at those times, I believed she may have thought that I would be better off spending the rest of my life with the Puritans of the sixteenth century.

In my uncle's workshop was an extra room with a sleeping mattress, and I slept there sometimes, at the request of my uncle. My relationship with Ada and her family was known to almost everyone, and I did not blame anyone who thought we were in love or that something serious was going on because it seemed obvious. My uncle was one of those who thought I was too deep into love to be saved, and he wanted to find out in a sneaky way. I was surprised when he kept encouraging me to

spend the night in the workshop, but I innocently believed he
had the right intentions. On one of those evenings, my uncle
came to the shop unannounced. I had a feeling that was not
the first time he hung around to spy on me, but he only came
into the shop on that night perhaps because Ada stayed longer
than usual as she came to pick up her mother's dishes. During
that visit, Ada wanted to talk about a few personal matters, and I
was very happy to be there for her, to listen and offer my advice
just as she had been there for me. But it was a shock to us when
my uncle quietly opened the door and tiptoed into my sleeping
room and, perhaps, was disappointed to find out we were in the
office sitting room. After he left without saying a word—and
evidently did not need anything from the shop, except to feed
his imagination—Ada and I looked at each other, not believing
my uncle could be so immature. If my uncle's intention was to
run into Ada and me in a compromising situation, he must have
been frustrated because the expression on his face indicated
he was discontent that he wasted his time or was embarrassed
for being childish. After that encounter, he started working too
hard to be very friendly and made insinuations that could only
come from someone who wished to turn his dreams into reality.
He called Ada my wife and always teased me about her. So, it
did not shock me that he joked about me running off with her
when I came back from Mass. I only smiled, which I am sure
frustrated him; I knew he would feel better if I confirmed his
assumption or exhibited some form of weakness. I may have
seemed too perfect for his liking and, that perhaps made him
uncomfortable. If only my uncle knew how bad I had been and
my wish to be a good young man, he would not see my honest
efforts as direct reproach of his way of life. I stayed with him and
his wife for six months before I returned home.

    The first indicator that I might get to go home for good was
the publication of the high school results six months after my
stay with my uncle and his wife. The reality of leaving, made me
wonder how much I would miss the work of resurrecting dead

car engines and healing sick ones, which I liked. My opportunity to visit home came when my uncle's wife made a trip to the village and brought back the news that my high school result was out and that everyone thought it was excellent. I had to go home to find out for myself, especially the details of the results. The eve of the day I left to go home, I went to Mass, and I prayed that things would improve between my mom and me. I wanted to believe my six months of being away from home healed the wounds inflicted on both sides and facilitated a fresh start for us. Within me, I was at peace, having asked forgiveness from God and having also forgiven my mom. I hoped that she had forgiven me, too. Father Paul came into my life at the right time. He put it in simple and practical terms the importance of reconciliation when he said during one of his homilies, that, "There can be no peace of mind and peace at home or in the world without reconciliation. It is important to make peace with God. But it is almost useless when you or I make peace with God and refuse to share that peace with others through the act of reconciliation. Forgiveness and peace from God should lead us to forgive those who did not treat us well and apologize to those we wronged, with the hope that they would find peace, too and forgive us." Hearing Father Paul's inspirational homilies made reconciliation effortless and the resulting relief and solace was priceless. My wish was that my newfound peace and maturity would help me win over my mom again.

When I returned home, I went to school and received my statement of result, which was as my mom had reported. My result was actually very good considering the fact that my last few months at home before the examination were tumultuous, and even when I left home to be with my friends, I partied more than I studied, contrary to what I had in mind. I wished my result was better though, and it would have been under normal circumstances. On my second night at home, my mom cooked my favorite dish, *ofe ukazi*, for dinner. It is a dish that includes some soup named after the herb *Ukazi*, with which it is cooked. Back home, a particular soup is often named after the herb or vegetable with which it is cooked. Apart from the herb, the soup is cooked with fish, beef, dried ground crawfish and more. The soup is eaten with processed cassava roots made into a carbohydrate pastry with boiled water, and it is a little denser than mashed potatoes. The processing of cassava takes tedious labor and a few days before it is edible. It is processed by being ground and left for two days to ferment. The fermentation helps to dilute its strong starch content, and while at that stage, extra starch and fluid are squeezed out. The fermented cassava is then cooked in a big frying pan until it crystallizes into tiny grains. It is then ready to be stirred in boiling water to make some pastry known as *foo-foo* and eaten with soup. The crystal cassava grains can also be eaten as cereal with milk, sugar, and nuts.

My mom cooked that painstaking and delicious meal for my benefit, maybe to welcome me home. Her gesture of cooking me my favorite meal may have been a way of saying, "I'm done quarrelling and moving on to things that unite and help us grow together."

After enjoying that delicious dinner that my mom cooked with a great measure of thoughtfulness and love, I showed her the official statement of the result I received from my school earlier that day as we sat under the porch in front of our family house. There was a full moon that night, and the sky was decorated with sparkling stars, which was beautiful to gaze at. As my mom held the official paper that stated my result, she said, "Udo, I'm happy you're home again. I missed you while you were gone."

"Thank you, Mommy, I missed you too, and I'm happy to be home," I replied.

She glanced through my result statement, which she had in her hand, and said, "You really made me proud, your result is good."

Her compliment was genuine, but I disagreed politely. "Mom, you call this good, but most of my friends made straight A's. If you had been nicer to me, I would have done far better than that."

My mom did something she had never done before; she asked for my forgiveness, which shocked and humbled me. She told me that she regretted not accepting my plea to let me study or trusting my judgment on what I thought would be the best. I cannot recall ever seeing that side of my mom, that is, her conceding that she had been wrong and rendering an apology. Maybe I had not seen it because she had never been wrong; she was tough and clear-headed, and she exercised good judgment in her decision-making process. She always proceeded with caution when she was not sure of what to do and would ask for help from her prudent friends and sometimes even from me before acting. I was so touched by my mom's candor in admitting that she was misguided that I apologized to her, too. I told her that I did not handle things well either and that I should have been more understanding or asked for her help with grace. I also humbly admitted that my leaving home was not an excuse not to study. She was happy to hear that if I were to do it all over again, I would have stayed at home and helped her as much as I could. I then shocked her with the story of my adventure after I left home.

"Mom, I did not read my books when I left home, and I almost got married," I said jokingly. If I intended the last part of my comment to get her attention, I succeeded. In the faint light given by the moon and stars, I could see her sit up in shock at what I said. My mom was shocked because when she heard the word *married*, she was not paying attention to the whole sentence but believed I had gotten married during my time away from home. She only relaxed when I said, "Mom, I was just kidding about the marriage part."

"I hope you are because I just survived a heart attack a second ago," she responded, and we laughed.

I then said, "If I find a good one, I'll bring her to you for approval and training."

"Let us be serious now, Udo." She attempted to change the subject by asking, "What do you intend to do now that your result is out?"

"Mom, I intend to go to the university, either major in aeronautic engineering or take the entrance exam to go to Nigerian Defense Academy."

"Those are lofty and excellent choices," my mom acknowledged. "A few minutes ago, you said you almost got married. So, I am not surprised you didn't include going to the seminary to know if you would be chosen to be a priest. I know that there was a time when being a priest was one of your dreams. I wonder what happened! Is it the girl you almost married?"

She smiled, and I did too, and I thought she really outwitted me. "Mom, I still want to be a priest, but I can't now. I'm really bad!" I contritely acknowledged.

"Udo, you don't give yourself enough credit. You're a good boy," she reassured me.

But I corrected her, "A *man*, Mom!"

"Okay, a man, but you're still my boy," she agreed, standing her ground, and then continued, "If you are not sure whether or not you want to be a priest, I'll make arrangements for you to visit my cousin, Father Ben. I believe he will help you with the process of discernment and the determination of what you wish to do with your life."

As was customary before I finally went to sleep, I thought about all I discussed with my mom and got hung up on one thing: the fact that my mom still believed that there was some good in me. It was striking, and I loved her more for it.

As my mom suggested, I went to stay with Father Ben who, at that time, was a pastor in Saint Anthony Parish, Mbawsi. That big parish had many outstation parishes and a convent where he also served. I went to Mass with him and offered my altar server assistance. I was surprised that I still remembered how to serve at Mass after being out of commission for so long, and Father Ben was grateful for the help I was able to provide. I only stayed with Father Ben for a few days to find out what a good man and a great priest he was. When I say a good man, I mean a really good man who shows transparent goodness even in very simple things and events. There was a day his chef miscalculated the number of people who would be eating at the rectory. It was on a Sunday, and we had gone to many Masses in the main parish church, mission parish churches, and the convent. We were very hungry and as we sat down to eat dinner, he observed that the food was not enough for the two of us, and his chef had already gone. He then said to me, "Udo, go ahead and eat, you need it more than I do. You're still a growing young man."

"Father Ben, what are you going to eat?" I asked.

"I'll fast tonight, and if I get hungry, I will snack on something," he replied with a smile. "I would cook for you if you don't mind although I might not be as good as your chef, but at least you won't starve," I volunteered.

"Judging from the starvation we are facing tonight because of the slipup of the chef, I don't know if I want you to cook, after you said you won't do better than the chef." He was laughing as he said that, and I laughed with him. He then added, "Don't worry, Udo, I'll be fine. Enjoy the meal, and if you feel guilty about eating my portion, pray two Hail Mary's for me. In that way, I would gain God's grace in exchange for my offered material food."

"Father Ben, I'll pray a full Rosary for you. I believe that will make me feel much better," I responded, but what I wanted to say was, "I'll pray a full Rosary for you because you're so kind and therefore deserve more."

I was so riveted by that ordinary act of kindness he showed because the circumstances made it an extraordinary sacrifice. He had worked hard all day, and if I was hungry, he must have been starving. He needed the nourishment to stay healthy and have the energy to do the Lord's work. That he did not put himself and his interest first showed the enormous strength of love and character he possessed. I loved him! His kindness and selflessness all the more reinforced my longing to be a priest.

On that night, as I sat across the dining table from Father Ben, I could not help but wonder about the changes that had taken place since the last time I saw him. The day he celebrated his First Mass was the last day I set my eyes on him. Seeing him again made me remember the incident of the woman he accidentally hit with the holy water bottle on that occasion. His seeming a little nervous as he sprinkled the faithful with holy water on that day was in total contrast to the calm, confident, and solid priest before me. Father Ben gave the best homilies with unrivaled clarity and richness. I particularly enjoyed the way he used stories to drive home the message of the Gospel and other readings. That method left his audience with meaningful and practical spiritual lessons they would always remember. I remembered his stories, and they led me back to the lessons he communicated. As I ate and wondered, Father Ben excused himself, and when he returned, he brought some smoked meat and some palm wine.

"I told you not to worry, that the Lord will provide. He just did."

When I finished eating, he offered me some of the meat and wine. As we enjoyed those, we talked about different things. At a time I thought appropriate, I told him how I enjoyed being at his priestly ordination and first Mass. I also told him how bad I felt for him when I saw the holy water bottle slip from his fingers. He made light of it, which brought me comfort, and clarified what caused the mishap. I came to understand that it was not nervousness as I had thought or imagined that caused the accident, but that the external part of the plastic bottle was wet and slippery. That explanation made better sense and removed any small leftover misgivings I may have had about the priesthood causing a person to have anxiety. I still believed Father Ben was a little nervous during his first Mass, but I did not press him on it because I had grown old and wise enough to know that anyone would have been anxious under those circumstances. He then changed the subject and asked me, "Daa Lucy, told me you wanted to visit to discern and explore the possibility of being a priest. Have you made up your mind?"

"Father Ben, let me think about it some more tonight, and I'll let you know tomorrow morning," I answered.

As I went to the chapel to pray that night, I thought about the many events and reasons that were making me lean toward wishing I would become a priest or dissuading me from hoping to become one. I reflected on some of the questions like the following: Does God really want me to be a priest? Is it a deep enough yearning that it comes from my soul rather than from my superficial self? Am I hoping to be one for the right reasons? Was my mom right when she said I was still a good boy? Do I have what it takes to be a priest?

My reflection on answering those questions led me to believe that I wanted to become a priest for the right reason, namely, to serve selflessly and make sacrifices in whatever way and wherever I would be needed. I also thought that while I still had a long way to go to be a better person, I am not completely damaged and, there may still be a few things in me that could be salvaged. I believed that if I could build on the spiritual and moral progress I made in Owerri City while I lived with my crazy uncle, that it would be a good step in the right direction. I did not have the answer to whether I had what it would take to be a priest. That answer, perhaps, may come to light as I progress in my formation in the seminary if I made it that far, or I may actually have to become a priest to find out. My visit to the chapel was helpful because I prayed to God and got answers to most of my concerns. Since things were not as clean-cut as I wanted, I asked God for a direct sign, which would be an indicator that my longing to become a priest was part of his plan. I told God that the way I would know he still wants me to consider the path to the priesthood is, if when I go to see the bishop, he tells me, without hesitation, that I had been admitted as a seminarian into the diocese of Umuahia. But, if he said something like, "Give me time to think about it or come in about a month when I will have an answer for you," then I would be certain the priesthood is not for me.

Early Monday morning, I told Father Ben that I had made up my mind to see the bishop in order to explore the possibility of becoming a Catholic priest. Since he was going to Umuahia City where the diocesan secretariat was and the bishop would be in the office, he asked me to accompany him. He told me to bring my statement of result from high school. While in the car heading to Umuahia, which was an hour's journey, we prayed the Rosary and talked a little bit. During the periods we were quiet, I would replay my reflection in the chapel in my head to make sure I was not missing a thing. I was concerned that I was moving too fast, but I believed the spiritual net of certainty I put in place by asking God for a sign would address my apprehension. I was thrilled that I might have an answer to my sole challenge to God as soon as we meet the bishop and then know whether or not I would still dream about being a priest. It did not matter to me whether or not I was acceptable to the bishop as a possible candidate for the priesthood. That was because it was going to be a huge sacrifice on my part to become a priest, and if I did not become one, at least I would be liberated from that enormous sacrifice. For the first son to pursue the vocation of priesthood meant swimming against the strong current of my culture. My people, and the culture we lived by, expected me, as the first son, to get married and maintain the posterity of the family. If I did not follow that cultural wisdom and expectation of my people, that might mean my having the support of my mom and only a few people. For me, all that mattered—and still matters—was what God wanted of me. If I knew his will, I would embrace it together with the required sacrifice. It was a great relief that I asked God for a sign to help me determine what he wanted of me. That act followed my personal tradition of bargaining with God. As you remember in chapter 3, I asked God for a favor before I would become a priest; the request was for him to let me skip school and make me knowledgeable at the same time. I would say today, after I look back at my life, that he did not grant me the waiver I asked for, but instead made me enjoy going to school and cherish reading, especially in high school. I could have accepted that indirectly fulfilled prayer as a sign that God was calling me, but many years had passed by, and many things had changed. Having grown older and a little rough around the edges, I did not think God would still want me in the capacity of a priest, so I asked for a more direct clue that would be clear and give no room for doubt.

We arrived at the bishop's office at nine o'clock that morning. Someone was with the bishop already, and we were third among those queued up to see him, and I did not know what to expect. The first time I was that close to Bishop Anthony Nwedo was the day I made my Confirmation, and I was only ten years old. In August, I made my First Communion, and in September, the Bishop was going to pay a visit to the parish, and whenever he visited any parish, kids usually received the Sacrament of Confirmation. But since there were a handful of children in the Confirmation class in my parish, the catechists picked some from my group who had just received Communion. Especially, those who looked grown or old and, taught us Catechism for a few days, gave us an ad hoc examination and presented us to be confirmed. One of the things we were told during preparation for the occasion was that the bishop would slap us on the cheek as a warning to be strong in faith and put up a good fight against Satan. Since the bishop was old and frail, I remember wondering how he was going to survive after slapping about eighty-five kids and why he would slap us instead of talking to us. At the Confirmation, it turned out to be a tender tap on the cheek, but I was nervous nonetheless. I actually was so anxious, I did not remember whether the bishop tapped me or not. He probably did, and the only proof I had was that I saw him tap other kids on the cheek. Nine years had passed since my confirmation, and as I rode in the car with Father Ben on the way to see the bishop, I thought to myself, *Boy, you have grown into a man since your Confirmation. You're not even nervous about seeing the bishop.*

My Confirmation Picture

When it was our turn to see the bishop, Father Ben told me to wait outside the office until he met with him first. I did not know why, and I was not in a hurry, so I waited. He stuck his head out through the half-opened door after about ten minutes and signaled that it was time for me to come in. Evidently, Father Ben had gone in first to tell the bishop why we were there. It made sense to keep the bishop informed and to know from him if that was the right time and place to address my admission into the seminary. I knew that was the reason, or part of the reason, he went in first because when I came in, the bishop called me by my name, and I was impressed.

"Vincent," he said, "I understand you wish to be a priest?"

"Yes, my Lord," I mumbled, stunned by the aura around him.

"Let me see your statement of result!" he said, extending his hand, and I handed it to him. He put on his reading glasses, looked, and ran his index finger through the official paper like he was searching for something in particular. Not knowing what it was, my heart skipped a beat. After about a minute, he broke the silence. "Is this your result?" he asked.

I believed he may have been impressed. "Yes, my Lord," I answered.

"Pack your bag and come here by this time next week to start your apostolic work." He was direct and did not waste time. I was still wondering if there was something more, almost as if I was regretting that the meeting was quick or that his decision came easy and that no condition was attached to my admission. On our way back, I did not speak very much; I was stunned! Although my prayers were answered in such an unambiguous way, I could not bring myself to believe I was not dreaming; it was too incredible to be real. The whole experience was ordinary yet fantastic in some way, and that night, I went to the chapel and thanked God for explicitly answering my prayers.

I stayed with Father Ben one more day before I returned home. My mom welcomed the news, which was not a surprise, and I informed her I was going to talk to two people about my plan. The first person was my uncle Dee Oriaku, my dad's big brother. I wanted to meet with him out of respect and, hopefully, get some moral support from him. He had his hands full with raising his own kids and caring for his two wives, and I knew from experience not to expect him to offer any financial help. The second person I wanted to talk to was Dee Lovet whom I mentioned earlier. He was very close to my dad and after my dad's passing continued to give my family unwavering support. Dee Lovet showed genuine interest in my well being when he helped put me in the best school. He even paid my tuition when the burden of raising us and putting us through school weighed heavily on my mom. Having his support would mean a great deal to me!

Dee Oriaku, my uncle, told me he did not support my choice and suggested that I join the police force or learn a trade and get married. I was not surprised at his opinion because he was not big on education. Besides, he probably thought that he should not be suggesting something that required financial commitment when he would not be helping to pay for it. I told him that I would consider his concerns and suggestions when I finally made a decision.

The response I received from Dee Lovet was both passionate and devastating. After I told him my wish to become a priest and that I had been admitted to the seminary, he was apparently angry.

"Are you out of your mind?" he asked in an outburst of frustration. I did not answer his question because I could see he was not happy with me, and I believed he was not expecting an answer because he continued, "You have a great future, but I'm afraid you're about to make a decision to throw it all away. I don't even want to mention the fact that Joe's posterity will be doomed, and you will be responsible for that."

He loved my dad and had great respect for him, so I was not surprised about his concern for my dad's posterity. "Dee, I'm not a priest yet. I'm only going to the seminary, and there's no guarantee I'll be a priest," I nicely offered, hoping my response would ease the disappointment he felt, but it instead made it worse.

"It takes about a decade to go through the seminary, that's ten lost years and lost opportunities! I don't believe you are using your brain right now. Come back to me when you are, and here is your cue: if you choose to go to the seminary, count me out. However, if you change your mind and decide to go to the university, I'll pay for everything until you graduate."

I thought the meeting with Dee Lovet was disappointing and went badly, contrary to what I expected. He stepped in after my dad died and helped us in every way he could. He was one of those who made my dad's passing less difficult. It would be painful to lose him not because of the material help I received from him, but because he had symbolically filled the space the loss of my dad created. He was like a dad to me, and I needed his moral support at a very crucial time in my life. He was not going to be happy if I made the choice to go to the seminary, and I was so conflicted. I did not tell my mom about the double defeat I had; instead, I told her they both pledged to pray for me. I wanted to save her from all the trouble and to personally reflect more on my choices, making an uninterrupted decision that I would own in every way. What I told my mom was true, both of them actually declared they would pray for me, but not for the reason you might consider. They may have thought I was out of my mind.

I eventually made the decision to go to the seminary because I was convinced that was what would bring me the most fulfillment, and I was not about to make God mad at me, either. I could not be in a hurry to give up on him, not after the sign he just showed me three days ago. Maybe I was truly out of my mind, as my uncle and Dee Lovet suggested, because God filled my mind up with the desire to long for him. Such a fascination with God has been known to make a sane young man seem crazy to the world. The second reason I made the choice to go to the seminary was because I knew I had my mom's support, and I presumed my dad was on my side, too, since he made the pledge to give his first son as a gift to serve God in the priestly ministry. I had great respect and love for my dad, Joseph, and because I had the least support from those I hoped in, I began a perpetual devotion to Saint Joseph and his wife, Mary. I prayed through them, asking for guidance. Before I left for the seminary, I bought a statue of Saint Joseph, which my pastor blessed for me, and I took it with me as I went to the seminary.

CHAPTER 7

Saint Joseph at Every Turn

*If you want to annoy your Guardian Angel, hide from him.
While you hide, keep in mind that you will be lost until you
make yourself visible to him and ask for help.*
—Father Udo Ogbuji

I arrived at the bishop's office at nine o'clock on a
Monday morning and was informed to wait for the arrival of
Father Nwabekee, the rector of the Immaculate Conception
Seminary, Ahiaeke, who also served as the vocation director
for my diocese. The rector, I understood, would be the one to
instruct me on what to do. He arrived forty-five minutes later,
and we loaded my luggage in the trunk of his car and headed
for the Minor Seminary. That was how unceremonious the
beginning of my journey as a seminarian was. Father Rector,
as we called him sometimes, was a very kind, gentle, and pious
man. After we drove in silence for two minutes and the traffic
was less congested, he started an invocation for our safe trip. "In
the name of the Father and of the Son and of the Holy Spirit,
Amen!" I joined in the prayer, making the sign of the cross.
Father Nwabekee, had his two hands on the steering wheel and
so did not physically join in the sign part, but I could tell he was
thinking and doing it in his mind. He continued, "We fly to your
patronage, Oh holy Mother of God, despise not our prayers in
our necessities, and always deliver us from dangers, Oh ever
glorious and blessed Virgin Mary." After the prayers were over,
he said, "Udo, I want to thank you for considering the vocation

to the priesthood." If Father Rector intended to win me over, he did. His piety, complimentary, warm, and caring features made him very likable. I smiled at him indicating I appreciated his kind words. He then continued, "The bishop gave me your credentials. After looking at your high school result, I thought it would be beneficial if you taught Geography and Integrated Science to the seventh through ninth grades. I know you went to a state-owned school and not the seminary, and so you may feel lost and out of place in the Minor Seminary at the initial time, but I believe you will soon adjust and begin to enjoy your stay."

I taught Geography and Integrated Science from seventh through ninth grades and enjoyed every moment of it. The minor seminarians, as I came to find out, were typical students except for the fact that they attended daily Mass and went to the chapel several times to pray. It did not take long before the students gave me a nickname. They called me Kawawa. I did not know what the name meant, but one of them confided in me, he indicated that they called me Kawawa because of the way I walked.

I enjoyed being in that seminary; it was a very serene and peaceful place to be when compared to the other institutions of learning I had attended. I was proud of my students and felt a sense of reward because they looked forward to the classes, which I tried to make interesting as well as informative. The minor seminary program was underscored by many prayer sessions during the day, evening, and night. I never prayed that many times in my whole life, but to my surprise, I began to enjoy those spiritual activities, especially the Sunday vespers (evening prayer), which were sung. I enjoyed it not because I sang with the voice of an angel; in fact, it was quite the opposite—but because the chapel was filled with joyful praise. Apart from prayers, I was edified by the communal spirit, the collaboration and bond of friendship among the prefects.

Just as there were things I liked about the seminary, there were some things I only accepted or did because I had to. One of those was how the seminary functioned like a military camp with rigid structures that had to be followed with precision and the constant threat of expulsion that hung in the air. I did not care for that aspect because that formation method could have made me—and perhaps others—do things mainly out of habit or fear. In such an environment, it was almost impossible to think things through or even enjoy doing them since they become habitual or done in a state of fright. Another reason for my dislike of that type of formation was that my personality was one that made me more productive and passionate when I did things not because I was obliged to but because I found it interesting and helpful. I have to admit, however, that a seminary without such provisions would be a disorganized place since there were others who had a different mind-set from me. Furthermore, I could not be certain that I would have been able to personally hold things together for very long without those strict structures and regulations that, in the end, proved to be both a guide and a challenge at the same time. I can see how such an environment with rigid regulations may have been useful to me and others; at least, it taught me to be a little more orderly and disciplined.

I did not care so much for the food served in the seminary; it could have been better, but that would rip an irreparable hole in the seminary's budget. That there were more than four hundred minor seminarians to feed, probably, made it a daunting task for the chefs who cooked the food and a pain for the rector who paid for the meals out of a meager budget. The nicest way I can say it, is that the food did not have all the necessary nutrients I needed. However, I ate what was set before me together with the other prefects, and sometimes, I augmented my diet with personal beverages I bought with my own money. It did not take too long before I began feeling the effects of poor nutrition, and it would not be the first time my health and life were in serious jeopardy due to the lack of proper nourishment.

The first time I experienced the terrible effects of malnourishment was a few months after my dad died. At the time, I was in third grade, and my aunt Daa Titi, my dad's older sister, came to visit my family. I asked my mom to let me go to the village with my aunt, where I intended to spend my vacation, and my mom gave her permission. I was supposed to stay with them until school resumed, but I enjoyed being in the village more than the city and asked my mom if I could enroll in a school in the village while living with my aunt. She reluctantly accepted my plea, fearing the extra burden I would put on my aunt and her family. Daa Titi was divorced and, for about sixteen years, had been living in an apartment with her three children. She struggled to provide for her family, and my decision to live with them did not help matters at all. We frequently ate cheap food that was comprised mainly of carbohydrates from the cassava and yam. Food with good protein and other nutrients were luxuries mostly beyond my aunt's reach, and soon enough, I became anemic. I had shortness of breath, loss of vision and, became very weak whenever I did something that required even the least energy. I did not know what was happening to me, but I thought I was seriously sick and dying, and I was too afraid to tell anyone. One of my mom's friends went and told my mom that if she did not bring me back to live with her, there was a great risk of her losing a son. My mom was not in a hurry to have me back because she hoped to teach me a valuable lesson about life, and I did not blame her for her seeming indifference. She let me stay till the end of the school year before she came to my aid. I did not have to go to the hospital in order to recover; I only had to eat well and stay in a cleaner environment, and my health was fully restored. It was a great relief to once again feel like the normal strong boy I was before I went to live with my aunt. That experience, despite being agonizing, taught me to appreciate life more and to cherish every privilege I had. I had even greater respect for my mom and became more thankful for how hard she worked to meet our needs as a family after my dad's passing. Living with Daa Titi turned out to be a boot camp I unknowingly chose for myself, and I learned a tough life lesson from my experience.

It was disturbing to me that after three months in the Minor Seminary, I started feeling the signs of anemia for the second time in my life. That malady brought me an increased feeling of abject helplessness, frustration, and even fear, since I knew that what I felt was caused by eating food that lacked proper nutrients, and I could not tell anyone. I remained silent because I did not want to appear to be complaining or seeking special treatment, and I believed that if others survived eating that food, then I could, too. I also did not want to risk being expelled, either, because I complained or was considered too sick or fragile to be a priest. In that situation, I had no energy to play soccer or any sport, and when I did, I had shortness of breath, felt dizzy, and was sick. I was so terrified of doing anything that demanded even the least bit of exertion. As I left for the seminary, I brought with me the Saint Joseph statue I had purchased, and I always prayed, asking Saint Joseph to intercede for me before his son and God. There were times when I could not avoid joining in a soccer match or other sports between the students and prefects, and during those times, I just kept playing the best I could, hoping not to collapse on the field. I could not help but think that my ailment could simply be taken care of if I had enough money to afford the beverages that were rich in nutrients to make up for what the food provided in the seminary lacked. If my uncle Dee Lovet still supported me financially as he had always done, I would not be in that situation. I had voted myself out of his favor when I made the decision (against his wish for me to choose another career) to go to the seminary. I could not tell my mom about my ordeal as I did not want her to worry about me because she had more than enough on her plate. She was still struggling to provide for my siblings amid dealing with other family matters that required her attention and financial commitment. The anomaly of my poor health taunted me through my stay in the Minor Seminary and even accompanied me to the Major Seminary the following year.

I arrived on the property of the Major Seminary on the fourteenth of October 1987. When I arrived on that joyous day, there were older seminarians in white cassocks that came to receive me and other new seminarians, and they were so kind and graceful. One approached me while I hauled my heavy luggage along.

"My name is Christopher," he said, and politely added, "Please, may I help you?"

My bags were heavy, and I should have been the one to humbly ask for help. His concern for my needs, volunteering to help with such grace and without being intrusive, made a great impression on me. That simple act of kindness instantly made me believe I was in the right place. Christopher took one of my bags, the heavier one.

"My name is Udochukwu," I introduced myself, and I was glad I did not have the extra weight of the bulkier bag while I talked and walked.

"I will help you settle in your room, Udochukwu, and if we have spare time, I will show you around the seminary."

He was so kind to me that I wondered if everyone in that seminary was as pleasant and if the first-class treatment was a onetime affair or part of the culture in that sacred institution. There was no way to find out because after that day of our arrival, we had no more contact with the older students, and the reason for that separation was that my class would be engaging in an intensive one-year spiritual program. There was a prevailing apprehension among the bishops and seminary authorities that some of the older seminarians would preoccupy the unassuming new ones with some advanced philosophy they may not be ready for. That is to say, they believed—and rightly so—that our fresh minds needed the spiritual disposition to better process and use for good purpose the complexity of philosophical courses. Christopher did show me around, but only a few places because we ran out of time and had to part ways. I was able to tell him how grateful I was before the final good-byes.

During my first two and half years in the seminary, the seminary was known as Bigard Memorial Seminary and, thereafter, was renamed Saint Joseph Major Seminary. It was located in a small town called Ikot Ekpene, which was a forty-minute drive from my home. The most striking thing about the seminary was how well-groomed the place was. After beholding the high-standard of cleanliness and orderliness in that place, I thought that perhaps the seminarians did nothing but clean up and polish every day. The next thing that marveled me was the serenity and peace I felt when I set foot on the seminary premises, which was far better than my experience in the minor seminary. I remember saying to myself, *I love being here. If anyone is not able to find God here, I can't see how he can find him anywhere.* The gate at the main entrance was large and beautiful and adorned with angels. On either side of the asphalt road that led to the campus were palm trees, spaced out from one another in exact measurements. All around the campus were flowers, trees, palms trees, and plants of different kinds and colors. They looked so fresh and good, no one would believe rich compost was not involved. It was a relief, though, to know that whatever was used to enrich the soil was not cow manure—at least, I did not smell any. The plants and flowers were so well maintained and manicured, you would think the persons in charge of trimming them stood by and waited to pluck the unwanted branches or dying flowers as soon as they saw one. The seminary, simply put, was beautiful! The first building I saw as I approached the campus was the academic house, which was a two-story structure with a basement. The basement housed the offices of the rector, academic dean, administrative dean, and some other priests. The first floor had two classrooms for the third and fourth year philosophy students. The second floor had two classrooms reserved for the second year philosophy seminarians and the freshmen. To the left of the academic building were the chapel and three hostels. The hostels were three-story buildings with basements. They were known as Saint Thomas Aquinas, Shanahan, and Saint Boniface hostels. When we walked toward the hostels, I saw the cafeteria, which was also used as an auditorium. Around that area were the student's kitchen, the infirmary, and two large soccer fields. At the back of the academic building were the priests' cafeteria and living quarters. A lawn tennis court and the school library were also located there.

The basement and ground floor of Thomas Aquinas hostel were assigned to us. We also had our own little chapel for prayers and Mass and a completely different schedule from the older seminarians. Each one of us was assigned a task, and mine was keeping the walkway tidy. The schedule of the weekday ran down like this: The student regulator rang the wake-up bell by five thirty in the morning. Morning prayers started by six, and Mass, by six thirty; breakfast was by seven thirty, and duties began by eight. Classes started at eight forty-five and ended by twelve forty-five in the afternoon, followed by midday prayer and lunch. Siesta was by two and lasted for one hour. Studies began at three and were through by five. We had sports every other day by five, for one hour, and on the days we did not have sports, we had manual labor to keep the premises thoroughly kempt. Six thirty was evening prayer, and seven was supper and recreation. We had night prayers at eight and two-hour studies beginning at eight thirty. Finally, lights out was by eleven at night. If you think reading this timetable is boring, imagine keeping and living it faithfully every day all through the academic periods for eight years—or nine, in my case. The weekend schedule was not that much different from the weekday; the only noticeable difference was that we did not go to class on weekends, which were usually more relaxed.

My first semester went so fast, and my results were mediocre. If I wanted to be an excellent student, I had to study more. There was no pressure to study more because most emphasis at that stage was on holiness of life and spirituality. I liked being in that seminary except for the food, which did not have sufficient nutrients, just like in the Minor Seminary. Once again, as a result of malnutrition, my shortness of breath and weakness continued, which kept me from things I enjoyed doing, like sports. That situation, I believe, may have undermined my body's immunity as I was no longer able to fight off diseases. That could have contributed to my getting sick during the first month of the second semester, and I was hospitalized for about six weeks. My mom offered all the love and care she could, and since there was no health insurance of any kind, the accrued financial debt was astronomical. The weight of the whole ordeal could not be any heavier on my mom. I knew she was hurting inside but on the outside she showed no sign of helplessness, frustration, or agony. One of the days she came to the hospital, I ate a large portion of the food she had cooked for me; that made her very happy because it was a sign that I was beginning to improve. I could tell she was more hopeful on that day because she not only stayed longer but talked more.

I took that rare opportunity and said to her, "Mom, thank you for taking care of me."

"I am happy to," she responded.

"How are you able to pay for my medication and the hospital bill?" I asked.

"I sold some of the gold your dad made for me, and if I have to sell all of them, I will. I don't want you to be worried about anything. I just want you to get well!"

I was very thankful to my mom who easily gave up her custom-made gold from my dad—a gift so unique and sealed with love by her husband—to save my life. Her thoughtfulness and selfless action will always tell the story of how much she was willing to give up for a son she loved. For me, at the time, it was not only gratifying but also regretful since the treasured gifts she sold were irrecoverable. The difficulty of meeting the financial obligation of my hospitalization was one thing, but the emotional toll it took on her was, I believed, beyond words. She probably had thought and asked: *What if my first son dies? Burying my husband was bad enough, should I have to bury my son, too?* Burying a child, I believe, is not an undertaking any widow should suffer! In the end, her invaluable sacrifice, strength, and courage paid off.

I was able to recover with the help and care of my mom and my medical team. Even as I recovered, my mom and I had to grapple with the prospect of my expulsion from the seminary. While I was sick, there was a matter that upset me more than my ailment. When I left the seminary, I was too ill to go home, so I checked myself into the hospital. I then sent for my mom, and when she arrived, I asked her to inform my pastor that I was in the hospital and to plead with him to let the bishop know. My pastor came to the hospital after a few days to visit me. During his visit, he informed me he had made my situation known to the bishop and that the bishop would come soon to pay me a visit. I spent many days in the hospital dreaming of the bishop's visit, a visit that never was! After I waited for a while, I sensed there was a problem and, sent my mom to see the bishop with a letter I had written. In the letter, I explained that I could not stay in the seminary because I got sick and, that I had the permission of the rector to go and seek medical treatment. I informed him of how serious my situation was, and that I had to go from school to the hospital bed. In explaining my condition, I hoped to also convey that I was incapable of informing him in person of my sickness. In a portion of my letter to the bishop, I gave him an update on how much I had improved and thanked him for his prayers and support. I was crushed when my mom came back with the news that the bishop was upset and opined that no one, not even my pastor, had told him anything about my situation. I was confused to say the least but began to believe the bishop did not pay me a visit all that time because he was disappointed in me for keeping him in the dark or unhappy with my pastor for the same reason. It also entered my mind that there may be an underlying issue that could explain the misunderstanding. My pastor confirmed to me that he did inform him, and I could not come up with at least a reason why my pastor may want to embellish the fact. The bishop was no longer young but close to retirement and, his memory perhaps was not as reliable as it used to be. It was saddening to come to the conclusion that my pastor may have informed him, and that I might be right to have thought that he forgot. He was a very good man, sharp and brilliant as he was holy; he was a great bishop! The thought that he was possibly at that stage of his life where we all begin to fall apart too quickly, underscored the deplorable state of human nature. Whatever may have happened, and whatever the reason, it brought a depressing feeling to have realized that the bishop was upset, and I prayed I would not be the grass that was compromised when two elephants played or fought. That is to say that if there was a disagreement between my bishop and my pastor because of me, it was possible that it could jeopardize my vocation to the priesthood.

After my recovery, I went to see the bishop and my visit confirmed my mom's report that he was unhappy. He told me to go back to the seminary and that he would, meanwhile, wait for the end-of-year report from the seminary authorities. When I arrived in the seminary, it was overwhelming to discover how much academic work I had missed and how much I had to study for the second semester examination that would start in a week's time. My friends were very supportive and of immense help and provided me with the lessons I had missed. I settled down to study, and to my surprise, my result was actually better than the one of the first semester.

The end of the academic school year always came with fresh worries for us as seminarians, because that was when we found out whether or not we would be allowed to continue our formation to the priesthood. My own worries came with a thick air of uncertainty because of my hospitalization, and I knew my report would not be good, and I only wished I knew how bad it would be. For all I knew, my ill health and subsequent absence from school was likely to come up again and that would not work in my favor. But because of what I had been through already and the fact that I had my mom's support, I did not panic. During the reunion, when all of us gathered to know from the bishop how we performed in the past academic year, I had my report read to me, and it was worse than I thought.

The bishop, looking very old and frail, sat in a comfortable brown leather office chair. The office desk covered the rest of him except for his bald head, crowned with the bishop's red skullcap, and his chest, which had borne many years of the diocesan burden. He wore a white soutane with red-silk trimmed hem. The office desk was shining with such a glow you would believe it was polished and buffed before each seminarian came in. I would have been surprised if it were not, because the bishop demanded nothing but holiness, excellence in all things, and cleanliness.

As I came into the room, which was as intimidating as it could possibly be—not only because of the main occupant, the bishop, but also the furnishings—the bishop quietly looked at a piece of paper I suspected was part of my report from the seminary. I did not interrupt him; he was so focused on what he was looking at, I doubt he knew I was there. I was startled when he broke the silence by saying, "Vincent, have a seat."

He preferred my baptismal name. "Thank you, my Lord." I stammered through the words. I carefully sat, hoping not to knock anything down because I was very nervous.

What he said next surprised me, "I don't understand this report. I may have to read it to you."

I was still quiet because I did not think he needed my permission to proceed. "'He is sick! If he has to come back, he will repeat Spiritual Year,'" He read it out loud and with a clear voice.

I did not understand it, either. There were many unanswered questions and unclear presuppositions. I had recovered from my ailment, so the opening statement on my report, "He is sick," was factually incorrect. I read from "If he has to come back" to mean the seminary authorities stopped short of recommending that I be withdrawn. That meant that they left the bishop to be solely saddled with the weight of making a decision on my case. Though the final decision of terminating a seminarian's formation falls within the bishop's discretion and jurisdiction, he sometimes preferred that the seminary officials gave him an indication of where they were leaning. The last part, "He will repeat Spiritual Year," was not funny. Repeating Spiritual Year would be pure torture; it meant I would be separated from my friends, wear a pair of uncomfortable white sashes on top of my white soutane to distinguish me from older students and, lastly, take the same classes over again and sit for the same exams I had already taken and did so well on.

I listened, was lost in my thoughts, and quietly waited for the verdict. At that point, I was truly overwhelmed by all I had been through and did not care which direction the pendulum swayed, favorable or not. In fact, I secretly wished I were expelled so the cloud of fatigue that hung around me from all the uncertainties and ordeals I had been facing would dissipate. As I waited and was lost in my thoughts, the bishop said, "You did well in your academic work, I see."

"Thank you, my Lord," I responded.

"You will hear from me before the reunion is over," he offered, and I thanked him again.

Waiting while the bishop considered what to do with me would have been a punishing suspense, but it was not because of the fact that I was no longer thrilled about being a seminarian. When the report came the following day, it was from the vocation director; it was oral and indicated that I go back when the seminary reopened.

It appeared God was not going to make it easy for me as I wished. I believed it would have been easier for me if I were withdrawn. Since it sounded like an unusual torment to go back and perhaps repeat Spiritual Year with terms and conditions that were unbearable. When the seminary resumed, I went to see the rector to know what my program would look like because my situation was unprecedented. He instructed that for the first semester, I would attend only the spiritual activities since I had already attended classes and took my examination. The rector also mentioned that the second semester would be different because I would join in all the activities, including the classes and examination. He was a very kind man and that was why we all called him Okuku, meaning "Father." As I left his office after the instruction, he called me back. He was still sitting down and peering at me through the top of his glasses while they balanced on the tip of his nose, and for a moment, I thought I was in trouble.

"Vincent, I believe you feel awful that you are repeating Spiritual Year." His voice echoed in his usual deep accent. "It might be a tough thing to do, but someday, you will realize how beneficial it was for you to do this and thank me for it. I see you are wearing a pair of sashes. That's a good step in the right direction. It tells me of your predisposition to embrace your challenges, even the least of them." He appeared to be smiling at that point. "I think everyone in the seminary knows you by now, and I presume you have learned a lot about spirituality, I, therefore, will spare you of wearing them."

That last part about getting rid of the sashes made me smile back at him. I somehow knew the rector wanted to seem stern as he looked at me through the top of his glasses, but he started laughing. He may have laughed because he observed my reaction when he made that exception for me. The rector was well aware of how much seminarians like me hated wearing those irritating sashes. The sashes were emblems of spirituality, but in our naïveté, most of us saw them as unnecessary leashes. The expression of relief on my face when the rector relieved me of wearing them was evident and genuine and, that the rector took notice meant he knew us well enough.

The rector was right about how beneficial repeating Spiritual Year would be for me. I had the whole semester to myself and spent my whole class and study periods in the library, researching different topics and courses, and I also read more novels than I can remember. There was, however, one course I could not pull myself away from, and that was Logic. I was not expected to attend Logic classes, but I went and never missed a class because I enjoyed it, besides loving Father Polycarp Ndugbu, who taught the course so well. I can certainly say that it was truly informative to read and research just for the sake of knowledge instead of being motivated to do so for the sake of passing examinations. Since I was prone to being anemic and having my body's immunity and defense against diseases compromised when my food was low in nutrients, the doctor gave me a medical report that required I eat highly nutritious meals and that I should be exempt from manual labor. After I joined the coveted club of those who ate special meals—which were well prepared, delicious, and rich in nutrients—I no longer had shortness of breath or got dizzy when I played soccer or any other sport. The next benefit I enjoyed was free association and interaction with older students, which the other Spiritual Year students were barred from doing. Modestly put, I lived like a prince. I could not believe that what seemed like my demise turned out to yield sweet dividends, which I relished. The joy and fortitude with which I accepted and dealt with my seeming plight made even those who did not know me, cheer for me. I would attribute my calm disposition as I faced my challenges partly to my decision to live my life a day at a time and, to hope that things would turn out well eventually. I believed that if things ended up badly after I had hoped for the best and made honest efforts there would not be any need to grieve or room for regret. I decided not to bemoan my situation but, on the contrary, to be joyful. If I was going to repeat Spiritual Year, it would be helpful to do it having fun. Being joyful and having fun while grappling with life issues conserves energy and inspires, besides drawing others to help us when we are in need. I sincerely thought that what I had to endure at the time was nothing compared to some of the things I had confronted in my lifetime. During those hard times it was comforting to appeal to past experiences which had ample evidence of God's sustenance and providence. It was also heartwarming to trust that God would continue to aid me and, for me to actually reap some instant little benefits even as I dealt with my situation. The most prominent of the blessings that I received did not come until the very end of my Philosophy program. If there were any remaining tiny, insignificant regret or doubt, that last blessing took it away altogether. I actually went and thanked the rector for recommending that I repeat Spiritual Year. At the end of my degree program in Philosophy, my final result was very good, thanks to the class I repeated the Spiritual Year with. That class was an exceptional class with many brilliant seminarians. The average score of the class was so excellent it overflowed to the not-so brilliant students, like me, in the class. The seminarians in my original class had such a poor result that their top students would have killed to have my grade.

The bishop helped to pay for most of the cost of getting seminarians trained and educated—except for the hundred dollars, or its equivalent, in naira for tuition, school supplies, books, and other personal effects. For those expenses, I depended on my family, especially my sister Helena, who took a job after high school as a clerk in a local community bank in my village. My family was still hurting financially, and my other siblings were in school and needed support, so I rarely went to my mom for money unless the matter needed urgent attention. Helena, my sister, I would say, was my small angel, and I called her Daa. That nickname, Daa, was born out of a big conflict and forced concession. *Daa* means "big sister" and could be used by itself, as a term of endearment, or added in a formal way, as a prefix before the name of an older woman when addressing her, because the culture demanded we do so as a sign of respect. Just as *Daa* is for women, so is *Dee* for men which meant "big brother". My sister Helena and I share the same birthday; we were both born on the fourth of December, but four years apart. For that reason, when we were growing up, I thought it would not be too much to ask or expect that she used Dee before my name or even for her to address me simply as Dee. I believed that the little recognition and respect, which my culture called for, would have been appropriate, but Helena did not observe that tradition when it had to do with me, and I considered it very disrespectful. When talking to her and using the power of persuasion would not work, we engaged in countless conflicts and quarrels. In fact, instead of Dee, she would call me Uretu (dirty little boy), the name my peers called me, and I hated it when I was a little boy. I would admit that, sometimes, I was the one that started the fight by calling her a nickname she did not like. When calling her names would not get her to close her ears, beg for mercy, or cry, I would sing for her a song she disliked, and that usually brought her to tears and victory for me. After a long period of feeling hurt from being denied my cultural privileges and, becoming weary of getting under the skin of my lovely sister, I found a different way of dealing with the matter. Instead of waiting to be accorded the respect I thought I deserved, I gently brought it out of her. I began to be nicer to Helena and addressed her as Daa (Big Sister). She felt uncomfortable and suspicious initially, but she started relishing it after she realized I was not mocking her, that it came from my heart and, that I loved her dearly. Some people who did not know us thought she was older when they heard me call her Big Sister. That was the nice little gift she got for defiling a precious culture. But seriously, we actually have become best friends, and she sometimes calls me Dee, and when she does, I enjoy it while it lasts.

One particular day, I had run completely out of money and had to leave the seminary to return home for all the pennies I could get for personal things and more. I stopped at the bank where Daa worked. Seeing me, she ran out and hugged me. "Udo, I'm so happy to see you."

The hug and welcoming words were therapeutic. "I'm happy to see you too, and you look beautiful, as always. Does the money you smell and touch have something to do with it?" I joked.

"They would if they were mine. Then I would not mind the pungent mildew-like smell and filthy bills of money that I swim in each day." The look on her face and choice of words were so funny, we laughed together.

"How is mom and everyone?" I asked.

"Everyone is doing well and behaving. Mom is at work, and the rest of us are in school. If you're hungry, we can go home, and I'll cook you something," she suggested after a brief update on the family.

"I was afraid you were going to volunteer to cook for me, but I also hate to lie that I am hungry . . ."

She knew where I was going with that and did not wait for me to conclude because she already got the message. She ran to my direction and nicely punched me in the belly as a warning against my tease. Her punch felt like that of a five-year-old. I did not want to taunt her anymore, so I bent down, pretending it hurt. While still in that position, I spoke like I learned my lesson. "Okay, I'm sorry. I'll eat your delicious meal." She then smiled, and I walked closer to her and whispered in her ears even though no one was around, "I'm broke!"

Daa had her many strengths and a few faults. Her cooking could fit in the strengths column as well as rest comfortably in her fault slot. If you are very hungry, you would want her in the kitchen because she can whip something up so fast, you would think it was a quick take-out from the store or restaurant. The food mostly tasted like a terribly cooked meal that was leftover and then warmed up in a microwave. I do not want to put down my own sister and her sincere service with regard to feeding us, but I have to admit that, at the time, she had much more to learn about cooking. When hungry though, none of us cared about the taste of her food; we were rather appreciative of her speed.

Daa hated cooking and, I would bet only a nickel that after many years—even after she improved on her cooking—that she would want to pick being a chef as a career. For all I knew she wanted the cooking to be over with even before she started. When we have had our fill and forgotten her being a life-saver, we would tease her for being a terrible cook. If we were not hungry, had time to burn, and wanted a delicious home-cooked meal, then my mom or Gloria, my second sister, were the preferred chefs. Daa did not mind my teasing at all; she fed me, her hungry brother, who was dying for a home-cooked meal, whether cooked in a hurry or in slow motion. I enjoyed the meal, and when I was ready to leave, she slipped an undisclosed amount into my pants' pocket, but I knew it was at least fifty percent of her salary.

"Is that my tip for eating your delicious meal?" I sarcastically asked with a mischievous smile. She rolled her eyes and called me Uretu (dirty little boy). I hugged her and whispered, "Thank you, Daa. I love you!" and left for the seminary.

I made many of those trips for the span of ten years I was in the seminary (nine years in Major Seminary, and one year of teaching after my philosophy degree). Daa patiently worked for ten years, supporting me. At some point, I only needed to show up at the community bank where she worked, and she would know why I was there, and without words exchanged, money changed hands. I would have lunch and go back to the seminary. She sometimes took her salary in advance just to make sure I was all right.

At the expiration of ten years, after I was ordained a priest, she wanted to go into the convent and become a nun. I told her she would have my blessing only after she went to the university and got a degree in anything she chose. In telling her that, I not only wanted her to have the best in life but also secretly wished she would get married at some point while in school or after. My reason for doing so was selfish. Since I was a priest and would not have any kids of my own, I was hoping to adopt her children. Despite my personal interest, I, however, was open to the fact that she may still nurse the idea of becoming a nun after graduating from the university. If that were the case, it would be a stronger indication of God's call of her. Another advantage offered by that period of learning would be the predisposition to make an informed decision after the maturity, knowledge, and edge the university education provides. There was no doubt that after she graduated from the university and insisted on joining the convent, she had a great measure of knowledge of the expectations and implications of her choice.

Father Ben, my mom's cousin, knew of my financial needs and regularly helped me out. Another source of help came when Father Ben invited me to accompany him to see a friend of his, who was also his benefactress. She lived in a city called Aba. When we arrived at the home of Mrs. Theresa Elechi Okekpe, it was striking to see how her two-story house, though old, was well maintained. It looked like it just got painted a day before we arrived. The only reason I thought otherwise was because I could not smell any paint. The interior part of the house bore witness to a detailed, conscious orderliness and unsurpassed cleanliness. The furniture, floor, and ceiling were all exotic, and from their looks, it seemed they never saw a day without a thorough cleaning and polish. I thought she had great taste and an ardent inclination for good aesthetics.

Father Ben introduced me, "Mama, this is Udochukwu Vincent Ogbuji, a seminarian in Saint Joseph's Major Seminary, Ikot Ekpene. Udo, meet Mama Theresa, a dear friend."

"Do you mind if I call you Mama like my adopted uncle Father Ben?" I humbly asked.

"I don't mind. In fact, I'll love it if you do," she replied. I believed that was how we bonded. The name Mama, even though used to address one's mother, can also be a term of endearment when used for someone other than your mother, especially for a woman old enough to be your mother. We had a very delicious lunch and, afterward, a great and longer visit.

Everything about Mama stood out in grace and beauty. Before we left Mama's home, she had a private audience with Father Ben. As we were ready to leave, she discreetly squeezed something into the palm of my hand, with the words, "I'll pray for you as you go back to the seminary."

"Mama, thank you. I pledge to include you in my prayers every time we go into the chapel in the seminary to pray, and we do so many times in a day. Thank you also for being so hospitable. I enjoyed your company and cooking very much," I replied.

As we went back home, Father Ben told me that Mama liked me and wanted to be my benefactress, too. She had informed him that she would like to help with my tuition and in any other ways she could. She also offered the prospect of adopting me as her son since she did not have a son that became a priest. I accepted her offer and, over the years, got to know and love her together with my other brothers and sisters from my second family. With Daa and Mama helping, I was not hurting too much financially. Even in theology, as my needs increased, the new bishop, Lucius I. Ugorji, provided me with enormous support and the financial help I needed.

If money was the only hurdle for me to jump in the seminary, it would be quite an insignificant leap. But many other dire challenges presented themselves over the course of time. I knew my written English well enough but did not speak much because I did not want to be ridiculed when I misspoke. I remember in eighth grade when two boys got into a fight, knocked down my desk, and broke it. I had to say something, and I could not speak in my native language since only English was allowed in the campus, so I said, "You've spoiled my desk!"

My disheartening observation did not stop the fight, but my desperate words certainly did. Most of the students believed that I had misspoken and started a mocking cheer, the first sign that someone had slipped and, soon after joyfully started singing a song with the intent to humiliate me. The song they sang was reserved for those who spoke poor English. It was ultra embarrassing especially when one self-appointed class representative came close to me when things were beginning to quiet down and said as everyone watched and listened, "Don't be a disgrace to this class. The right word is *spoilt* not *spoiled*."

Spoilt in British English is the past tense for *spoil*. I wish I knew then that saying *spoiled* is correct in American English perhaps I would have used that as a cover to save face. Because of that embarrassment, I vowed not to speak out again in public. However, my self-damaging resolve was reconsidered and disavowed in ninth grade when I took the advice of my English Literature teacher. His piece of advice was that if we wanted to improve our spoken English, we had to listen to great speakers, devour English literature, and most importantly, use the language in speech. He also opined that even when we made mistakes and were laughed at, we should not quit speaking in English because the more we practiced, the better we become. It is not just the English language; it is true with every other language. He also warned that if we refused to speak because our classmates would make fun of us if we fumbled, some day, we may have to speak not in a classroom setting but as grown men. If we did not learn by speaking and are corrected now if there is need, we may face more painful and embarrassing experiences in the future. My teacher was right when he also said that the correction from our fellow students stayed with us all through life. I agree with him because I believe I would have to be dead before I forget the word *spoilt*, even here in the United States, where I can use *spoiled*. I tried to follow the advice of my teacher for many years, so I spoke in English openly, without fear of being laughed at. I got corrected in high school many times when I committed a blunder, and I was never ashamed, but benefited as I learned and improved.

Before I went to the seminary, I believed I had conquered my struggle with the English language. At least, it appeared I spoke it better and more fluently, but then I suddenly discovered how unsure I was about my spoken English. My confidence actually began peeling off when one of my dear friends started being very protective of me—or should I say, tried to be his brother's keeper. He wanted the best for me, but he sometimes went about it the wrong way, and it made things worse for me. Whenever I misspoke in the slightest way, he made sure he corrected me, and a number of times he did so with a few people present. Even when I spoke out publicly and my speech was impeccable, if he perceived it as analytically provocative in the smallest terms, I got a long lecture from him on how I could be expelled for my blunt remarks. He did not mean harm, but his corrections—especially the ones he made in public where he implied he was disappointed in me, unknown to him and, of course, me—were wearing down my sense of self-worth and self-assurance. At the time, I hardly knew it was a problem or how bad it was, so I let him play the role of a concerned friend, which I believed was his intention. On my part, I viewed his intended help in the same spirit of a friend helping the other, and that it was for my own good although I noticed that my confidence was gradually declining. The day it occurred to me that I had a bigger problem and needed help was the day I had a frightening mishap in the chapel during evening prayer. During the time of intercession within the evening prayers, the seminarians were allowed to add three more personal intercessory prayers to the official ones in the breviary. You can either read your prayer from a script you wrote down or say it extemporaneously. I chose the latter, to pray on the spur of the moment. In the middle of my off-the-cuff prayer, which progressed smoothly, I remembered my friend was sitting close by and that if I made any mistake, I was going to be reminded of it and chastised for it. I suddenly became nervous and frightened and went blank. When the students did not continue to hear from me, they responded, saying, "Lord, hear our prayers," thinking I was through. The Lord was watching out for me because, at the point, I lost my train of thought; the prayer I was saying, though short, sounded like a complete one. Only I knew I still had something to say, which I could not remember, and the situation could have been very humiliating.

My eroding confidence, I thought, would soon bring more torment and disgrace if I did not get a handle on it. Seeking guidance, I went to the spiritual director and related to him the story of my strange slip-up at evening prayer. He then asked, "Why were you afraid?"

"I don't know, Father," I responded. At the time, I actually did not know or saw any correlation between what was happening and my friend's attempt to correct me. Then what the spiritual director said next helped me to connect the dots.

"I want you to think for a minute and see if you can remember when your gradual loss of confidence started and what you think caused it."

After I thought for about three minutes, I linked it to my friend. I arrived at that conclusion because I believed I overcame my stage fright in secondary school and was doing well in the seminary until some point. Without a doubt, I narrowed my detractor to my friend when I replayed the incident in the chapel in my head. In doing so, I remembered I progressed very well until I thought about what my friend would think of or say to me in the event I tripped. It was then that my cognitive self gave way to fear.

I told the spiritual director that I thought my friend may be partly responsible, and he gave me the best advice. "You have to be aware of one thing about life: that no human being is free from making mistakes. Not even your friend who tries to correct you. So, even when your friend is present, express your opinion like he's not there. Tell your friend to come and see me, and don't be afraid to misspeak. Remember, we all do. You'll be surprised how many more people will show understanding or kindly forgive you because they identify with your being human."

I did not know what the spiritual director told my friend when they met. I never asked, but I am sure he told him not to confront me any more when I made a mistake because after I visited the spiritual director and my friend also did at his request, he never corrected me again. I did not really care whether he tried again to correct me or not because I had secretly resolved, and was personally determined, not to let him, anyone, or anything undercut my self-confidence again.

The next challenge that presented itself to me was my love and responsibility to my family. Growing up in a family where each person, beginning with my parents to the least of us, mostly denied themselves every luxury and sometimes sacrificed even the basic necessities of life to keep the family together, demanded that I try to do my part whether I am a seminarian or not. Being the breadwinner of the family, my dad worked every day, even when sick and in excruciating pain, to provide for us, but he did not complain. He left behind a beautiful example and had the right attitude that, perhaps, laid the great foundation for us all. It was not all sacrifice, though; once in a while, my dad would give himself, my mom, and the rest of us a treat. I knew of a time he visited the village and went by the farmers' market and bought a whole leg of a large goat, which was more meat than we needed, and dragged it home. My frugal mom was not amused at all. While my dad was ready to start a party, the look on my mom's face seemed to say "If you were a child, I would spank you for behaving very badly."

But instead she gently protested, "Dee Joe, this is too much meat. We don't need all this! You know we have to save some money to complete the house in the village and send these kids to college."

My dad responded in his usual funny easygoing way, "Lucy, you worry about too many things, which sometimes can be a good thing. Let's forget about all the worries and celebrate tonight. Make for us some tasty hot soup with part of that meat and open up that rich red wine I have been saving because you kept me from drinking it. If you quit being mad at me and lighten up, I'll dance with you tonight."

My mom, at that point, laughed and was so happy that she forgot she had been slightly mad at my dad and the reason why she was.

He then concluded, "Lucy, let us celebrate our lives and blessings tonight, okay? How many times will I have to remind you that the good things we enjoy while we are still alive, may be the only material reward we share before we are gone! It is wise to keep in mind the sacrifices we have to make. Even as we do that it won't be a bad idea to celebrate our successes so far. Please, may we give ourselves a little treat tonight, so as to be in a good spirit to take care of these 'naughty' kids and each other." He was laughing heartily as he was convinced he had smoothened out any reluctance left in my mom with his humor, gentleness and forthrightness. My mom did not stop laughing because she continued to be fascinated by his charm, and the truth he conveyed. There was no room for disagreement that night, so we celebrated. We all had a great time, including my mom who only smelled the wine and was hesitant to dance until the festive magic broke down her defenses.

My mom sacrificed everything when she decided to stay a single mom in order to care for us after my dad died, although she was still very young and had many suitors who were very serious about marrying her. She may have made the decision to remain unmarried partly because in a patriarchal society where we lived, my mom marrying another man would have automatically made the only brother my dad had the executor of his estate. The prevalent culture would have expected us to trust my uncle to manage my dad's property while caring for us and to hand it over to me when I was old enough to take over the administration. My mom did not believe in that arrangement and I would not either if I were her, especially since my uncle did not seem to have a genuine personal interest in us. It was possible that if my mom remarried and we lived with my prospective stepfather, we would have, perhaps, lost everything. That my mom stayed single meant that she remained the executor of my dad's assets, and she has been a very good manager. She knew how to run the family's affairs with very little! My mom understood when to be stingy and when to be generous and how to put a smile on our faces. Her decision to choose us instead of another husband required enormous sacrifice, and that thoughtfulness and selflessness she showed by giving up what she would have wanted, became a redemptive act that saved the family.

My sister Helena also sacrificed as I noted earlier in this chapter, and so did my other siblings in their own little ways. When my dad passed away, a vacuum was created, which culture and circumstances demanded that I fill. My mom was instrumental to my adjusting quickly to that new role—she did so by relying on me for different things and even entrusted me with much more as I grew older. She would not do anything unless she had my opinion and blessing. I felt directly responsible for everyone's safety and well-being. There was no phone, so I had to go home every other week. One of the times I had gone home from the seminary, my little brother, Henry, had rheumatism that had twisted his arm out of balance. My mom, already battling with too many responsibilities, was confused on what to do, and the best she knew to do under the circumstances was to take him to a chemist store. That was a small local store that sold medicine to the sick; sometimes the owner of the store was the only "doctor" the villagers knew. When I saw the condition of my brother, I knew it was not a case for the village "doctor", and I took him to the hospital. As it turned out my brother's situation was much more complicated than it seemed, and he would have lost his arm if I did not visit home. The need to go home grew, and I began to visit more frequently, and I have to be honest to admit that my going home became a habit I began to enjoy very much. That habit was conflicting with the expectations in the seminary, built upon the principle of leaving everything to follow Christ, including family. The more I progressed in my seminary training, the worst things got. I was not supposed to leave the seminary premises without permission, but I did many times because I knew it would be a waste of time to go to the seminary authorities and ask to be permitted to go home for personal matters.

The final problem that fundamentally threatened my hope of becoming a priest and further compounded things was my feeling of unworthiness. The closer I got to being a priest, the more I had reservations about being one. I suddenly started feeling a strong sense of falling short. I began to entertain the thought that Catholic priesthood and the attached condition of celibacy was a vocation for perfect men or angels. I knew I was not a perfect man or an angel, so there was no need to keep hanging around the seminary. I could not help but wonder why I was still in the seminary and what I was doing in that place when the dream of a nice girl and cute kids (a wonderful family of my own) flooded my brain. My fantasy, I believed, cancelled the idea of being a priest and made the thought of celibacy an ideal beyond me. Once I was convinced of my unworthiness of Catholic priesthood, I wanted to leave the seminary, but I could not get myself to do it. I could not leave because I had unanswered questions like, what if God was really calling me and I gave up on God because of my nagging desire? I had to be sure God did not want me before I left; upsetting God was the last thing I wanted to do. I, therefore, sought for a way to find out what God wanted of me while I stayed back in the seminary. After many earnest prayers said in search of answers, I got none, and with no clear way of knowing what was in God's mind, I started engaging in some behaviors contrary to what my bishop, teachers, and of course, myself expected of me. My hope was that I would be caught and expelled if God did not want me as his priest. As strange as it sounded, I would have felt better or preferred to be expelled from the seminary than to leave on my own. One of such bad behaviors I adopted in order to be expelled was a conscious effort not to pay attention to my studies, classes, or lecturers. I remember being in class, bored out of my mind and wishing I could be somewhere else. I got out my pencil and a blank sheet of paper while the class was going on and began to draw one of the seminarians. I chose one of my friends whom we called G.O.D. He was a good sport and enjoyable to be around and, would even be the first to make fun of himself. I drew a cartoon character of him. His lips were big in real life and I gave him much larger ones and with attitude. I proceeded to highlight his broad nose, which I twisted a little bit for a desired effect of teasing and taunting. I sketched his pear-like cheeks and small flat forehead, which shone like three electric bulbs. I was faithful in drawing his small receded eyes and, his fluffy hair that would make a good nest for squirrels. All that gave him a laid-back expression that was true to him. I sketched everything with care to bring out an exaggerated representation of him, with the intention of getting anyone who saw it to laugh. I passed it on to the next person who sat with me in class; he looked at it, then turned and looked at G.O.D and laughed silently. When done, he passed it to the next person.

Before long someone chuckled out loud, and the professor sensed something was wrong, and my drawing ended up in his hands. I was not expelled but was asked to clean all the toilets in Saint Boniface Hostel for two weeks as my punishment.

The next destructive behavior of mine was leaving the seminary many more times, and for days, without permission from authorities. On one such day, I encountered the administrative dean who hesitated at first to approach me because he thought I had permission since I came in through the main gate of the seminary. Seminarians who left without permission did not dare come in through the main gate to avoid being caught. Although he believed I was authorized to leave the seminary premises, he asked—maybe to make sure—but was shocked when I told him I left on my own accord. Because I had come in through the main entrance to the seminary, and did not panic even when I saw him, but boldly walked in and greeted him, the look on his face was that of a man who was trying to solve a perplexing puzzle. The next question that he asked me proved how confused he was. "You mean to tell me you don't have permission to leave the seminary?" Not waiting for an answer, he continued, "Come and see me in my office tomorrow by eleven in the morning."

I did not lose any sleep that night over my impending appointment but, on the contrary, relished the outcome—which was possible expulsion. Finally, I could actually have my freedom, and it would be tomorrow, when I would probably be told that the seminary is not the place for me.

As I knocked at the door of the dean's office, I was surprised that he was standing there, waiting for me, and actually let me in. "Have a seat, Vincent. I'm finishing up with a report, and I'll see you in a minute."

I almost started singing for joy thinking, *That must be my expulsion report*, and hoping he would hurry to get through with it. I knew packing my things would not take that much time especially with friends helping me; we might even have time to celebrate and share a bottle of wine before I said my final good-byes.

Father Dean's voice brought me back to reality. "You want something to drink?" he gracefully offered.

"I'll have a big bottle of beer," I joked and chuckled. He wanted to laugh so hard but suppressed the laughter and smiled instead. I then said, "I'll have soda or water."

He was trying to be serious but could not help himself, and concluded, "You're in so much trouble and probably need the beer, but I want you to be sober because we have serious matters to discuss." We both laughed. He came out of his living room still laughing—but with no letter, report, or anything in hand—and asked, "Vincent, let's be serious. Why did you leave the seminary without permission?"

My instinct told me that he really liked me and wanted to help me. But I was not sure I wanted his help, and if I continued letting my guard down, I thought, he was going to drag me into the church and ordain me a priest. My reply was guarded, "I don't know, Father."

"Do you want to be expelled?" he asked.

"If you believe that is the best thing for me, I will happily accept your decision," I responded.

What he said next surprised and disappointed me at the same time. "I am not going to expel you, Vincent, go and see the spiritual director."

What he told me was not what I expected to hear, nevertheless, I thought seeing the spiritual director and opening up to him might turn things to my advantage. I did not think he would want me in the seminary when I told him about the battle going on inside of me. He would probably close his ears when I told him how much I thought about having a girl in my life. I knew caring for my mom and siblings was not that significant, so I would leave that out of our discussion.

The spiritual director was nice and welcoming, and he thought I was there to see him because of my stage fright. "Are you still frightened of your little friend?" he joked.

"No, Father, it is the other way around now. I think he is the one frightened of me." He chuckled, and I smiled. "Father, thank you for your help, you made the fear incident so easy to resolve."

"You did all the hard work, Vincent, and I am proud of you. I am still praying for you and I hope you will invite me to your ordination in two and a half years," he concluded.

"I'll invite you if I don't get married by then." It was meant as a joke but it fell flat. He did not laugh, and the look on his face was not that of disappointment but a man who was stunned, maybe waiting to understand the issue before he spoke. "Father, I was sent by the administrative dean to see you. I left the seminary without permission," I volunteered.

"Do you mind sharing with me why?" He said and leaned forward eager to hear everything I had to say.

"Father, I have been leaving the seminary without permission in the hope that I will be caught and expelled. I don't just want to leave on my own because if God really wanted me to be a priest, I don't want him to be mad at me for leaving. But I'm conflicted. I feel very unworthy of becoming a priest. I think of girls and want to be married to a good one. I am beginning to worry that this is not something someone this close to being a priest should be thinking or feeling. My belief is that this is a vocation meant for angels, and I'm not one."

When I was done, he looked at me and smiled, a smile that said "What you just told me is easy to solve."

Then he asked me a question. "Do you think I'm worthy to be a priest?"

"Yes, Father!" I answered. "You're cut out to be a priest. Don't you know what the seminarians call you?" Without waiting for him to ask, I proudly told him, "We call you 'Spirit'. That is because we believe you are a very good and holy man and cut out to be a priest."

"No, no, stop, Vincent!" he protested. "I want you to know that I have my own struggles, too. God doesn't call us because we are worthy, but to work in and through us despite our unworthiness in order to bring his salvation to his people. I want you to pray about your vocation. Do the best you can and try to do the right thing. If in the process you are expelled, at least your conscience will be at peace since you gave it your best and didn't succeed."

His words of wisdom were what I needed to hear, and he left me in awe and wonder of his insight.

During the period I struggled with making a decision on whether to become a priest or not, I hardly had a good personal prayer life, and even my communal prayers with the other seminarians were lifeless and came off as mere rote. Faced with those uncertain times, I wished I still had my former roommate, Martin Edward Ohajunwa, whom I adopted as my brother in the same seminary with me. He had been sent at the time to a different seminary by his bishop to study Theology. The reason I wished he was close by was because he had clarity about why he was in the seminary and prayed like he did. His love for and joy in the seminary rubbed off on me while we were roommates, and in many ways, he loaned me the support I needed as my brother and friend. All we shared, all I learned from him and more, came to life more after I discussed my situation with the spiritual director. The result was that I improved on my behavior and prayer life and rediscovered my favorite saint, Joseph. I dusted off his statue on my reading table and persistently had devotion to him, asking him to protect and direct me like he did his son, Jesus. That I love Saint Joseph and, that he meant so much to me is evident in many ways: my dad, whom I adored, was named Joseph and my parish church together with the seminary I attended were named after Saint Joseph. Lastly, my thesis on Theology was titled "The Role of Saint Joseph in Salvation History." With Saint Joseph at every turn, I was finally led to God's plan through his help, intercession, and protection.

Picture with Martin Edward while we were roommates

CHAPTER 8

Apprenticeship

Love is at its finest and truly fulfilling when it seeks nothing for itself, and the more daunting the sacrifice in love, the more rewarding love is.

—Father Udo Ogbuji

As my third year of Theology was coming to a close, I knew my priestly apprenticeship was about to begin. My ordination as a transitional deacon was a few months away and, being a deacon meant I could be of assistance to the priest at Mass. I would also be able to administer the Sacrament of Baptism and witness to weddings, among other duties. I had many years to reflect on Catholic priesthood, but as I got closer to becoming one, it became clearer that even if I had endless time to contemplate and conceptualize the depth and breadth of the priesthood, it would not be enough. There were a few questions I wished were answered, but after nine years in Major Seminary, I knew it would require going into God's mind to find the answers. I proceeded with the belief and hope that the conundrums would be resolved after I became a priest because there would be an actual experience and a realistic proof of the legitimacy of my concerns. I was aware that if the muddy subjects were not rectified before or after I became a priest, I may have to pray a lot more since I would need the help of God to live with them, like what Saint Paul did when God told him, "My grace is sufficient for you" (2 Corinthians 12:9). Even though, at that point, I was leaning more toward accepting the gift of priesthood and the sacrifice it would demand, I still approached that divine venture with measured caution. I tried, on a few occasions, to slow myself down in case I was moving too fast.

The last attempt to talk myself out of becoming a priest or trying to get someone else to do so was the eve of my diaconate ordination. I was getting ready to leave for the bishop's house for the incardination ceremony when my mom came to check on me.

"Mom, you have a minute?" I asked.

"Sure! What do you need?" she graciously responded.

I began with this question: "Mom, you know I will be ordained a deacon tomorrow, and you support me, don't you?"

She was very happy and celebrating the wonderful moment so much that she was oblivious of the hidden trap I was laying for her. Smiling, she answered, "Yes, I do, of course."

My next question, which revealed my mischievous plot, turned my joyful and smiling mother into a subdued and somber woman. "You realize that after tomorrow, you won't have any grandchild from me?"

The force and impact of the reality was sudden and so overpowering that my mom broke down in tears. I felt some relief that, at least, my greatest fan was about to agree with me that I needed to reconsider my decision to become a priest. My mom seemed to have realized that her tears gave the hint she, herself, was having second thoughts about the commitment I was about to make. Not intending in the least to discourage me, she stopped the flow of tears and appealed to the toughness and wisdom she had always shown in difficult circumstances. "Udo," she said, "Of course, I would love to have grandkids, but it is not my decision. I'll support you, no matter what your choice is."

Boy, I said to myself, *here I thought you were about to make my decision much easier by encouraging me to reconsider becoming a priest.* But, on the contrary, she threw the whole weight of that decision back at me and gently rubbed my nose on the rough surface of the fact that it was my life and responsibility. I made the decision to go to the cathedral to be ordained a deacon.

The diaconate ordination Mass at Mater Dei Cathedral, Umuahia, was as solemn as could be, and the reception afterward with family and friends cheered my heart. Everyone was happy for me and asked me to pray for them and that they were praying for me. I was treated like royalty, but there was nothing special about me because I did not perceive or feel that anything changed, especially physically; I was practically the same person I was before the ordination. Although I believed there was an inner transformation, I somewhat hoped for, perhaps, a recognizable change in me that would attest to the reality of the spiritual gift and grace I received. The reason I missed the beautiful and recognizable changes around me on that day was because I played the elephant. The elephant does not see something close to it, and I clearly did not take note of the great joy that filled the air, which everyone, including me, felt. I had a few days to assist my pastor as a deacon before I returned to the seminary, and on one of such days after Mass, I had a simple but deep revelation. On that day, as I stayed back for a private prayer, I reflected on my diaconate ordination ceremony and my concern for the absence of a noticeable sign or change in me. My reflection led me to the most subtle and important realistic sign of the day, which I missed while waiting for something extraordinary. What I overlooked was the joy and fulfillment I felt, which was beyond what anything material could give. That fine discovery led me to one of the inscriptions I decided I would print on my priestly ordination souvenir, if I made it that far. The quote I chose from the Bible was "You have given my heart more joy than they have when grain and wine abound" (Psalm 4:8).

As I went back to the seminary, I observed that I enjoyed being in the seminary much more than I ever did before. I rarely went out of the seminary for any reason, even to go home either with or without permission. I found myself discovering the seminary anew and was firmly drawn to the profound tranquility, peace, and many spiritual benefits the seminary offered. My renewed passion for the seminary grew to the point that I wished to be permitted to stay in the seminary even during short holidays. I attributed my newfound love for the seminary to the overflowing bliss from my diaconate ordination, which had opened me up to enjoy the beauty I had previously ignored. My fondness for the seminary was also because it offered me a place of escape and preparation for the predictable difficulties priestly ministry would pose. After I spent a little time with my pastor as a deacon, I realized how much more knowledge, wisdom, fortitude, and God's grace I would need; and so I devoted the rest of the period I spent in the seminary imbibing those attributes. It did not matter what made the seminary suddenly a delightful place for me to be; all I knew was that I enjoyed being there and no other place. It appeared God had something in mind when he opened my heart to behold the beauty of the seminary because after I was ordained a priest, my first assignment was to teach in the seminary.

When I first got the news of my posting after my ordination to priesthood, I thought it was a mistake. If anything, I surmised I was ill-qualified to be teaching seminarians who would be priests when I felt that I did not know any better myself. I could practically teach anything academic if given a textbook and a syllabus, but formation of seminarians for me was much more than academic work. It first required guiding the young minds to discern if they have a calling to the priesthood. Training seminarians also entails helping them to have a true sense of the privilege of what it means to be priests and the selfless sacrifice it demands. Furthermore, their being formed must also include supporting them in their determination to carry out the will and mission of Christ with dedication and devotion. Doing these things and more for the seminarians would not be easy, especially since I was only beginning to find my priestly bearings and still had unanswered questions. Being a human being, I am aware that there is only so much I am able know regarding my relationship with God—as it concerns the priesthood. That is because it falls within the level of the spiritual, which can be murky sometimes, and always demands faith, which is also a supernatural mystery. Since serving God in that elevated capacity is an intense spiritual endeavor, it does not help matters that the physical part of man interjects itself and, sometimes, makes things a lot more difficult. Hence, it was a little upsetting that a few months after I was ordained a priest, my hope and need for resolution to my unresolved matters were not realized. In the light of that, I fine-tuned my expectation with regard to my assignment. I no longer accepted my assignment mainly as an opportunity to teach seminarians but as a spiritual provision that would continually help me form and inform myself. With that in mind, I believed my first mission of teaching in the seminary may not have been a bad idea after all. I began to understand that ten years in the seminary was hardly enough for the wisdom I desired and to have some complicated issues resolved. I was, therefore, thankful that heaven gave me the gift of my first mission, which became a special form of apprenticeship to prepare me for the work ahead.

My first ministry as a priest was to teach at a Spiritual Year Seminary in a little town called Ozu Abam. It was a place for an intensive one-year spiritual program for seminarians from my diocese. My bishop sent minor seminarians there after they have completed high school and also served for one year in a parish or any other institution in the diocese. My own Spiritual Year Program was in the Philosophy campus of a major seminary. But several years later, my bishop (and other bishops) built a separate seminary just for Spiritual Year Program. It made sense for those young men to be prepared mentally and spiritually in that unique seminary before they are sent to study Philosophy in the major seminary. My bishop's strategy, I am sure, have saved a few vocations over the years, that otherwise could have been lost in the philosophical wilderness of wonder.

When I arrived at my post of duty and looked around, I thought to myself, almost aloud, *How stunningly beautiful this place is. I'm truly lucky to be here!* That seminary was located on top of a small mountain, and you could see up to five miles of green vegetation of hills and valleys. It was the rainy season but a clear sunny day, so those visible five miles looked like a rich, fresh, delightful vast green blanket. It was gorgeous and a wonderful sight to behold. During my first night, there was a full moon, and the stars looked so close to Earth, it could not possibly be real, and I thought I could reach out and touch them if only I grew taller. There was also a sweet breeze that was cold enough and blew strong enough to keep the mosquitoes away while offering a welcoming bliss. The seminarians had not returned for the academic year, so the seminary was quiet and very peaceful, and I hoped never to go anywhere else. I knew that was wishful thinking, and it did not take too long before my fate changed.

My primary assignment in the Spiritual Year Seminary was to teach Scripture, Psychology, and Liturgy, and I very much enjoyed that privilege. We had fourteen seminarians, and they arrived three months after I did. There were only two priests, the rector and myself. For three months, as we waited for the seminarians to return for the academic year, Father Rector and I had each other, and it did not take long for us to bond as brothers and as friends. For the one academic year we worked together before he was relocated, I felt at home with him and had the opportunity to ask him some of the unanswered questions I had about different issues. One such question was the reality of human sexuality as it relates to the Catholic priesthood and celibacy. I was delighted that he felt at ease to give me his honest reflection on that topic after having lived it for four years as a priest. His openness about that perplexing issue—which almost everyone considered a taboo, though no one said so, and many tactfully avoided or barely addressed—made me have greater respect for him. The brief answer I got from the spiritual director (as I narrated in chapter seven) was one of the rarest, most direct and revealing I heard personally about a priest's struggles. The priests, as I knew them, seemed to have all their problems resolved and were doing perfectly well. I cannot say with certainty that the spiritual director was referring directly to struggles with human sexuality because his exact words were "I have my own struggles, too." So, it could have been anything. His short revealing response was very useful and seemed enough at the time. There were questions I wished I had asked him, but I did not ask them probably because I was too timid to do so or did not know the best way to frame them. Such questions would be the following: Does the grace of God erase or help suppress human sexual feelings? What happens when one becomes a priest and feels that smothering sexual urge or falls in love? Could sexual longing be overcome completely at some point with age, effort, and grace from God?

I did not blame anyone who stayed away from that subject, priests and seminarians alike, since it was an uncomfortable topic to discuss and had to do with people's private lives and feelings they wished to keep to themselves. It was possible that part of the reason it was avoided by the seminary authorities was because they hoped that life's experiences would be the best teacher for us in that matter. Moreover, it was a delicate area to venture in, and they wanted to tread very carefully so as not to scandalize us.

The closest anyone came to addressing the issues surrounding celibacy was at one of the retreats we had in the seminary, moderated by a newly ordained bishop. To say that one of his memorable comments—which by extension was a piece of advice—had set the seminary on fire would be an understatement. He said that if any of his seminarians had not experienced the love of a woman, he would not ordain him a priest. Some priests among the staff members were furious because they felt somewhat betrayed. They may have thought, *We have worked so hard to keep these young men on a tight leash, and here comes someone in authority, a bishop, who is supposed to cement our grip but, on the contrary, is undoing our many years of labor. He is about to unleash the floodgate of orgies in the seminary!* Some of the frustrated priests may have been confused, perhaps wondering if the bishop's threat would also be extended to very good seminarians who, for reasons beyond their control, did not have the opportunity of experiencing a woman's love. It was unfortunate to witness the unintended interpretation and reaction to the bishop's honest opinion by some of the priests. I did not believe the bishop was sending us on a hunt; his intention was not to misguide us or encourage us to engage in a behavior unbecoming of seminarians. What I understood from his statement and entire retreat was that he wanted his seminarians (and us) to not only imbibe spiritual, academic, and common-sense knowledge but also hoped for them to be streetwise, balanced, and mature. If they never experienced some basic human social habits, how would they know how to react when they have to minister to the faithful? Women are clearly in the majority among the faithful and often more dedicated in church functions. It is, therefore, easy to imagine how uncomfortable it would be if a priest did not know, to some extent, how most women think (their psyche) or what he may feel or expect when a woman he is attracted to is present and how to handle the situation. He would most certainly be like a fish out of water.

The story told about two monks not only highlights what good training, experience, maturity, and prayer can accomplish but also underscores how destructive ignorance and immaturity can be. Two monks were on a local road walking back to the monastery when it started raining. The rain was so heavy it flooded the local river and overflowed its bank, destroying the bridge that served the community. As the two monks approached the river, they saw a girl stranded, wet and crying on the other side of the river. With the bridge broken, she could not cross over, and it was getting dark.

Monk A said, "Let us get over to the other side so we can help her."

Monk B responded, "How in the world are you going to help her? Our rules in the monastery say we should not come in close proximity with any girl."

Monk A knew it was getting dark and that there was no time to argue the laws before justifying a good deed that needed to be done, and urgently. He thought there would be plenty of time later to debate what was appropriate as prescribed in the law, but at the moment, it was time enough for a charitable work. He quickly went over to the girl and gently carried her across the river and bid her good-bye.

As they proceeded on their way, Monk B said, "Did you see how her clothes were stuck to her body?"

Monk A answered, "No."

After they walked in silence for a while and were almost close to the monastery, Monk B asked yet another suggestive question, "Did you feel anything when you carried her?"

Monk A could not bear it anymore, so he said to Monk B, "That young girl needed help, and after I helped her, I left her across the river. From all your questions, you have been carrying her in your mind ever since. I brought her to safety and left her beside the river."

If seminarians never experienced the love of a woman, how are they able to exercise self-control or know if they can stand the strong current of human passion or measure their level of discipline? The bishop may have thought that if his—or any—seminarian was making such a lifetime commitment, it would be beneficial for him to have some real-life experience of the sacrifice he would be faced with if he made it to priesthood.

I was among the many seminarians who understood the message the bishop was trying to communicate and was grateful and respectful of his valuable advice, honesty, and openness. It was out of total misunderstanding that some priests took offense at what the bishop said, and the same can be said of the seminarians who were scandalized. It would also be a fair assessment to say that attitudes like those or anticipation of such misinterpretation helped to drive the conversation and resolving of issues like that deeper into oblivion. Those who had the courage to discuss it, did so with caution so as not to be misunderstood, cause scandal, or avoid shame; and in the process meaningful debate, valuable lessons, and hands-on training were lost.

I did recognize, however, that every person's situation was different, experiences varied, the level of spirituality and individual strength were not shared equitably among people. I also, in some way, understood the complexity of the ministry of a priest. We cannot reduce the priestly ministry to simply guarding celibacy since it's only but one among many other tools adopted by the church to aid the priest in the ministry. Christ's ministry is quite larger than celibacy; to reduce it to celibacy or place celibacy above it may lead us to the miscalculation of what our mission as priests is. That is to say that, as priests, if we lack the proper perspective, we may use up our energy and time trying to preserve our celibacy and, in the process, compromise Christ's mission, just like Monk B, who placed the monastic rules above the demands of charity. When we act in that manner, we lose everything, including the celibacy, since our strength and priority are misplaced, like Monk B in the story. Monk B, even as he decided to obey the monastic rules with total disregard for the demands of charity, could not stop himself from thinking of the girl lustfully. What he preoccupied himself with as the girl received help was evident in his line of question and his being consumed with what Monk A felt. It would not be far from the truth if one argued that he sinned in his mind over and over again because, apparently, his imagination was going wild. Consequently, his not letting the principle of charity guide his actions stalled the success of his monastic life in that moment and instance. That was because charity is the center of Christ's mission, it informs it, breathes life into it, and grants it the right sense of purpose. The ministry of a priest essentially has everything to do with Christ and belongs to Christ, who called us to minister in love on his behalf among his people. Celibacy, therefore, should be lived every day as far as humanly possible and with God's grace, as a sacrifice of self-denial that should lead to a bountiful expression of God's love. When seen just as a rule to be obeyed, celibacy is bereaved of God's love or lived in the absence of the practice of charity, and this renders it counterproductive in Christ's ministry.

My summation about celibacy after seminary formation and listening to many opinions and assessments of some knowledgeable priests is that my living as a celibate means carrying out Christ's will to the utmost of my ability in love, with a humble attitude through God's grace. That at the end of each day, I may have the courage and humility to ask God to accept my sacrifice and self-denial, though imperfect it might be, and to bless those he touched through me. Celibacy is a life lived as a human and, hence, may continue to be perfected in Christ each day, but may never here on earth be rid of the elements of limitations and unworthiness. The letter to the Hebrews made sure to state this fact very clearly: "Every high priest is taken from among men and made their representative before God, to offer gifts and sacrifices for sins. He is able to deal patiently with the ignorant and erring, for he himself is beset by weakness and so, for this reason, must make sin offerings for himself as well as for the people" (Hebrews 5:1-3). In spite of a priest's human limitation, God has a way of spiritually enriching his people as was echoed by Saint Paul when he said, "I planted, Apollos watered, but God caused the growth" (1 Corinthians 3:6). Armed with that knowledge and conviction, I proceeded to live out the gift of service and sacrifice as best as I could, trusting in God's mercy and grace.

After my first anniversary as a priest, one thing became clearer: the fact that human sexual feelings do not go away because one became a priest, and the passage of time does not erase or ease it up. However, my reflection helped me understand that I should not see this part of me as a burden or try to pray or wish it away. If that part of me was completely gone, that would mean that, for me, celibacy as a sacrifice ceases to be. The reason is because every true definition of sacrifice retains the aspect of something offered or given up. One can only sacrifice what he possesses and has the willingness and ability to give up without any inhibiting or propelling pressure. The nonexistence of that natural feeling indicates the absence of temptation or trial and, consequently, the lack of opportunity in this particular case to win victory for God, to work with the grace of God, and to make the power of God most manifest. God told Saint Paul that he would not take away the thorn in his flesh; his reason being that his "grace is sufficient, for power is made perfect in weakness" (2 Corinthians 12:9). The best I could do, I imagined, was to cooperate with the grace of God and hope that his power would be made perfect in me.

As I anticipated, the seminary was a great place to start my priestly ministry. It was a delight to teach those young curious minds, who reminded me so much of myself, and I had enough time to pray, read, reflect, and play. I considered my being sent to that seminary after my ordination to the priesthood an invaluable gift and hoped I could stay longer, unaware that God had something else in mind for me. I received a call from the bishop's secretary who informed me the bishop wanted to meet with me to discuss some matters. That would be my first official private audience with the bishop since I was ordained a priest. Since the bishop was the one that requested the meeting, and I was not told exactly why, I was left to speculate on what he wanted to talk over with me. The first thing that came to my mind was that he wanted to know how I was doing after a year and a few months of my being a priest. I also thought about the possibility of a new assignment but did not think that would be the reason since the rector and I worked well together, and I had not taught in that Spiritual Year Seminary long enough.

I knew the matter was a very serious one when, instead of the office, the bishop chose to meet with me at his house. That venue was special; it was reserved for very special occasions and most confidential issues. His steward led me to a large, simple but, tastefully furnished living room. The upholstery was covered with soft burgundy-colored leather. Though comfortable to sit on, I appreciated the cushion's firmness, too since I had no problem sitting in an upright manner; slumping in the bishop's couch was not how I intended him to find me. He seemed happy to see me because he smiled when he walked into the room, and I was glad at the opportunity to see him, too. With the heartwarming smile came the words, "Vincent, how are you today?" Without waiting for an answer, he added, "Come with me."

After I got up and followed, with the bishop leading the way, I responded, "I'm doing well, my Lord." I breathed heavily as I tried to keep up with him while I talked. We were soon climbing the staircase, I was going to ask the bishop how he was doing, but I knew that had to wait. I did not know my way around; I was climbing the stairs for the first time and would fall over if I did not pay attention. He led me into a room that was large and shaped like the letter L, I could tell that it was his library/study. The large room had half of the walls covered with bookshelves containing books of different sizes, shapes, and colors in them. The part of the room that did not have bookshelves had an office desk and a chair. The last part of the room was a den with a center table and five comfortable chairs, and that was where we had that high level meeting.

As we both sat down, he said, "Father Vincent, we will have lunch after this meeting. So I will get to business quickly before our meal gets cold." We both made eye contact, like we agreed on the last point, and smiled. Then he proceeded to tell me there was a difficult task he wanted someone to help him accomplish. I was waiting to hear what it was when he said, "I need two priests who will volunteer to help out."

"My Lord," I said, "I do volunteer if you believe I can be of any use. If you eventually choose me, I promise to do my best to justify your choice and I will pray and hope that my best will be good enough."

"Since you said yes to helping out, I will be sending you to the United States. Bishop Andrew McDonald has asked me to send him two priests. So you and possibly another priest I will see later today will be sent to the Diocese of Little Rock as missionaries." He smiled.

I had no doubt the last word, *missionaries*, sounded a little bit strange and funny at the same time to him, and to me, too. That was because we were used to the church in the Western world sending priests to Africa to help in the work of evangelization. The scenario of returning the favor by sending some priests to those who brought us Christianity underscores the fact that we took the lead of missionaries and watered the seed of faith they planted in our midst. In doing so, we had grown in number and the vocation to the priesthood had remained robust. Therefore, the gesture of sending priests to the United States would be a kindness extended, with a harmless sense of pride. We should, however, be mindful of and learn from the shrinking vocation and the faithful in the larger part of the Western world. It could help us tap into the factors that made the growth among us possible and avoid the reason, or reasons, for the decreasing vocation in the Western world. The ultimate joy and lesson for any Christian everywhere is that this missionary exchange bears witness to the reality and benefits of the charity embedded in our spiritual and pastoral interdependency. Another lesson of that exchange is that it shines light on the oneness of the church and how God grows and sustains his church in unimaginable ways. If the Saint Patrick Fathers from Ireland and other religious congregations from other parts of the Western world never came to us in Africa to preach the Gospel, we would not have known about Christianity or grown in number as to help fill in for the shortage of priests in the United States and other places. Just as we spare some priests today to help out, it is possible that, someday, we may need help again, and I have no doubt God will supply through others if that day comes. I understood why my bishop smiled, and I smiled back at him, even though I was still trying to digest what he told me concerning a new mission for me in the United States.

During lunch that afternoon, and for many days, I wondered why the bishop chose me. There were, I was sure, many priests more competent and qualified than I was. I had only been a priest for eighteen months before this meeting with the bishop, so my experience in the ministry was hardly enough. The only ministry I had been largely exposed to at the time consisted of teaching in the seminary, and it sounded like my mission in the United States would be in the parish. Subsequently, I could not but wonder how different and difficult switching from teaching in the seminary to working in the parish in a foreign country would be. I also reflected on how much effect the differences in culture and other factors would have on my ministry. I tried to keep my thought in the positive realm because I knew it would be futile and frustrating to worry about the unknown factors that would surround my new assignment.

The reality of what to expect came to light when I arrived on a cold Thursday, on November 25, 1999, at Little Rock National Airport, where the temperature was about thirty-five degrees. When I left home, the temperature was ninety-three degrees; hence, the harsh cold weather and contrast was truly felt when I stepped out of the airport building and its controlled temperature. As we got to where Monsignor Frank Malone parked his car and spent a few minutes putting my luggage in the trunk, I felt like I was in an industrial freezer. My bones were aching either from exhaustion, from flying for sixteen hours and several hours of waiting for my connecting flight at the airport, or from the cold weather or both. I remember thinking, *If I do not get to some warm place, I am going to freeze to death.* I was happy when we got into the car, and it was warm.

"Father Vincent, welcome to the Diocese of Little Rock. You will stay with me and Father Tom Elliott, my associate, at Immaculate Conception Church, North Little Rock, until the bishop sends you to the parish where you will minister."

I was appreciative of his kindness, and I told him I was. "Thank you, Monsignor."

"How do you pronounce your last name?" he asked.

"My last name may look strange, but it's easy to pronounce. The *G* is silent, *Ogbuji* is pronounced 'Obuji,'" I explained, trying to encourage him not to give up. There was a brief moment of silence, and then I asked, "Monsignor, is it always this cold?"

"Yes, during winter, and it will get colder tonight." He answered.

The thought of the weather being colder was inconceivable and sounded like another planet incapable of sustaining life. I have never been to any place so cold, and it did not help to hear that it would get colder.

Monsignor quickly got me out of that scary frozen world my mind tried to grasp and was trapped in, when he announced, "Today is Thanksgiving Day."

"Why is today a thanksgiving day, and what do you do on this day?" I asked.

"The fourth Thursday in the month of November is a day reserved for thanking God in the United States. We also celebrate the day visiting with family and friends. There is also a lot of cooking and eating. The food includes deep-fried turkey, dressing, and gravy and more," he elaborated.

"We have a thanksgiving too, celebrated by different towns and villages on different dates. So, in my country, it is not celebrated as a national holiday like you do," I offered, but did not elaborate.

I left out the details when I talked to Monsignor because it was a long, boring, and complicated narrative. I am going to attempt to describe the thanksgiving celebration in my village, and at any point it gets too boring, you can turn to the next page. It was actually a celebration that began with my forefathers who practiced the indigenous religion. Yam (not sweet potatoes, but a special root crop) was the most-valued crop during the days of my great-grandparents and grandparents, and only rich farmers could afford to cultivate that root crop because it took a lot of resources and manpower to grow. My grandfather was named after that crop. So *Ogbuji*, my grandfather's name, means a great farmer of yams (wealthy one). He was married to four wives, because having many wives at the time provided many benefits, among which was economic necessity or prosperity. Mechanized farming was not part of my grandfather's age, so to have or maintain a big farm required marrying many wives and having many children who would help provide the needed raw human energy. The soil was plowed and tilled with hoes while the planting of the yams was done with bare hands, and your hands better be tough for the hard labor.

Thanksgiving in my town is called Iri ji (New Yam Festival). Even though yam was mainly eaten during that occasion, it was much more than eating and drinking. The head of each household, usually a man, sacrificed the first fruits and chicken to the gods and ancestors who opened the sky for rain and made the soil fertile for bountiful harvest. The New Yam Festival was normally scheduled by each village on a day they considered their day of rest. Instead of seven, we have eight days in a week: *Eke, Orie, Afo, Nkwo, Ekeugwu, Orieukwu, Afoukwu,* and *Nkwoukwu.* My village's day of rest is Afoukwu, and that is the day Thanksgiving is celebrated, at the end of the harvesting season. When Christianity came, and Thanksgiving was Christianized, it was celebrated on a Sunday that falls on Afoukwu day, at the end of the harvesting season. With the influence of Christianity, unlike my ancestors who sacrificed their first fruits to the gods, the community brought their first fruits to the church, to offer to God and to be blessed. After church services they went home, cooked a good meal and celebrated with friends and family.

The two weeks I stayed with Monsignor and Father Tom, were ones of intense internship and crash courses on American culture, social life, and subtle differences in the ministry of the priest here in the United States and that in my home. The next morning, as we went to Saint Anne Church (a mission parish covered by Monsignor and Father Tom) for morning Mass, Monsignor asked, "Would you be open to preaching a short homily?"

"Yes, Monsignor," I accepted his offer but wished he had defined *short* because my *short* homily was about ten minutes. Back home, weekday homilies would last for twenty minutes.

"Father, that could have easily passed for a Sunday homily," Monsignor said with a smile, and I knew it was not exactly a compliment but that my homily was longer than he expected.

"Monsignor, I hope I did not disappoint you?" I pleaded.

"No, you didn't. The content was okay, but it lasted a little longer. Weekday homilies should only last three to five minutes and Sundays, eight to ten minutes."

If that is the case, I thought, *I have got a lot of work and editing to do.* After the Mass, we went to Waffle House for breakfast, and I would have to admit that some of the items on the menu were completely strange, so I made a choice of omelet and toast, which were familiar to me and, I hoped, were safe, too. In our company were two of Monsignor's friends; one of them asked me to take a bite out of the food he had ordered, and I did; it was delicious, and I told him it was as I thanked him. This part of the story sets the stage for the most humiliating thing that happened to me the next day during breakfast.

For dinner, we went to a Chinese restaurant that happened to be a buffet arrangement. I arrived in the United States barely twenty-four hours earlier and did not have a clue on how eating in a restaurant that served buffet worked. I filled my first plate and when I was done eating, Monsignor said, "You can get another plate if you are still hungry." And I did.

As we ate, I asked him, "Monsignor, how does the restaurant keep track of how much we have eaten, and how do they know what to charge us for the food?"

"It is a buffet," he explained, "which means you pay one basic amount, and you eat as much as you want."

What I said next became a punch line, which Monsignor has not failed to use whenever he wants to tease me or refer to the funny things that happened during my early days in the United States. I said, "If that is the case, then, the indigenes of China must be very generous."

I can still remember how loud he laughed, and we still laugh today whenever he tells the story. My response was based on my presumption that only Chinese restaurants had the buffet phenomenon, which sounded too fantastic, like a deal you could get only from "Soup Kitchen" or "Second Blessing".

My second day in the United States was highlighted by an embarrassing incident at breakfast. We went again to the Waffle House, which I appreciated since I knew my way around the menu. I was, however, going to avoid any thing exotic until I was familiar with the food. I ordered an omelet and toast, exactly what I had the day before. But Monsignor's friend, who had asked me to try part of his meal yesterday, said, "Father, you said you liked my food you tried yesterday, why don't you order it?"

Well, I did. I thought that when my ordered meal arrived, only the side dish I had from Monsignor's friend would come with my food. When the waitress brought my food, it included the main course of the meal with all the side dishes. She also got me the main course and side dishes of the meal Mike had talked me into ordering. There was so much food and not enough space at the table, and the picture was a very discomforting one, not exactly what I intended or hoped for. What Mike said next, even though true and an attempt at humor, made me wish it was all a dream. "Father, it looks like you can use an extra table." The waitress dragged up an extra table, and we had three tables put together, and my food filled a table and half. I have never felt so humiliated in my entire life. I actually lost my appetite and was quiet through the whole ordeal. I ate as much food as I could, but what was more painful was pretending I enjoyed it and actually had to tell a white lie when Mike asked me if the food was good. As I ate the food, I wondered what a waste it was when there are many starving people around the world. That dominating thought, guilt, and embarrassment did not make the food taste right. The silver lining about that incident was that I learned the wisdom of asking for clarification when I am not sure about something.

I tried to follow the instruction Jesus gave to his disciples as he sent them on their mission to preach and took a few things, leaving out some essential items, like my shaver. After a few days, my hair fiercely grew out to protect me from the cold weather. A week without shaving left me looking too rough around the edges and badly in need of facial manscaping. Father Tom took me to Walgreens, where I got most of my immediate needs. I cut my hair, shaved my beard, spiritually prepared myself, and waited for Father Phillip to come and take me to Saint Edward Church, Texarkana, where I was assigned to minister to the flock.

The drive from Little Rock to Texarkana with Father Phillip was mostly quiet, except when I asked him a question or he had one for me. He also broke the silence when he wanted to tell me about a certain landmark or place. When we got to Benton, he pointed out, "This is my hometown, and someday, we will drive up to see my mom."

"Thank you, Father Phillip. That is very kind of you."

As we got closer to a rest area, he asked, "Would you like me to stop at the rest area?"

"What is a rest area, and what will we be doing there?" I asked.

The name *rest area* made what the place was used for obvious, but I still had to ask. I would rather look dumb asking than encourage him to stop and not having any reason to do so, thereby wasting time.

"When you are on a long trip, the rest area will be a place you can stop if you are tired and need to stretch out your legs or take a nap. You can also stop there if you need to take care of number 1 or 2 or both." When he was mentioning number 1 or 2, he was laughing boisterously, with a little twist of mischief. From the nature of his laughter, I believed I had an idea of what he meant, but I still did not want to presume to know.

"What are numbers 1 and 2?"

"Bathroom visits!" He briefly confirmed what I thought.

I liked Father Phillip! He was kind to me and, exercised patience and understanding, even when I kept asking him questions like a six-year-old. He also had a sense of humor, but you have to cut through the dry walls of his personality, to get to the layer, rich in humor, buried deep, inside of him.

We made a stop at Wal Mart when we arrived in Texarkana, and what happened revealed his dry sense of humor. We stopped to get toiletries, and at the shampoo section, I carefully read each product, hoping to find a magic one that would keep me from getting bald faster than I was. Father Phillip, meanwhile, stood by, watching and wondering what I was doing. Finally, he asked, "Are you looking for something in particular?"

"Yes, I'm looking for a brand of shampoo that can help my hair grow," I replied.

"Good luck with that!" he sarcastically said, as he bent slightly to show me the top of his head, which, unfortunately, was wearing off like mine. "Why don't we come on a day when we have time to burn, so you can have a thorough search?" He meant it to be funny, but he was not laughing; however, I sensed the humor and smiled.

Our next stop was the Police Traffic Department in Texarkana. "In February, I'll be going on vacation," he announced. "We have to get you to start driving because you will be taking care of the parish while I am gone."

We went into the police traffic office and picked up a driver's manual and inquired what days the test was taken. The written and driving tests was taken 9:00 AM to 5:00 PM every day except weekends. I read half of the manual that night before I went to bed and completed the reading the next day. I knew I had to read it again before I took the written test.

My first three months of apprenticeship in Saint Edward Church, Texarkana, were dotted with drama and learning. The rest of the additional two years before I was relocated did not have as much drama, but it was interesting nonetheless. The next day after I arrived, Father Phillip took me on a tour around the parish. First, we went to the church office, and he introduced me to four members of the staff, who were very happy to see me. He showed me my office, which was clean and had good looking, modest furniture that I would need. I thought it would make a good place to study after office hours, and two days later, I went to try it out. I unlocked the door with the key I had been given, opened the door, and walked into my office. I overheard something beeping, but since I did not know what it was, I ignored it and settled down to read. The beeping sound turned into a loud piercing alarm, and I actually thought the office was on fire, but it was not. I did not know what was happening and was confused. As I came out from the office, two police cars pulled up. Before the police men could approach me for questioning or arrest, Father Phillip hurried to the scene and, in-between his gasping for air, identified me as his associate pastor. "He is a priest in the parish who just arrived from Nigeria." I was unaware the office had an alarm system and certainly did not know the password or even how to operate the system. After that unfortunate incident, I found out everything I needed to know to avoid the police from showing up again.

Father Phillip also showed me around Saint Edward Church, which, to say the least, was magnificent. I thought the beauty of the church was a testimony to the rich architectural taste of those who lived the Catholic faith before us and the profound sacrifice they were willing to make. The stained glass windows were bold and delightfully aesthetic to behold, and my favorites were Saint Joseph and the Holy Family. I could not wait to celebrate my first Sunday Mass in that church. Although I looked forward to my first Sunday Mass there, I was, at the same time, apprehensive. I knew my accent may pose a little problem. My accent was born out of an unusual marriage between Igbo, which is my first language and native tongue, and the British English. Consequently, I knew that upon my arrival in the United States, that my English would not sound British. I surmised it would sound like a unique blend of Igbo and British accent. I knew understanding me clearly would, therefore, require patience on the part of my listeners and time to improve on my part. On my third day in the parish, I went to the meeting of the Youth Ministry. I met many of the youth members of the parish for the first time and was surprised at how much they understood my English. One of the kids had asked me, "Father, how did you get here?"

I teasingly answered, "I walked!"

The youth members thought that was very funny, and their laughter was a delightful confirmation. I eventually told them about my long flight to the United States and other things of interest I could remember, and I had their full attention through the whole narrative. Since they listened with unfading fascination, I began to think we understood each other perfectly well until one of the youth members, actually the youngest among them, asked me, "Father, what did you eat on the airplane while flying over here?"

"Rice cooked with some cabbage." I was pleasantly interrupted by a hearty laughter because my thick accent made my *C* sound like a *G*, so instead of hearing *cabbage*, they heard *garbage*. I noticed that almost all of them laughed, except two younger girls, who covered their faces with their tiny hands to indicate they overheard something that sounded so foul, they wished not to see. It was not difficult for me to know they heard *garbage*. I tried to clear up the confusion, but under the circumstances, my *cabbage* still sounded like *garbage*. They laughed with me all the louder but also got the right message. At that point, I thought that more communication with the parishioners would not only help me pronounce words as close to an American accent as possible but would help them understand me better, and vice versa. I once again had to put to use what my junior high school English literature teacher told us about ways to perfect our spoken English. That in addition to learning our grammar and vocabularies, we should listen to good speakers and try to speak a language if we wish to have good command of it ourselves. I bought a talking dictionary, watched the news and good programs on television, and observed my friends and people give speeches.

The language barrier was weighing heavily on my mind as my first Sunday Mass in the parish approached because I was expecting nothing of myself short of perfection. I had a major question that kept resounding in my head: What if I am not understood by those who attended Mass? I prepared for the Mass and my homily as best as I could and was happy with the result, but then I got trapped in the doubt of the form my delivery of the homily would take. I was torn between giving it off the cuff or simply reading it. Since I was ordained a priest, I had never read my homily. Our homiletics professor in the seminary recommended we write our homilies down and read it to the congregation. I did not rigidly follow all the rules he taught us, at least, not the one on reading from the script. I had to apply the general rules or tailor them to my talent and personal way of communication. The few times I tried to read it as my professor recommended, it came off as a horrible lecture that went bad, and I believed I helped many in the congregation find a reason to fall asleep. The benefits of speaking from the heart extemporaneously led me to preach without reading from the script and to lecture in the seminary during my first assignment without looking or reading from my notes or textbook. It was not easy or seamless at the beginning, but it got easier with more work, and my efforts may have paid off since my students looked forward to my lectures as well as homilies.

As I argued with myself whether or not to read the homily as I prepared for my first Sunday in Saint Edward Parish, it occurred to me that either of the two methods made sense under the circumstances. I thought that reading from the script would help me speak in a measured way, slow enough for the faithful I was meeting for the first time to understand me. Reading it would also minimize the possible element of stage fright that may happen on my first outing. Before I slept, I finally decided to preach from the pulpit and read from my written homily. However, on the Sunday morning, a few minutes before the Mass started, as I put on my vestments and silently prayed, I changed my mind and decided to preach off the cuff. I was persuaded to make that final decision, bearing in mind that I did not want to read my homily simply because I lacked confidence in myself or thought the worshipping community would not understand me. If I did read it for those reasons, I would never have the courage to deliver my homily the way I knew best.

After I read the Gospel, I carefully walked down the steps of the sanctuary and hoped not to trip because I was nervous. When I arrived at a suitable position, I stopped and smiled at the congregation, announced the theme of my homily and initiated the prayer of the sign of the cross. During the gesture of the cross sign, they all joined in and that was the first signal I got that I was understood. The next thing I said brought about such unexpected laughter that completely surprised me. "After I read the Gospel and I looked at you, I was so afraid I wished I could run away. You know why?" Some shook their head, some said no, and I continued, "Because this is the first time I am preaching to a large crowd of whites!"

The energetic laughter, the cheering, and evident fascination was unbelievable. It was exhilarating to know they understood me and that I could take them with me to explore the word of God. My choice of not reading my homily from a script paid off on my first Sunday in the parish and many more Sundays. I was confident I had mastered the art until after about a year and six months I had been in the parish. The hitch on that day humbled and taught me that I still had a lot to learn, especially the lesson of relying more on God's grace than on my personal skill. That Sunday, I had been preaching, and everything was going smoothly. I had four points to make, and I made the first, second, and forgot the third. I stood there and looked at the people; I tried to smile but could not and hoped to remember the third point, but I had no luck. I did not speak for about thirty seconds, which felt awkward and like forever since I had been speaking fluently before the unintended pause. When I could not remember the third point and could not keep quiet anymore, I exclaimed, "Oh, my God!" The whole gathered congregation started laughing, and I laughed with them. They probably laughed because they thought I was using God's name in vain when, indeed, I was in trouble and was calling on God for help, and he did help. As the people quieted down after the laughter, I said, "I forgot the third point I was making, but after you laughed with me, I remembered it." My explanation made them laugh some more. After that day, I thought about what I did wrong and what I should do to avoid incidents like that or what I would do if it ever happened again. I decided to rely more on God, and if it occurred again, it was best not to be quiet but to keep talking. That strategy worked, and the only time it happened again, I had left Texarkana, and no one noticed.

There was a clearer flow of communication between me and the faithful after the few months I spent in the parish of Saint Edward. I could note that we asked each other to repeat what was said less frequently. I attributed that to my interaction with the parishioners and my being able to learn from each experience. One of the days I attended the Youth Ministry there was a deliberation about the youth going on a mission trip. After the meeting, I was on my way to the rectory when the youth minister approached me and asked, "Father, will you go on a mission trip with us?"

"I will be happy to," I answered. Even as I indicated I was willing to go on the trip, I knew I had to talk it over with the pastor first and have his blessing before I was sure I could go. Well, the news went around the parish and to the pastor that I was going on the mission trip with the youth even before I talked to him about it. Needless to say, I spent some quality time explaining how I made my convenient arrangement without consulting with the pastor. After that incident, I learned to speak a little more clearly and without ambiguity about my position on any issue so as not be misunderstood. I later went on the youth mission trip to San Antonio, Texas and it was rewarding on different fronts. I celebrated Mass each day throughout the duration of that mission trip for the young adults and chaperones from Saint Edward and other parishes. The youth and adults who went on that trip as if to return the favor, taught me more about the American culture and southern accent. It was also truly fulfilling to help a family in need! We engaged in the renovation of a house for a poor single mother with four kids under the supervision of a particular local nonprofit organization. Before we started that project, the house was in a deplorable shape, but after we refurbished it, it looked new and livable. The joy of being part of that worthy mission was validated by the sincere gratitude of the woman who owned the house. Her smile and sense of relief as she thanked us will forever live in me. Her four kids were not less grateful; I will always remember their excitement and joyful screams when they saw the surprises we had for them.

After the mission trip, I stayed back in San Antonio to attend a three-day workshop on courses related to American culture, language, pastoral care, administration and priestly ministry in the United States. It was at that seminar that I became acquainted with the subtle differences in pronunciation and meaning of some words in American English and how it varies from British English. I learned to use the words like *hood* instead of *bonnet*, *windshield* and not *wind screen*, and *glove box* instead of *pigeon hole* as it relates to cars. When someone thanked me, I should not say "Don't mention" but say "You are welcome." I learned to address the bishop as "Bishop" and not as "My Lord." This last one I had to seek to be exempted from it. I humbly asked Bishop Sartain if he would let me address him as "My Lord" since that was how I addressed my bishop in Nigeria. At first he hesitated, and I pleaded some more, "Please, my Lord, it will be my honor to do so, and I will keep in mind the reverence your title and office demand."

We both laughed, and he said, "Okay, Udo."

During that workshop in San Antonio—attended by extern priests and newly appointed pastors—Father Phillip had the opportunity to speak with my sister, Helena, who had called to check on me. As they conversed, Helena asked him how her brother Udo was doing.

After their conversation Father Phillip said to me, "Helena, didn't call you Vincent, she called you a different name when we talked."

"Yes," I admitted, "she called me Udo. That is my first name and Vincent is my baptismal name." I explained.

That was how Father Phillip found out that my name is Udo and that it means peace. Before he made this discovery, he and everyone in the parish, addressed me as Father Vincent. After that revelation he started calling me Udo, and I called him Big Brother Phillip and, soon, everyone in the parish preferred Father Udo.

I wish I had been to that workshop sooner; I would have been able to avoid the embarrassment I faced in the local airport in Texarkana. It was about six months after I arrived in the United States, and I was flying to Dallas to visit Dee Austin, Irene, and their kids. They are the family I have here in the United States; we are from the same village. They bought a ticket for me to fly to Dallas to spend some time with them. That visit was truly needed! Although I pretended I did not miss home, the fact was that I did, and being with Dee Austin, Irene, and their kids filled the vacuum my leaving home and missing my family created. Well, at the airport in Texarkana, as I checked in my luggage, the girl at the desk asked me a few questions about my identity and destination. After that she dabbled into series of other questions like "Is this your bag?" And I answered yes. The question that followed was "Did you give your bag to anyone?" She spoke so fast that I did not understand her questions, but instead of asking her to repeat what she said, I answered yes. I am glad Big Brother Phillip was standing close to me and clarified what my response should have been when he said, "He did not give his bag to anyone." From then on, I learned to say, "I beg your pardon" or "Excuse me" when I did not understand what was said.

I had no doubt that, with effort and passage of time, my communication with the people improved tremendously, but there were a few incidents that made me think that I may have to keep working at it much longer. Megan was about nine years old, and as part of her religious lessons, her mom asked her to read the words of consecration the priest used during Mass. She read, "He took the cup filled with wine. Gave it to his disciples and said, 'This is the cup of my blood of the new and everlasting coconut."

Megan's mom was shocked and confused about what she heard, so she asked her to read it again. When she got to covenant, she said *coconut* again. Then the mom said, "Megan, why do you read *coconut*, instead of *covenant*?"

Megan replied, "That is what Father Udo says at Mass."

Another episode has to do with my friend John, who was in his late seventies and always came to tell me how beautiful the Mass was. I had been in Saint Edward Church a little more than two years and had only two months left before I left for Saint James Church, Searcy, where I had been given a new assignment as pastor. John came to me after Mass as he usually did, but on that particular occasion, he said something different. "Father Udo, I enjoyed your homily very much! I was able to hear you very clearly today. You have improved on your English."

Before I could thank him for his compliment, another man, who came to greet me and overheard what John said responded on my behalf. "John," he said, "Father Udo has spoken the same way since he came to the parish. I think it is you who have improved on your hearing." I was surprised at what John said next.

"You are right, Peter, I forgot, I got a new hearing aid yesterday!"

We all laughed so hard.

Living and ministering in a country other than mine came with a set of challenges, as I had anticipated. I started first by eating whatever was set before me. It was not too long before I found out that I should have treaded more cautiously. About four months after I arrived in the United States I started having stubborn and fiery heart burn. At first it would quit after a short time, and then it took a bad turn, and not even the over-the-counter medicine my friend Mil recommended would stop it. Since no normal medicine could put that acid reflux to rest and the burn was unbearable, especially at night when it kept me from sleeping, I had to devise a way, even though crude, to get needed relief. I drank a lot of water, put my index and middle fingers into my mouth to induce vomiting, and that stopped the heartburn until the next day when I would eat again. When it seemed everything I ate made me miserable, I took a more drastic measure; I stopped eating altogether for two days except for boiled potato and drank just water, and without any medicine, my acid reflux was gone. After that breakthrough, I ate only vegetables for a while and was free from my troubles for some time. But after three months, I went out to eat lunch with a friend, and later that night, my heartburn came back. Three months of freedom from heartburn made me almost forget what it felt like to have it, but the excruciating burn that gnawed and stabbed at my esophagus brought back the bad memory of that painful experience. I had to think fast on what I did differently that afternoon at lunch, and I traced it back to the lemon in the water I had at the restaurant. I also found out after a few months that fatty food was another culprit.

Part of my duties as the associate pastor in Saint Edward Church was to help run the Outreach Center where we offered help like food, clothing, and money to the needy. One afternoon, I left to eat lunch at the rectory. I was just going to have a boiled egg and bread with a glass of chocolate drink. I had only one egg in the refrigerator, and I decided boiling it in the microwave would be quicker. I took a cup, filled it with water, and with the egg in it, I put the cup in the microwave for six minutes and then went into my room for something. You now know the rest of the story! I heard a loud explosion and ran back into the kitchen, and what I saw simply wore me down. The door of the microwave was flung open, and there were tiny pieces of half-boiled egg spattered everywhere. I spent almost all afternoon cleaning the kitchen and, if I might add, on an empty stomach. Needless to say, I learned a valuable lesson about the microwave, which, until I came to the United States, I had not seen or used. After setting off the egg bomb and cleaning up after myself on that very day, I went ahead and read about the safe operation of the microwave. Following that incident I have had to read the manual of everything, even the tag on the comforter before I spread it on my bed.

On the same day of the microwave mishap, I learned a hard lesson on the difference between steak and stew meat. Having fasted all afternoon, I was determined to give myself a deserved treat for dinner. I was going to cook some stew and eat it with rice. I cooked the stew with some beef I had found in the refrigerator. After cooking, I was enjoying dinner when Big Brother Phillip came back. I told him I had used the meat I found in the refrigerator to cook and that I saved him some. "Udo, those are steaks," he said. "I was planning to grill them this evening for us. Steak is not used for stew—there's stew meat. I will show you next time we go to Albertson."

What he said did not make that much sense to me then, but now, I know better. Big Brother had bought some New York strips, and I used two out of the three to cook some stew. Thank goodness he had at least one left to grill for his dinner. That night, we drank some beer together. There was something he said, and I laughed, and my laughter made him laugh longer and louder. When he stopped laughing, he said, "You look like the Grinch when you laugh."

"Who is the Grinch?" I asked.

"I can't tell you. I will have to rent the movie for you to watch it and find out."

I watched the cartoon character of *The Grinch*, with him and, I was glad I exercised restraint and did not hurt him. I thought the movie had a good message and was funny. However, I did not look anything close to his outlandish and exaggerated comparison. I was happy to have Big Brother Phillip as one of those who helped me during my apprenticeship phase in the priesthood because he had many things to teach me, and we worked well together. The fact that within my first two months in the Parish, I passed the written and driving traffic tests and, was able to drive to care for the parishioners—while he went on a badly needed vacation for two weeks—was proof that Big Brother Phillip was a great mentor, and I tried to be a good apprentice. Maybe, that was the reason why I received a surprising phone call from Bishop Sartain which changed my status.

CHAPTER 9

The Lion's Den

Your staying alive may not be guaranteed in the lion's den
when you play a fearful prey, but you may survive with a few
scratches by being a fearless, helpful and a playful friend.
— Father Udo Ogbuji

Most of my phone calls came through the office line, and the secretary would transfer the call to me if it was an urgent matter but would take a message if otherwise. So when the private phone in the rectory rang after working hours, I was sure it was Big Brother Phillip. In fact, the voice at the other end of the phone could not be more distinguished from the coarse voice of Big Brother. It was the deep clear baritone voice of Bishop Sartain who called out, "Udo!"

I immediately recognized who it was and happily answered, "My Lord!"

"You are doing very well today, Udo, I can tell by your voice."

It was a genuine compliment from his Excellency, and I generously replied, "Yes, My Lord, I am. It partly has to do with me getting excited when I heard your voice."

After a brief laughter on my forthrightness and intent to tease, the bishop was ready to talk about the business of the Church. "Udo, I have some important news for you. I am appointing you the pastor of Saint James Parish, Searcy; Saint Albert Parish, Heber Springs; and Saint Richard Parish, Bald Knob. I would advise that you don't tell anyone until we are ready to announce it. You can talk about it with Big Brother Phillip since I will tell him, too. Before I forget, Udo, Searcy has a Hispanic community, see what you can do for them."

"My Lord, I am humbled! Do you feel confident entrusting me with this much responsibility?" He knew I was being modest and was not expecting an answer, and he was right because I did not wait for one, but added, "I will do my best to justify your trust in me. Thank you, my Lord."

"You're welcome, Udo. Say hello to Big Brother and take care."

"I will, my Lord. You take care of yourself too, and please keep me in your prayers."

I considered it a great honor to have been appointed a pastor because I had only been four years a priest; two in my country in a seminary, and the other two I had spent here in the States as associate pastor in Saint Edward Parish, Texarkana. In some ways, I questioned my competence, but I convinced myself that I would do my best, and I prayed that God would bless any humble contribution I would make.

In my four years of priesthood, I had discovered that one may only prepare to the extent a human being can and rely on the help of God for those awkward moments that could not have been predicted, planned, or trained for. As I waited for the official day of my ministry as a pastor—twenty-fifth of June, 2002 to be exact—I prepared spiritually and mentally. I did not have any illusions about the difficulty of the herculean task ahead of me, because the facts and stories coming out of the post of my pending new assignment could scare the cassock off the most courageous priest. The least of my worries was that Searcy appeared to be the capital of the Church of Christ denomination, and the fact that they have a big school there, called Harding University, was proof. Some fanatical members of that church whom I had met during my life's journey, thought and alleged that the pope is the Antichrist and that all Catholics are going to hell. Even Big Brother Phillip joked that I should watch out since some of them may attempt to challenge my belief or even try to convert me. He did not have to tell me because I have had the occasion of having a long, heated chat with one of their ministers, who believed he had a reserved right to make me join his Church after he learned I was a Catholic priest.

That encounter with a Church of Christ minister happened on a flight while I was returning from my country, Nigeria, after a month's vacation. As I sat wishing that the plane en route to the United States would take off, Tim came and sat beside me after he stuffed his hand luggage into the overhead compartment. Tim was an acquaintance I met at Port Harcourt International Airport, Nigeria, as I waited to check in my luggage. While I was at the airport departure area, he approached me and introduced himself as a Church of Christ minister. After he showed interest in me, I told him my name and that I was a Catholic priest returning to the United States. Unknown to me, and I guess to him, we were going to sit together in the same plane. As we boarded and waited for the aircraft to take off, I wished for nothing more than for us to be airborne so I could sleep until I woke myself up. I had been so busy the last four days saying good-bye, wrapping my vacation up, and packing my bag, I was sleep deprived. Besides being drained by all the preparations before my departure, the emotional toil of leaving home was smothering. I was simply exhausted and could barely keep my eyes open. As soon as the pilot announced we were cruising at a safe altitude and speed, and was expecting a smooth flight, I felt a light tap on my shoulder. My eyes were closed, and I folded my arms around my chest ready to sleep. Since the tap was light and my eyes were closed, I did not know it was Tim. He tapped me again, this time harder. I opened my eyes and turned to look at him to know what he wanted, and he said. "Udo, you said you are a Catholic priest, do you know that you have not been saved?"

My brain was too dull to process his question fast enough or to know what he was talking about. The only thing I knew to ask was, "How do you mean?" I was still looking at him, hoping for a simple, short answer, when he dabbled into the Bible, starting from Genesis; and I surmised he was going to make his way to Revelation and some more before he stopped. Since I thought it would take a while, I decided I was not going to keep my neck twisted so I could look at him and listen until he was done. He had spoken for about six minutes, and in that time, my neck had taken as much strain as it could, and my eyes were hurting from lack of sleep and were pleading with me to shut them. In that situation, I did not have any choice but to interrupt him with a request. "Tim, I am very tired. I can't keep my eyes open because they are hurting from lack of sleep. I am going to keep them closed while I listen to you. I don't want you to think that I am ignoring you, okay?" He talked for about an hour and a half while I painfully listened. I would admit, though, that it was remarkable how much of the Scripture he memorized and how much time he must have put into it. My suspicion was right because he eventually found his way through the wilderness of the book of Revelation, and as soon as he was done with spilling the quotations, he seemed not to have much to say except to vilify and condemn me and everyone who is Catholic. The exact words he used were, "From what I have said thus far, you can see that all Catholics, including you, are going to inherit hellfire—a place of eternal punishment. Now is the time for you to repent, to accept Jesus Christ and be saved!"

At that point I thought I had heard enough and taken unwarranted religious abuse from Tim, and I politely told him that it was time for him to listen. "Tim, let me begin by asking you these simple questions: Have you ever been in a Catholic church or known what the true Catholic teachings are? Have you ever put to test the truth and integrity of what you heard about Catholics? Have you read any Catholic documents to know what She teaches? Have you ever met or dealt with a Catholic priest?" His answers were in the negative to all the questions. When it became clear to me that his assumptions were recklessly presumptuous, and that his judgment was based on the biased, twisted facts he was fed, which he blindly accepted as true, I continued, "Tim, we met about two hours ago in the airport in my country when you introduced yourself to me, and we barely know each other. So, what gives you the right and religious authority to play God and tell me what my fate will be in the afterlife? Even more insulting is your pretending to either read the mind of God or know better than he does by prejudging his judgment of the people I serve or millions of Catholics who are doing everything humanly possible to do the will of God." I paused and took a sip from the drinking water I was served.

After that, I continued, "It's impressive at face value to see how you were able to quote the Bible, though there is no way I will know whether or not you quoted them correctly. But let us accept the fact that you have a great art of memorizing the Bible, what use is that when you are incapable of practicing the simplest thing it demands, which is charity? It's like building an airplane that can't fly, and I hope you remember what Jesus said: 'Not everyone who says to me, "Lord, Lord," will enter the kingdom of heaven, but only the one who does the will of my Father in heaven. Many will say to me on that day, "Lord, Lord, did we not prophesy in your name?" . . . Then I will declare to them solemnly, "I never knew you" '(Matthew 7:21ff). You seemed to have failed in the least way of showing charity tonight. In addition to that, you condemn people whom you do not know their belief and their sincere effort to serve God. Even if you know what they believe in, does that give you the religious authority to sit in judgment? Did you not read the portion of the Bible—the chapter seven I quoted above, that verse one says 'Stop judging that you may not be judged'?"

I took a short break to let it sink in and, Tim sat quietly and looked so remorseful. I felt sorry for him and almost stopped beating him. But I still had a few more things to say, so I did. "I was in dire need of rest and tried to sleep, but you woke me up against my will. I was respectful of you and listened for a few minutes until I could no longer keep my eyes open. I told you how tired I was and how my eyes were hurting from lack of sleep, but you were neither considerate nor sympathetic. You were determined to have me listen to you, for more than one hour, until I could not take it anymore and stopped you. If you failed to show kindness to me, even the least of it, when you are trying to convince me to join your church, how do you expect me to believe you will be charitable to me when I am already a member and there is no need to court or persuade me? We have got about nine hours to fly, why could you not wait for an hour or two for me to get some needed rest first? I had the right to my peace of mind and to worship as I choose, and unless I permit you, you have no right to try to proselytize me, and if you felt moved to do so, I would expect you to be polite and ask for my permission. If you seek so much as to preach charity and fairness, why did you not show it by respecting my rights and privacy?"

At that stage Tim was becoming weary of all the mounting evidence against him and the steady, massive mental blows that he received—not knowing when and if they would stop. But I had one last point to make: "I guess your unspoken claim in trying to convert me is that your denomination is superior to mine. I would think that if anyone is seeking a denomination of Christianity to join, he would want the church that is original. Perhaps one that has a rich teaching and tradition with unbroken succession since the time of the twelve apostles of Christ, and that church, is the Catholic Church. I believe you are aware that your church was founded in New York by Joseph Smith, Jr. in 1829. So, what makes you think I would leave my church for yours? If you want me to like you a little more, and if you want to be successful in the future, you have to be nicer, unbiased, respectful, and humane. You do not have to accept what others believe, but you can show tolerance, and if you appreciate who people are and treat them with dignity, even if they do not accept your belief system, they would be enriched by the grace you show. Why can't you just preach Christ crucified, the abounding remarkable love of God for us, and our call to demonstrate that love in the least of all we do each day? As much as you talked, you could have saved your breath and used half of that time and energy to practice charity, and that would have been far more convincing!"

Tim did not talk for most of the trip and, when he did, he deliberately avoided religion. That he learned a lesson from the experience was evident in the fact that he spent the rest of the journey being really kind to me. When we stopped in Atlanta, he gave me his business card and asked me to keep in touch.

As I was saying before I digressed, it was not a hidden fact that the parishes I was about to be sent were uniquely tough for priestly ministry. Some priests and some members of my new parish knew and even joked about that. I remember a parishioner who approached me a few months after I arrived in the parish and teased me to make light of the situation, "Father Udo, you will need a lot of prayers, our parish is a 'priest-killer-parish'. I'll be one among many people praying for you!" He said, and we both laughed as I thanked him for his prayers and pledged to pray for him too. History and evidence have a way of corroborating facts, and in this case, they amply did so. My third predecessor did not remember his name by the time he left the parishes, maybe because he was ill, but I also believe that the heavy weight of the ministry he engaged in pushed him over the edge. My second predecessor easily sailed through every burden of proof until his fifth year, when he began to get dizzy and even slumped for some unknown reason. I was told he went to the doctor, and the results from tests were inconclusive, and he was placed in another parish to rest. After about a year, he was well and strong enough to go back into active ministry without taking any medication or getting medical attention. My immediate predecessor lasted about eleven months before the transfers were announced. His short tenure may be an indication of nothing, but I nevertheless wondered how out of the ordinary it seemed.

I have to be clear in saying at this point that I was not in the least discouraged or intimidated by any bad news, true or manufactured, I learned about my new parishes. But on the contrary, I was drawn to the positive aspects and the benefits the parishioners could tap into despite their internal problems, the somewhat hostile environment, and the strong rivals they faced. What I saw was how those difficult challenges and daunting ministry could prepare and make them stronger and better Christians and the leadership role I could bring to that spiritual endeavor. I knew that the faithful, and whoever their pastor would be, would need acquired toughness and tenacity to survive the unmatched rivalry from the giant churches and not-so-friendly people surrounding them. However, what made the situation more painful was that the parishioners' struggle for survival was not just restricted to religious matters. In Searcy, there were instances where some Catholics had to constantly look over their shoulders in their workplaces for simply being Catholics, and they were judged more by their religious tenet than by their qualifications and performance at work. Despite the parishes and my work appearing more exigent, I believed that in working hard and working together, God would turn things in our favor. Moreover, I get bored when any task I am performing is not demanding, and being bored is not a situation any priest—or any person for that matter—wants to find himself in. Therefore, I relished the adventure and mission, and looking back on it today, I think the bishop was led by the Spirit to have assigned me to a fitting place that was not boring for a single second of the almost five years I was there.

The drama started unfolding from the point it was announced that I would be the new pastor in Searcy, Heber Springs, and Bald Knob. About two weeks after the announcement, I received a surprising letter from the chairperson of the Parish Council in Searcy. In some way, you might expect such a letter to be a welcoming one that expressed hope and desire to work together. Maybe it did, but barely and indirectly. The only clear part was Peter instructing me to sign an attached document meant for the pastor, for the approval of the expansion of the existing church in Searcy. It was, to say the least, a shock because I still had about two months before I officially became the pastor; even a person who is brain-dead would know something was not right. I had many questions I wanted to ask, such as: Why would the present pastor not sign it? Why could it not wait till I get there? Does he realize that anything I signed would not be valid?

My conclusion after I read that letter a few more times and reflected on it was that there was a misunderstanding of some sort, so I wrote Peter, the chairperson of the Parish Council a short, nice letter. I meanly thanked him for introducing himself and told him I looked forward to working with him and others. On the request to sign the document, I told him to be patient with me and wait until I made it to the parish first, and then we could address the church expansion and other looming issues. I was surprised that his reply to my reply was even more demanding than the first; it was like a superior instructing a subordinate on what to do. My first reaction was to ignore the second letter and believe we could settle the matter when I arrived in the parish and become the pastor. But, I also thought that if I did not reply, it may come off as me being rude, or he might see my non-response as an indication of weakness on my part. I decided to exercise restraint and not reply, hoping we could discuss it when I get there and that it did not matter what he thought of me. He called after a week and left me a message, reminding me he was still waiting for my reply with signed documents. As much as I hated it, especially that early, I wrote him an official letter and laid bare some facts that had been ignored. My letter read somewhat like this:

Dear Peter,

Greetings in the name of our Lord Jesus Christ!

After carefully reading your letter and reflecting over it, I have the following response:

While I appreciate your passion and dedication and have taken note of your statement about the urgency of my signing the document you sent me, I will defer signing it until I officially take charge of the parish as pastor. My decision is based on these obvious reasons: I will want to take a look at the project I am approving of. I will also want to know how the agreement of expanding the church by fourteen pews was arrived. If I sign the document now, the only reason I will be doing so is because you asked me to. I do not want to be a pastor or leader who bases his judgment of signing on to a project of this magnitude solely on the reason that the parish chairperson asked me to do so.

Furthermore, any document I sign now is invalid because I am not officially the pastor. In addition to being invalid, it is also disrespectful to the present pastor, who is the pastor until the twenty-fourth of June. If you still believe it is urgent and necessary to have my signature on that document, then I must have to consult with the bishop to give me advice on how to proceed.

God bless!

Yours truly,
Fr. Udo

I did not hear from him on that matter again, but I knew that, sooner or later, we would be addressing our unresolved issue again.

The secretary to the parishes also wrote me a letter; she was graceful and congratulated me on my new assignment. She also informed me that she was resigning as secretary of Saint James Church, Searcy, effective, 24th of June. That would be a day before I arrived to assume the position of the pastor. I read her letter, thought long and seriously, and prayed earnestly before I decided on what my response to her would be. Before my determination to reply to the secretary's letter and encourage her to continue to hold that secretarial position, I received another letter from the parish chairperson, Peter. In that particular letter he informed me that his wife was open to working as the parish secretary; which meant that if employed she would replace the secretary who sent me her resignation letter. I did not doubt his concern to make sure the parish had a secretary in the event that position became open and was grateful that he—and perhaps his wife—was willing to make the sacrifice. The little concern I had was the picture it painted of the parish: the image of an exclusive family business. He was not only the Parish Council chairperson but also the Financial Council chairperson, and if his spouse were to become the parish secretary, then the imagery would not be a representation of the church I know. To say the least, the church is a community where everyone is supposed to participate in every facet of the parish, and no talent should be left untapped. I would have been out of my mind to let the secretary go! Her leaving before I arrived meant utter disaster for me—and maybe the parish—who would rely on her, since, she likely knew the inner workings of the parish more than any other person. So I wrote her a letter and tried to persuade her to stay until I arrived, and then she could resign if she wanted to. She was considerate and agreed to stay.

My predecessor, Father Jim, and I scheduled to meet two weeks before my new assignment began so we could go over a few things in anticipation of the handover. Father Jim was a very kind, gentle, and wise man. He showed me the church, the hall, and the classrooms for religious classes and also gave me a tour around the rectory while he told me all that would be helpful as I minister to the parishioners. As he showed me things in the rectory, he took me to a corner with piles of letters of petitions written against and in favor of the Director of Religious Education. He told me I was free to take them with me; I declined to do so but, instead, suggested he keep them for me since I would go through them when I officially took over. During that meeting, I asked his opinion on the expansion of the church and the requests made by the parish council chairperson, Peter, for me to sign the document needed to facilitate the undertaking of the project. I was delighted and enlightened by the useful pieces of advice I received from him. I was even more grateful to him because he not only gave me his honest opinion on where he stood as far as signing the document was concerned but also the circumstances that informed his position. I came to learn that he was not privy to how the decision was made with regard to expanding the church building; meetings were held without him being present. Peter may have been scheduling meetings and deciding what to do on behalf of the pastor and the parish—and may have been doing so even before Father Jim arrived. That, I was sure, would pose a problem, especially as it seems the chairperson was already testing the waters by trying to tell me what to do and, indirectly pointing out who was in charge. I could easily see why Father Jim appeared somewhat relieved that he was being transferred. The more time I spent with him, the more the fatigue that lay inside of him slowly revealed itself. The sign of weariness was evident in his blinking his eyes too frequently and occasionally leaning on the wall for support. My interpretation of his external gestures was possibly incorrect, but that was the impression I got.

As my friend Father Okey and I got into the car to drive back to Texarkana, we took our seats and strapped in, and I was ready to turn on the car's ignition when my friend gently held my right hand, smiled, and said, "Listen to me, I know you don't get easily rattled, but I listened to Father Jim closely and hoped for a single good news—there was none! Most of the things he said make this place sound like the lion's den. There is enough trouble here for a whole army of passionate priests. I hope you don't disappoint me by resigning in the middle of this mission. I believe God will see you through."

My friend wrapped the reality as he perceived it in such great humor. Even as we laughed heartily because he was funny, I received and was thankful for his words of encouragement and promised prayers.

When I looked at the mountain of work before me and the challenging circumstances surrounding it, I knew I had to be a shepherd from the outset and apply that same spirit in all facets of my leadership, even in the administrative realm. But the problem was that, up till then, I did not have any actual experience on how to be a shepherd, so I prayed a lot and hoped that God would help me. Even as I prayed and thought very hard on how best I could serve as a shepherd, I got very close to blowing it on my first weekend in the parish. There were five Masses during the weekend—three on Saturday: 4:00 PM in Saint Richard Church, Bald Knob; 5:30 PM at Saint James Church, Searcy; and a 7:00 PM Saint James Church, Searcy, Spanish Mass. At that time, Father Jim (from Jonesboro, not my predecessor) came to help out with the Hispanic Mass, but I knew that, at some point, I would celebrate that Mass since it was my intention to minister to all the members of the parish. There were two Masses on Sunday—at 8:00 AM in Searcy and 11:00 AM in Heber Springs.

After the 4:00 PM Mass on Saturday in Bald Knob on my first weekend, I was driving over to Searcy for the next Mass when I missed Exit 42, which was the last exit on Federal Highway 67/167. I had to drive to the next exit in a small town, McRae, to turn around. I was very late, twenty-five minutes to be exact. Being late on my very first weekend in the parish was not the good beginning I wished or prayed for. I started the Mass with an apology, and when I told the story about why I was late, they thought it was funny, laughed and were very forgiving. In fact, their love, grace, and forgiveness became the backdrop of my first address to the parish before I concluded the Mass: "We are a family, and no family can survive without the spirit of love, which demands constant grace, reconciliation, and collaboration. I am happy to be accepted as a member of this welcoming family. I am also impressed and inspired to identify among you those fine qualities that sustain any family, namely: understanding, love, and kindness—all of which I enjoyed this evening. Even after I kept you waiting, you forgave me. Instead of laughing at me for being ignorant and clumsy, you laughed with me. I promise to spend every day getting to know each one of you and to minister to you in the spirit of love and sacrifice—as exemplified in Christ, whose love we all share. I will spend each day offering earnest prayers for our family in general and each one of us in particular. All I ask for are your prayers that I may model my life and ministry for you after that of Christ our Good

Shepherd. We have so much to pray for, so much to learn from each other and, so much work to do. Let us therefore go forth in that collective spirit of love and dedication to work for God, aided by his grace and guidance!"

That speech was followed by a spontaneous ovation, which I thought was an indication of their acceptance, gratitude, love, and readiness to work together as a family. If I said they made me feel at home, that would be an understatement, since they made me feel in every way like a family member.

The joyful reception I received soon gave way to a heap of thorny and crippling problems that had to be addressed. Part of the leadership structures, as I came to find out, gave rise to and exacerbated some of the serious issues that were strangling Saint James Church. Resolving those matters required difficult adjustments, which I intended to prudently implement. I had to exercise caution, though in that endeavor because somehow I knew that going too quickly would be counter-productive and suicidal. "I can't come to a place and turn things upside down too quickly, even before I step my foot in the door. If I did, things could become chaotic and overwhelming for the parishioners and myself," I thought aloud.

The faithful had to be prepared for the changes to come and part of that preparation included communicating the reason for changes in a clear and convincing way. I had to first know the community: what their vision, aspirations, strengths, and weaknesses were. I knew it would be useful to study the strata of the parish population, and that it would entail the knowledge of whether there were more younger couples with kids in the parish or more older faithful or whether the parish was made up of other groups or a mixture of all. The data resulting from the census would be helpful as I wished to determine the many human resources available to work with and how to manage the different aspects of my ministry so the people would benefit more. For instance, if there were 90 percent retired and older couples in the parish, the ministry could lean more toward caring for the elderly and visiting the sick and the dying.

Even as I identified the potentials in the parishes and gradually harnessed them for their benefit, I somewhat understood the problems that may get in the way and had to be resolved. I had to learn the origin, potency, urgency, duration and how far reaching each problem was, in order to be in a good position to address it. The matters I thought needed immediate attention and should be handled first were what I called the DRE saga and leadership restructuring in Searcy. I had to find a way to strengthen and unite the leadership, which I believed could not be done unless I was present in all the meetings. While I was studying the minutes of the previous meetings and thinking of an appropriate time to set up a meeting with the Parish Council and, subsequently, Financial Council, the chairperson approached me after the 8:00 AM Mass on a Sunday and said, "Father, we are having a parish council meeting by nine thirty this morning."

I could not believe what I heard, and it was hard to process. I tried to appeal to the voice of reason; I asked questions to get enlightened and, only said what I thought was helpful. "Peter, I would appreciate it if I can be present at this meeting," I offered.

The surprises did not dry up; his reply was, "Father, Sunday morning after Mass is the only time members are able to attend meetings. Since you are going to Mass, I will take care of things at the meeting and give you the report later."

At that point, I knew we needed to work on understanding each other and our responsibilities better, and so I made a direct appeal, "Peter, I hope you don't mind if I still insist on being present at the first parish council meeting to be held while I am your pastor. If for no other reason, at least, to meet and know the parish leaders, thank them for their services, and pledge my intention to work closely with them. Peter, if I heard you well, you just informed me that you are incapable of persuading the members of the parish council to assemble at any other time for meetings except on a Sunday morning. In the light of that, I will be scheduling a meeting of the parish council, and when I do, I will let you know."

I did schedule a meeting, and every member of the parish council was in attendance. I was grateful that they did, even though it was on a Wednesday evening. I believed my giving each member a courtesy call and gracefully asking them to attend, partly helped to do the magic.

I had read all the letters written to my predecessor for and against the Director for Religious Education, Kandy. My summation was that her fans had many nice things to say about her, but her detractors passionately disliked her, and it was reflected in their petitions asking to have her fired. To be fair in my assessment, it would have helped to have the perspective of some members who were not biased, but neutral. But time was of the essence; the religious education classes for the kids were to begin in two months. Since Saint James Church, Searcy, was made up of mainly young couples with kids, that problem was going to have a far-reaching effect. When I reflected over the magnitude and depth of the case, I knew that how I handled it may, to a greater extent, define my success or failure as a pastor. I invited Peter, the chairperson of the Parish Council, over to discuss what he knew, thought of, or could suggest concerning the matter. He had an interesting perspective, and his words were short and to the point. "Father, whatever you do, do not fire her! If you do, the parish will be split into two."

If Peter was right, then the situation was more depressing than I thought. It did not make any religious sense that the unity of the parish depended on Kandy remaining the Director of Religious Education, even if she was doing a poor job. I had to hasten my findings to see where it led me, and I also planned to rely more on the teachers who did not write a letter for or against her. The reason being that I already knew the sentiments of those who wrote, and those who did not write may not have had a vested interest and may furnish me with objective information.

I personally called the teachers who did not write any letter in favor of or complained against Kandy in the hope of knowing their views. I believed that speaking with them in person and individually rather than over the phone would yield better results. It was also likely that meeting with them as a group may discourage some of them from being completely frank in telling their side of the story. So I started making calls to know how possible it would be to meet with each of them; I had called three of the teachers, left a message for one who was unavailable, and scheduled an appointment with the other two. When I called the fourth teacher, I introduced myself, told her of my hope to resolve the turmoil plaguing our Religious Education and that I needed her help and that of the other teachers to resolve the issue. I expressed my wish to meet with her, if she would not mind, to discuss the matter. Her response left a bitter taste in my mouth and a painful knot in my belly.

"Father, I am not meeting with you, and not after all the news about sexual abuse of kids by priests!"

I was so stunned all I could do was apologize. "Sorry, I bothered you. It was not my intention to upset you. In any case, my invitation of meeting with you is still open in case you change your mind. But instead of my office, we will meet on the parking lot because of your concerns." My response, which was a painful practice of charity—an awkward attempt at humor and a gracious effort not to sound condescending—appeared to have enlightened her on the implications of her response, and she apologized. "I am sorry, Father. I have had a bad day!"

What I did next was unlike me: I stopped all the calls I was making, went to the back of the rectory, and cried like a baby.

The last time I remember crying in that manner was at my first Mass. On that day, everything was smoothly working according to plan until the time for final blessings. As customary, I blessed my pastor, all the priests, seminarians who attended, and then, I blessed my mom. As I did so and prayed off the cuff, the smooth-flowing prayer hit a bump as I tried to incorporate my dad, praying, "May God give eternal rest to my dad, Joseph, whom I know would have enjoyed this day more than everyone." I did not know if it was just me or the tears rolling down my mom's cheek that induced my sobbing. My sobbing was subdued at first as I intended to avoid a drama at my first Mass, but the pressure of the compressed emotions inside of me was too intense. It felt like I would implode if I did not cry. When it became most unbearable, I started crying. My mom was also without success in her effort to remain strong as she knelt at the altar trying not to cry. She seemed to be suffocating every time she made an effort to quit sobbing. After several failed attempts, she let go, and we wept together for a fine man we both knew very well and loved most dearly. In an attempt to comfort my mom, I leaned forward and hugged her as we cried. When the faithful in the church witnessed the hug, they began to clap and cheer as if to join in and share in that unique moment that only happens once in a lifetime. When that sweet embrace was over, and I looked into my mom's eyes, I observed her smiling and so was I, and I then proceeded to conclude the prayer.

The commandment the patriarchal culture made me—and I believed many other young men—falsely observe that only girls cried and, that any public show of emotion or public crying by a man was considered a sign of weakness was broken on that day. For the first time in my life, I was not ashamed to cry and before an audience, but on the contrary, I felt great relief and calmness. I actually did not have time to understand why it felt so soothing when I cried at that moment. Perhaps it was therapeutic because the congregation thought it was a beautiful expression of love and showed support, or because I was in that spark of life where nothing else made sense except what I did, or because it was one of those things about life no one can explain or understand.

Late that afternoon, after that ominous call and the upsetting outcome, there was nothing I thought to do but cry, and cry I did! As I groaned, I fantasized about how my burden would quickly dissipate if I called the bishop and told him the mission he entrusted to me was beyond what I could handle. I knew things would be bad, but that daunting load exceeded what human tolerance could accommodate. While I cried and bemoaned my misery, I had a feeling for some reason that it was not particularly fitting to cry or get disillusioned. As I tried to contemplate the rationale behind my grief, a voice within me, which sounded like my dad's voice, said, "Are you crying like a little boy because a girl beat you up!" I could not believe myself; I actually started laughing. When I got tired of laughing, I kept smiling and asked myself a series of questions and attempted to answer them.

How long have you been in this parish? *Two weeks,* I answered.

Is that enough frame of time to have an accurate assessment of a place? How many people have you met? I could not answer this last question because I barely met anyone.

Why do you try to paint an unrealistic picture with a wide brush a person on the phone handed you, especially when two other previous teachers you called were extremely nice to you? It was troubling for me to think that I was beginning to act like, and was not any better than, the parishioner who caused me pain because I was mentally condemning the whole parish for the action of one person and, thereby, committing the fallacy of overgeneralization.

My misguided thought of judging the whole parish by the act of one person, who even apologized as quickly as she slipped, made me realize how, in unguarded moments, we can misjudge people or lump them together unfairly; and I immediately forgave her. My going from the emotional to the intellectual and then to the spiritual, left me with the understanding that my problem may be that I was working too hard and in a hurry but without God—and that my approach could only yield frustration. I came to the conclusion that it was God's work, and that I should let Him work with me. That I should be patient and give God some time and see how things would fall into place at the right time. With that unusual theophany, I happily went back and made the rest of the calls.

After I read the letters and listened to the teachers I thought were neutral, I requested to meet with the Director of Religious Education, Kandy, and was happy when she agreed to the meeting and arrived on time. We spent the first forty-five minutes trying to know each other and, it was by my own design, because I genuinely wanted to get to know her. I asked her about her family, her career before she worked for the church, things of that sort. She also asked me about my family, about Nigeria, and my ministry here in the United States; and I liked her. After I felt we knew each other well enough, I proceeded to discuss with Kandy, one of the parish's prevalent problems, hoping we could solve it. I politely asked, "Kandy, would you mind telling me about your position as the Director of Religious Education and the challenges you have had to grapple with?"

Her first sentence was shocking and revealing. "Father, I know you have heard so many bad things about me and that you are probably prejudice—"

We were having a good meeting, and I did not want her to mess it up with unsubstantiated damaging assumptions, so I interjected, "Kandy, what have we done for almost an hour since you arrived here?" I did not wait for an answer but continued to finish my thought, "I have been kind to you. I served you and your little boy soda and snacks, and we have been visiting. At this point, you know me better than any other person in the parish because I chose to talk about myself with you, which I don't often do. I have shown you a sincere personal interest, because I appreciate the sacrifices you make for the parish and our kids as you serve in the capacity of the Director of Religious Education. I also know how hard it is to be in the leadership position, and I don't think I have in any way treated you like I am biased. On the contrary, I have shown you hospitality, respect, trust, and kindness. Can you tell me your side of the story without prejudging my opinion and what informed it?"

She then apologized, and I listened to all she had to say. All she said confirmed the accounts of those who liked her and attempted to rebut the allegations of her assailants. The bone of contention in my judgment hinged in some way on the misunderstanding and lack of patience on both sides. There was a repudiation and rejection of Kandy's method of leadership and good intentions when she insisted on the Baltimore Catechism being the textbook to be used by the teachers when teaching the kids. If there was good communication and perhaps a little accommodation from the outset, maybe a resolution would not have been far-fetched. But with the prolonged quarrels and bitterness that ensued, the water of collaboration was muddied, making healing and trust much more difficult to come by.

After I appraised the magnitude of the situation, I knew it would take more time to sway things back to balance, and time was not a luxury we could afford. Unfortunately, we had less than two months to make all the necessary arrangements before the religious education classes started. But even with the pressure of time, I was willing to be thorough and fair to all involved, especially the kids. My next line of questions to Kandy was going to determine how mentally prepared she was to handle the strong current of dissent. "Kandy, let us assume you are in my position as the pastor, how do you think this problem can be resolved?"

After she thought for a short time, she answered, "I don't know, Father."

"I agree with you—this is not an easy problem to resolve, especially with the limited time we have. Do you still want to remain the Director of Religious Education?" I asked.

But again, her answer was even more revealing. "Yes, Father, but only if you will shield me from my enemies."

"Your position as the director of Religious Education I am able to restore, but I don't know about shielding you from those who do not agree with you. That is because the teachers are supposed to be under your leadership, and you have to work to reinstate their respect for you and the confidence of some of the parents who no longer want to entrust you with their children. Furthermore, my predecessors were not able to secure that kind of protection you're seeking from me. I would be giving you a false hope if I pretend that I would do any better than they did. Why don't we do this: since we cannot work out all the problems now, give me a few days to pray and to mull over all we talked about—the magnitude of the problem, the possible solutions—and I will get back to you." With those words and more by way of thanks, I said a short prayer and adjourned the meeting.

After two days of sustained mental tasks and prayers, I settled on a decision that would offer a temporary solution. The Parish and Financial Councils had decided not to pay Kandy her salary for the last month before the end of the school year when the squabble peaked. I persuaded the councils to reconsider that decision since Kandy made me understand she continued to lend her services to the parish despite the commotion. I pleaded with them, arguing that not paying her for the work she claimed she had done, in my opinion, would further complicate the already-brewing animosity. After the councils reconsidered their decision and agreed with my point of view, I wrote her a letter with an enclosed check to cover her payment for the last month she said she worked. The letter read as follows:

Dear Kandy,

Greetings of peace in the name of our Lord Jesus Christ!

I am writing to first thank you on behalf of the parish for your services. I believe that your acceptance of the position as the Director of Religious Education and the enormous work it demanded could not have been possible without sacrifice from you and your family. Find enclosed the check to pay for the last month you indicated that you worked.

I had two days to reflect and pray over the problems that had plagued and threatened the religious education of the kids and unity of our parish family, and I believe in our being able to get this behind us; however, it will require time, understanding, reconciliation, and healing. I am happy we share the view that this problem is not an easy one to resolve. I know that the difficulty in addressing this issue lies in the broad and deep hurt on either side. During our meeting, you indicated your willingness to continue to work for the parish as the Director of Religious Education but on the condition that I shield you from those who disagree with you. You did not revoke that condition, which I know is beyond what I am able to do.

In the face of this daunting problem and limited time to resolve it, I have a proposal that I am going to adopt as the first step toward reconciliation, healing, trust, and peace and, in the process, build a good working relationship and better religious education for the kids. As strange as it might sound, I am going to volunteer to direct things as far as religious education is concerned until the dust settles. I am going to need your help, and I will call you in a few days, so, we can discuss the details and implementation of this proposal. Once again, thank you for all you have done for the parish. I still have confidence in you; otherwise, I would not request your help. I am also hopeful that we can turn things around working together.

Remain blessed and in God's love together with your family.

Yours truly,
Fr. Udo

My letter to Kandy was well received—at least, that was what I thought. Because when I called her, she was graceful and stated her intention to assist me, so we scheduled to meet the next day by 4:00 PM. By 3:00 PM, she left a message on the office phone: "Father, I have decided not to meet with you. I am resigning as the Director of Religious Education, and my family and I are requesting that our names be taken off the parish list because we are no longer members of Saint James Church, effective immediately."

I did not receive Kandy's voice message until about 7:00 PM, and for three hours, I waited and wondered why she did not come until I listened to it. I regretted that she resigned, but I also felt a sense of relief because I knew she just made things a whole lot easier for me. I called a meeting of the teachers and told them about my decision to be the Director of Religious Education until healing and harmony was restored. I also informed them of the arrangement I had hoped to work out with Kandy until her resignation and how much I would need their help. Since classes were to resume in a month, that meeting with the teachers turned into a working session. On that day, we were able to forecast the number of students for the year, determine the number of teachers needed, and in addition, we picked out the needed books, and we also determined what school supplies would be needed and other things that may be required. God came through for the kids and the parish; classes resumed without a hitch, and after three months a new Director of Religious Education was hired.

I did not need a diviner to tell me that the somewhat unproductive unilateral power the Parish Council chairperson had enjoyed was going to pose a problem, especially as it was my intention to work on restoring things according to the laws of the diocese. I was hoping my intended changes would lead him to share part of the leadership position he had borne alone. To make that transition as smooth, and as peaceful as possible, I decided to start by organizing a seminar for the whole parish leadership and any member of the parish who wished to attend. The seminar was twofold: the first part focused on the structure, guidelines, and the duties of the Parish Council and other leaders. The second part dealt with how we could have a parish with great vision and substantial growth. That seminar was conducted by Deacon Bo, who did a spectacular job of enlightening all in attendance. The knowledge from that seminar fostered understanding and soothed any discomfort that could have resulted from adjusting to the needed changes. How difficult it was to eventually have a Parish Council and

Financial Council that were structured according to the diocesan regulation made me wonder how much more taxing it would have been to do so without the seminar.

A month after we had the seminar, I decided to start implementing the guidelines of the diocese with regard to the parish and finance councils. I also formed an exploratory committee I called Development Committee, and its members were tasked with the vision and growth of the parish. Since Peter was both the chairperson for the Parish Council and Financial Council, I wrote him a letter thanking him on behalf of the parish for his service, letting him know that at the next Financial Council meeting, I expected him to relinquish his position as the chairperson of the Financial Council. In the letter, I explained that my decision was based on the diocesan guidelines and recommendations, which stated that a person should not serve in both positions. The reply I received was not exactly what I expected; it read something like this:

Dear Father Udo,

I am writing you this letter to inform you of my decision to resign from the positions of Parish Council and Financial Council chairperson. My first reason is that I can see the chaotic situation for which I was given these positions starting again. The second is that I want to pay more attention to my personal spiritual life.

After reading Peter's letter, I was very sympathetic and, at the same time, thankful to him. I was thankful for his services because, rightly or wrongly, he had been in those leadership positions for many years, which demanded a lot of sacrifice—and he had tried to hold things together. There was no doubt he believed in the help he offered the parish, which I acknowledged, and that he was very passionate with his obligations as the chairperson of the parish and finance councils. I was sympathetic because he did not realize that his help was not going to gender a permanent solution. The trend of his leadership was like sweeping the dirt under the carpet, and it was easy to predict that it would certainly creep up some day. I did not agree completely with his assumption that if he gave up being the Financial Council chairperson while he was still the Parish Council chairperson, the problems for which he was asked to take up the two positions would resurrect again. Let us assume he was right, then, his prediction of the problems showing up again meant that for those many years he led, the issues were never resolved—the cracks were merely covered with wallpaper. I was also sympathetic because he was not able to see with me the abundant human resources in the parish and the need to put them to good use.

It was not just him; the trend of one person juggling too many leadership positions and functions was widespread. You only needed to read the parish bulletin to find out how apparent it was. At the back of the parish bulletin were a few names of parishioners who held certain leadership positions in the parish, and there you would find, for instance, one person holding five positions at the same time: Choir, RCIA, Adult Religious Education, Hispanic ministry, and a paid position. She worked her heart out even more than Peter and never realized how much help she needed. I did provide her help by gradually involving more people and relieving her of all but one of those religious duties. I wished she did not get discouraged or disliked me too much, after I effected those changes which brought her relief and ensured there was progress in the parish. I truly admired and appreciated her passion for and devotion to the Lord's work. But I also wondered how any human being could carry out that many religious duties and do them very well. If anything, hanging those pious functions around her neck could have slowed her down and, perhaps put the parish in some form of a snag. I am sure there may have been people willing to volunteer or contribute to the good of the parish but became complacent because those positions were filled. It was my hope that my strategy would keep the parish life from the stagnation it could have been suffering because of that abnormal tradition.

This was my reply to Peter's letter:

Dear Peter,

I am writing to acknowledge the receipt of your resignation letter. I have to start by thanking you from my heart for all your sacrifices and services to the parish as the chairperson for the Parish and Financial Councils and in many other ways. I accept your resignation based on the reason that it will benefit your personal spiritual life. I respectfully disagree with you that the problems you resolved will resurface again. Even if they do, that would give us some challenges to work on together as a family, to help us grow stronger and be blessed for them.

There are some facts that always remain true; the first is that no parish on earth is completely rid of problems. The second is that as a family of God's people and as individuals that make up this family, from the least to the greatest, we all have some responsibility toward the parish. Each of us will be affected by the outcome of our contributions; we will all share in the blessings of our hard work and also share the blame if things go badly because of our negligence. The last fact is that we are doing God's work and not ours and, therefore, should be open to let him use us as he pleases. Sometimes we are not the ones to determine when to help, in what ministry, and how; otherwise, it would not be a call.

God bless you and your family.

Even though I told Peter that I had accepted his resignation in my reply, I did not want to lose him. I knew he was a good man, meant well, had a lot to offer the parish, had sacrificed so much for the parish and done well under the circumstance. But unknown to him, he was caught in the web and burden of power, and after being in that euphoria for a while, he may have lost touch with reality just like any of us would have.

I had in mind to talk things over with Peter, so I called and invited him over to the rectory. I was aware of the misunderstanding and misgivings that hung in the air and, therefore, decided that making our meeting a "beer summit" would not be a bad idea. With the wheels being as rusty and squeaky as they were, it was time for me to show the softer side of myself and my willingness to work things out more smoothly. I knew that prayers would bring divine help to enable us to work in harmony, and we already had that. But I also needed something that would bring out the little "happy boys" in us who could agree to work together, and what on earth can do that better than a good beer? The snacks and few bottles of Heineken beer we had worked; we talked about everything except parish work for at least two hours and laughed. We actually got to know each other better and agreed without words not only to work together but also be friends. When it appeared we had exhausted all there was to know about each other, I said, "Peter, I wanted to use this opportunity to personally thank you for all you have done and still do for the parish at different levels. I am sorry if you felt hurt or misunderstood my request of you. It was not my intention to upset you, but to work with you. I actually have something in mind that you could do for the parish, and you are best suited for it. If you don't mind, I will plead with you to continue to head the Parish Council until at a time when the parish is ready for Parish Council election. I will let you know at the right time when the leadership position I have in mind for you is ready."

That leadership position, as he came to find out, was being a member of the Development Committee. I thought he would be happy with that offer since he was very passionate about expanding the church, and he was.

When I arrived in the parish and saw how so few volunteered for everything, I immediately started appealing to parishioners to volunteer. First, I preached about participating actively in the parish when the theme of the scripture readings permitted. I also challenged members to not only be present during liturgical celebrations but to also help out in different ministries. I furthermore encouraged them to attend social events, both educational and recreational. That summon helped to boost the parish life in different ways and levels. I announced that whoever was interested in any position or activity in the parish—for instance, Lector, Eucharistic Minister, Choir, and more—should call the church office.

I did not wait to see if they did call or not; in fact, I cannot recall that anyone did. I had to personally ask anyone who came up to me to say hello what they were good at or wanted to do for the parish and, I pleaded with them to volunteer when they indicated where their interest lied. That was far more successful, so I was happy that I did not sit back and hope they would take out time in their busy schedule and call the parish office. Surprisingly, many relished the privilege of being personally asked, but I also quickly gained a reputation. Whenever someone tried to approach me, his/her friends would give a warning bark by way of tease: "Be careful, Father Udo will talk you into becoming a volunteer!" And there was usually a hearty laughter that followed. I was happy to be a good sport especially since my cobweb of volunteerism promotion caught many.

It is a proven concept that all work and no play makes for a dull parish and parishioners who want a reason to stay home. I came in June, and while doing my best to take care of liturgical, pastoral, and spiritual needs of the faithful, I thought of a way to improve on the social well-being of the parish, too. I believed a parish with a vibrant social life radiates some lively energy, and when that energy is combined with deep genuine spiritual energy, an unstoppable force for good in God's name is produced. I did not see the need of inventing a completely new social event since we needed to put something together quickly for the beginning of fall season. We chose to have a parish picnic, and it was my wish to make it the most fun—ever.

To have a superb occasion meant good planning, but the Parish Life Committee that would plan the event was, up till then, a one-woman committee. I, therefore, had to strengthen the Parish Life Committee by adding four more members. During the meetings, I sensed the members of the committee were concerned about the possibility of low attendance at the picnic.

"Father Udo," one of them spoke on behalf of others. "We have been in this parish long enough to know that only a few people will attend. Let us plan it on a small scale."

I could see they already contemplated failure even before we started planning, and I did not blame them because low attendance was all they had known for a long time.

My response was, "I want us to plan something fun and big."

The look on their faces when I insisted was something like: "Is this priest from the moon?" They knew I was not backing down when I said, "Prove me wrong! Let us give it our best and blame me if a few show up."

I made sure I was at each meeting to help guide the course of events, and we appointed one of the members as the communication person. She was to inform and update the faithful of what we were planning and how far we had progressed. To get the parishioners more involved and engaged, the committee asked them for suggestions on what they wanted to see incorporated in the plan. You would be surprised at how many valuable contributions parish members made; many volunteered and many asked in what ways they could help. Involving the whole parish in the planning phase added the benefit of each parishioner feeling a sense of personal ownership and great excitement. The smile on almost every one's face spoke of their appreciation and belief that their expectations would be met. We actually had more volunteers than we needed, and that in itself was a new record and a sign we already succeeded, at least in part. That was what I hoped to see—genuine and lovely excitement even at the planning phase because such characteristics make for a great festivity. That the faithful wanted to be a part of the picnic in anticipation, meant that they had in some way already embraced the outcome, that their attendance was somewhat guaranteed—since they already loved the preparation, it was easy to predict that they would have fun in spite of how things turned out. I believed that that joyful, loving sentiment would carry them through to the end, and it did. Many came after the event and complimented me, saying, "Father, we never knew there were this many people in the parish; we have never seen anything like this!" I, however, told them to thank God and those who put it together. Some enjoyed the festivities, while many met new people or made new friends, but in totality the whole ceremony was a phenomenal success!

In case you are wondering, I enjoyed the occasion very much. Earlier during the picnic, I met a family who just moved to the parish, and I took time to talk to them so as to get to know them. I made sure they felt at home, and I only left them when there were parishioners who had interest in them. But while I visited with that young couple, Kate, their daughter and the only child at the time, was busy trying to hide from me. She hid at her mom's back, obviously shy but also curious. She would stick out her head to watch when I laughed or said something she liked. Mom and Dad tried to get her to say hello, and that made her hide even more. I thought asking her to be my friend would make her warm up to me, but that made her want to crawl back to her mom's belly.

It was wonderful to witness the love and joy that filled the air as I greeted everyone in attendance in the hope to know many, if not all, my parishioners. The celebration was a fun fair, like the rodeo was in town except, in that case, it was better because it was a family celebrating in love. The joy emanating from the festivities was infectious; every one smiled or laughed, and all wanted to celebrate. All afternoon and part of the evening, I had been a greeter, but the air that spoke of merriment was too strong to be ignored, so I joined the people who played different games. My choice of game was the sack race; it appeared to be more entertaining running while inside a sack. I wore a big sack for the race that covered me from my feet to my chest. Apart from me, there was another adult and three other kids who ran the race. Candies were the prize for whoever finished first, and I had my eyes on the prize, not because I ate candies, but for the thrill of the win and then to give the candies to Kate or some of the kids. I did not think I would be a fast runner in the sack, especially since that was my first time to do so. I was right; the sack slowed me down more than I anticipated! The race barely began before I found out that it required a special skill to run with my legs partially restricted by a big bag. At first I jumped like a frog and was not fast enough. The kids in the competition knew their game and were beating us the adults by a substantial margin. The only thing that brought me comfort was that the other adult was behind me. I moved faster and actually passed one of the kids. I pushed myself a little harder, determined to win, and that was when I tripped and fell. My heart was beating so fast, and overall, it felt good to just lie there on the grass. I lay there motionless, enjoying the moment, with everyone's attention on those still in the tournament and many fans cheering. I believed the fans for the front runner shouted the loudest. My eyes were closed as I lay there, but something made me open my eyes, and whom did I see running toward me as fast as she could? Kate. As I saw her approaching, I closed my eyes, and when she got to me, she rocked my feet—which were still in the bag—with her tiny gentle fingers which I slightly felt. I guess she tried to wake me up, thinking I had fainted. While she tried to resuscitate me, she kept asking, repeatedly, "Father, are you okay?" When I sensed she was about to start crying, thinking something serious had happened to me, I opened my eyes and assured her I was okay, and then I rubbed it in. "Kate, I thought you didn't like me?" She grinned and I believed she was happy that I was alright.

The sex-abuse scandal by some Catholic priests was a big shock to me and, I believe, many other priests who know how much more sacred it is to minister to the young and innocent children. The natural instinct to protect the young and innocent and, what Christ said, "Let the children come to me" (Matthew 19:14), lend credence to this fact. It was not only devastating to watch it play out on the news but also crippling to have your own parishioner remind you of it as I experienced during my first two weeks in the parish as pastor. In the face of those ugly incidents, it became increasingly difficult to decide how best to minister to those young friends of Jesus. For instance, I had always after Mass while greeting the faithful paid special attention to the kids. I would kneel to hug them and ask them to be good kids and bless them. But the constant bombardment of the airwaves with the news of some priests' child abuse, in addition to the teacher rubbing it on my nose, made me reconsider if I should even be hugging the kids or paying special attention to them under any circumstance. I was happy I made the determination to not let all the distractions keep me from putting my heart and humor into caring for God's children. Kate's kindness, and some of the other memorable experiences, sustained me in my resolve to give them the best that I could offer and to witness how rewarding it could be.

The first way I thought to be there for the kids was to visit them at their classes during religious education. It was always an interesting adventure to make such visits; the teachers were always happy to let me teach for a few minutes, which I enjoyed. Apart from teaching, some of the most precious gifts would be painting with the kindergarten class and sometimes singing and demonstrating the "Father Abraham" song with them. I would say with certainty that the constant prayer of those beloved young friends of mine were answered and that their pure, protective, caring, sincere love was so visible and priceless.

I have a few stories to tell about my personal experiences with these beloved friends of Jesus, who happen to be my friends, too. Angel was one of my little friends who would always say hello after Mass. She was shy and hardly said anything but sat quietly beside me any time there was a parish function. Once we were having breakfast cooked by the Knights of Columbus after first Sunday Mass. I was having a quick breakfast before I left for the next Mass in Heber Springs. B.J., one of the parishioners, was sitting across the table from me, and he kept playfully talking about how mean I was because I refused him something. Angel quietly sat beside me as she always did while B.J. continued with his mocking accusations. I needed an advocate, so I asked Angel, "My Angel, is Father Udo mean?" She slowly shook her head in disagreement, and that was very comforting.

On a certain Wednesday, I was in the office when a parishioner arrived with her young son. As they took their seats and we visited for a few minutes, I waited to hear the reason for their visit. The mom spoke up, "Father, my son told me he wanted to see you."

Then I asked her, "Do you know why?"

"I don't," she replied. "Maybe he will tell you. I'll be in the car for ten minutes, and I'll come back to check on you both."

After the mom was gone, we sat quietly for a while before I broke the silence: "How are you today, Kewood?"

"Good, Father!" he answered.

"Have you been a good boy?"

"Yes, Father," he replied.

When I ran out of questions to ask, I then inquired about the reason for his visit. "Kewood, your mom said you asked to see me, you want to tell me why?"

Then I heard some of the finest words in my life: "Father, I was missing you, so I asked my mom to bring me to see you."

I have only had a few moments when I was at a loss for words, and that was one of those times. I could only say, "Thank you, Kewood. That was really nice of you."

We sat in silence for a moment, and I looked down at his black shoes, which looked good but showed signs of ugly scratches and could have used some shoe paint and polish. So I offered, "You want me to take care of your shoes for you?"

"Yes, Father," he said.

I put some black finishing on the shoes and then applied black polish, which made them look like new again. When he saw them, he was grateful and so delighted; that was the first thing he showed his mom when she came back for him.

The next time a mom visited my office with her son, it was not for pleasantries. That was during the height of the Iraqi war, and the youngster told his parents that God was causing all the death, disaster, and wars in the world. He was disturbed and could not sleep, and worst of all, did not want to attend Mass anymore. Thus, I asked him why he thought God did all the bad things that were happening in the world. His reply was, "Father, I don't know. I thought God has power to stop them."

My answer to him was, "God created us to be free to choose him. When we choose him, it means we choose to love others and to do charitable deeds. If we choose him, he will help us, through the power of his grace, to do good instead of evil. When we refuse to choose God and choose evil, all we do is fight wars, try to hurt instead of heal people, because we don't have peace."

From the look on his face, I knew that either he was unconvinced or my short sermon was a little over his head. I, therefore, took the liberty of using his personal experience to drive the point across. "Do you remember when Mom told you and your little brother not to mess with the superglue she uses for her artwork?" He nodded, and I continued. "After your mom went to run errands, do you remember your little brother climbing on to the table, not once but twice, to play with the superglue, and twice you persuaded him to get off the table and leave it alone?" Again he nodded, still curious about where I was going with my probe. "Then as you went into your room for a few minutes to take care of a few personal things, your little brother again mounted the table against your advice and smeared the superglue all over his fingers, which became glued together, and he ended up in the hospital emergency room?"

This time, he did not nod but said, "Yes, Father," as if he wanted me to hear him clearly and not confuse his nod to mean no, or for me to know how much he disapproved of his brother's action.

Then I asked him, "Do you think your mom is responsible for what happened to your brother?"

"No, Father!" he answered.

I pressed him to know why he thought his mom was not responsible, and he told me because his mom made it clear to them several times the danger of touching the superglue and tried to hide it from them. Then I asked him, "Are you responsible for what happened to your brother?"

"No, Father!" he answered.

"Why do you think you are not responsible?" I asked.

At that point, he was almost overwhelmed by the evidence against his assumption that God was responsible for the bad choices we make in this world. So he offered, "I told him, I warned him, but he wouldn't listen!"

I therefore concluded, "You see, as your mom was not responsible because she told you the right thing to do, tried to discourage you by hiding the superglue, and you're not to blame because you tried to dissuade your brother twice, but he wouldn't listen, God is not responsible when we fight wars or hurt others. We are the ones that make those bad choices instead of making the good ones, like your brother did. We are, therefore, responsible for our actions and the harm or destruction they caused."

As a pastor, I wondered how the kids could benefit more from Mass. I knew if they had scripture readings and homilies that were tailored for them, they would understand, enjoy, and benefit more from them. Since I already had too many Masses for the weekend, I worked out a program where the kids had liturgy of the Word ministered by Deacon Bob concurrently with 8:00 AM Mass. During that service, kids read the first and second readings of that Sunday; reading the Gospel and preaching the homily was done by Deacon Bob. He was very wonderful with kids, and they adored him. I was truly pleased with how he ministered to them, and their parents enjoyed the Mass without being chaperones until during presentation of the gifts, when the kids brought the gifts to the altar, received a blessing, and went back to sit with their parents.

The next thing I did was to schedule a weekday Mass for kids on Tuesday evening. Before now, all the weekday Masses were by 7:30 AM and had never been changed as far as people could remember. So my changing the Tuesday Mass time to 4:00 PM so the kids could come and Friday Mass to 12:00 noon so working parishioners could take twenty minutes out of their lunchtime to attend Mass did not go smoothly. Some who came to daily Masses—only about seven people came regularly—threatened not to attend weekday Masses unless I changed the time for Mass back to 7:30 AM, and some made their disappointment known. I could understand why they were not very happy with my decision to change the time for Mass. I knew the change would alter what they were used to and required an extra effort and sacrifice on their part. But I could not accept the reasons for their disagreement. They argued that the time of Mass had never been changed and that the kids would not come because they never came to weekday Masses. There was no need for things to remain unchanged if the prospect of change would spread the benefits to more people than just the privileged few. I encouraged the faithful to attend not only the Sunday Masses but also the weekday. I was conflicted about persuading them to attend weekday Masses while, at the same time, having all the weekday Masses at 7:30 AM when workers are heading to work and kids are going to school.

After the Mass time changed, we had about the average of thirty people on Friday noon Masses, and for Tuesdays, we got much more. My secret was, I told the kids that if they came to Mass on any Tuesday, I would have a surprise for them. I kept my promise; every child who came got a holy picture, and those who answered my questions correctly received extra gifts. As news spread on how much fun the Mass was, many more kids also came. However, there were kids who wanted to come, but their parents were not able to bring them. So I told those kids, "If you want to come to Mass and your parents won't bring you, cry and scream like you do when you want a new pet or toy." The number of attendance increased some more.

One of the parents had dropped off her son for Mass, and you could tell she had a lot on her mind and was about to go and run other errands. I thanked her for bringing him.

She replied, "Father, you don't have to thank me, I didn't have any choice. My son wouldn't quit crying until I promised to bring him."

My reply was, "I told them to cry if that would get them to Mass."

And she said, with an air of sarcasm, "Thank you, Father!"

Before I let her go, I pulled the last punch. "You're welcome! I know you would rather be somewhere else, and it may well be that you have very important errands to run, and I won't keep you from attending to them. You're a grownup and I don't care so much about whether you come to weekday Mass or not, as I care for him coming. If he has that hunger to attend Mass, we should encourage and help in every way we can to encourage him."

I could not help but note that she started coming regularly to the weekday Mass and with her son.

Changing the times for some of the weekday Mass was rewarding in many ways; the number of attendance increased even for the ones in the morning that I left unchanged. Maybe after coming at other times, some realized how beautiful it could be to attend Mass and made extra sacrifices to come in the morning. The spiritual benefits were invaluable, and the kids cared for me in their own angelic ways. They never failed to pray for me, and I knew because they told me in letters, drawings, and word of mouth. They gave many symbolic gifts too, like Mary, one of the little girls who came to weekday Mass with both parents and little sister. I always told her I liked her red hair. Once, during children's Mass, I told them that being as young as they were, the sky should be their limit on how much they could learn about God and how much they could excel in school. I also made them understand that when they become as old as me and their parents, it gets increasingly difficult to have time to learn many more things. That is because the older we get, the more the number and harder the problems we have to attend to. I also told them that one of the indicators for the guys that they are getting to that age is when they begin to get bald like me, and the kids all laughed, thinking it was funny. But I noticed there was a little girl, Mary, who sat at the second pew in the church who did not laugh, and I wondered why because she looked rather concerned. The following week after the Mass, Mary handed me an envelope, but I did not open it until I got to the rectory. What a surprise! In the envelope was a lock of beautiful red hair. Mary had a haircut and told her parents she wanted to replace my fallen hair, to reverse my age, to be younger, so I could learn many more things. Her love and care actually made me feel a lot younger, and hopefully, her prayer has helped me to learn more and be a lot wiser.

When my friend Father Okey said that what he heard about my place of ministry made it sound like the "lion's den," he meant it as a joke. A joke that somewhat underscored some of what he was told about the place. What I experienced was not the "lion's den," but a great family I was fortunate and happy to be part of in good times and difficult ones. In that family, there was such outpouring support, kindness, and love, and we were able to accomplish a lot for the Lord together that I hope to write about someday. Even when we had little misunderstandings, they were always out of passion for the Lord's work. Our harmless family misgivings, were, I believed, always resolved out of Christian love. We also learned a lot of lessons from such experiences which led to further growth. Having said that let me now relay some of my adventures in the "lion's den."

CHAPTER 10

The Challenges of a Cleric

Humor can serve as the sweet grease that eases the squeaky pain caused by life's challenges.

—Father Udo Ogbuji

I first wish to clarify why I tell the stories you will find in this chapter. The stories were remarkable moments in my ministry as a priest, which ranged from happy to not so happy and from conflicted to paradoxical. Some were times I was beaten down or situations when I felt lost or helpless but surprisingly triumphed. Others were moments I felt like a clown or embraced the clown in me to calm the brewing storm. During some of those unpredictable life episodes, I made concerted efforts to remain sane by not trying to find intellectual explanations since that would not make sense in those cases. What all these transforming experiences had in common in spite of how unpleasant, unprecedented, and intellectually challenging—or challenged—were that they all provided unique opportunities that I learned from, and they mostly yielded helpful results.

The registration list of the parish of Saint James, Searcy, indicated we had 250 families, but only about 220 were active members. Some families had moved while some quit coming to church. Mindful of the example of the Good Shepherd, I went in search of the lost sheep. I was determined to initiate reconciliation and, perhaps, bring back those who had left. Through homilies, seminars, spiritual and social events, I also put together some structures that would foster unity, peace, and love. It was important that I embarked on that mission after a ten-month period of getting to know the faithful who were entrusted to my care, because my observation revealed a few instances of animosity in the parish and the devastating pain it caused. It is not out of the ordinary to see some of these behavioral traits in parishes. In fact, they exist wherever you have a group of humans who are bound by sets of goals and relationships. Those anomalies call to mind the scourge of human imperfection and the need to address them, where and when possible, especially, among God's people.

The family feuds I witnessed in the parish were fueled, it appeared, by strong dissent and active cliques in the parish. Each small group had a unique perspective on how things should be and espoused certain spirituality or religious orientation that was not bad in itself. I was inclined to think that the seeming chaos I observed was a result of unharnessed talent and improper channeling of the abounding energy in the parish. That may be part of the reason some members stopped coming to church. Although I was aware of that situation—the cliques and their disagreements with one another—my strategy was not to break them up but to slowly bend each group until they all converge. I knew that it was often counter-productive to force people to be friends or dictate to them whom to be close to. Even if you have the power as a parent or pastor, you can only preach acceptance, kindness to all, and love of neighbor. I understood the cliques were deeply entrenched, and that any attempt on my part to break them up would consume so much time and energy and may result in more division and monstrous pandemonium. My desire and goal after appraising the complexity of the circumstances were to design an overall plan that would, in a web-like way, connect all the circles of friends and facilitate communication between them. I believed that once there was dialogue, there would be understanding, tolerance, and maybe, acceptance. To achieve that goal, it was vital to include in every committee, if possible, a representative that was very well respected in his/her group. At the same time,

I had to appoint a chairperson who did not particularly identify with any defined group but was respected by all. My fantasized approach and its application paid off. Everyone felt included, and the mutual coexistence brought some degree of harmony and love—the ripe atmosphere that helped us to reap the rich human and spiritual resources we had.

My search for the slacked members did not yield the expected abundant result. Only one family among the three who told me they would come back to the church actually did. There were two other families I went to visit who, by all accounts, sent signals that indicated I was not in a Catholic camp and was not welcomed. It made me wonder why they agreed to my visit when I called on the phone and inquired if I could come to see them. It took me three years to realize the unfriendly treatment I received was indeed a royal reception when compared to the hovering ill sentiments I was oblivious to but came to know, thanks to the First Presbyterian Church pastor in Searcy. He revealed to me a disturbing reason why some members of Saint James Parish left and joined his church. I did not know what brought us closer; probably the hunger to stay true to the spirit of ecumenism, but we had lunch together when our crowded schedules would permit. On one such occasion after we had eaten and gone to his church to visit some more, he made what should have been a shocking revelation. He told me that when the news of my posting reached my would-be parishioners, some families from Saint James parish began to attend his church. When he asked them why they left the Catholic Church to come to his church, they informed him that they could not stand or accept a black man being their pastor. It was deplorable that something of that sort could be attributed to even one Catholic in Searcy! I also learned that Heber Springs—where my second parish was located—was not completely free of prejudice. The city had a terrible reputation, and a past history that attested to a group of individuals who tried to terrorize some people they considered different. I was told that there was a time in the past, when signs were put up warning Catholics, blacks, and Jews not to stay in

Heber Springs after sunset. One would like to believe that such behaviors died with those who perpetrated them. Although those hateful sentiments are almost nonexistent, there was one incident that occurred while I was still there. I was told there was a black family who moved to Heber Springs, and after a few months, their house burned down when they were away from home. The incident may have been an accident, but there were suspicions, and the family actually left town after that possible hateful act.

My attitude toward those whose judgments are clouded and, who think in racial terms is that of pity and forgiveness. How can anyone think that way, unless such a person is ignorant or feels a deep sense of insecurity? My reaction, which mirrors clemency for people who carry out such terrible racial overtures, might be attributed to my being a Catholic priest, and part of my job description is to forgive. It may also be because I had been through so much and seen much worse in my lifetime, therefore, those incidents seemed as nothing in comparison. Another plausible reason could be that I never walked in the hurting shoes of the black Americans who still have the blisters from the burden and memory of racism.

The First Presbyterian Church pastor was surprised when I laughed at his revelation of an apparent racist comment from some fallen Catholics. He looked at me as if to say "You should be upset. I can't understand why you are not." I then told him what I thought: "If those families left because someone who is not of the same race as they are was appointed their pastor, then, they had been in the wrong church all this time—I doubt that the Catholic Church can afford their demand. The Church is universal. It belongs to all people, and everyone is welcomed. They have no authority to choose who should be Catholic or what race a priest has to be to qualify as their pastor. Their leaving Saint James Parish, though unfortunate, may have turned out to be a blessing for me. If they were still members of Saint James Parish when I arrived, with the kind of mind-set they had, they probably would have been among those who would have made my work and life most miserable."

After that sad revelation that bordered between ridiculous and sadness, I wondered whether the two families who were not very nice to me were among those who went to the First Presbyterian Church because they did not want me as their pastor. If they were, how much of a clown was I to an audience who had already made up their minds not to laugh? Those thoughts and families quickly evaporated from my mind and did not offend me because I was unaware of the identity of the actual families. It helped that I did not know their identity or sought to know, even though I sensed my pastor friend was willing to tell me who they were. I am quite sure this is where the saying is so true: ignorance is bliss. I am not sure how much difference it would have made if I knew who they were; I am inclined to think I would have seen them for who they represent—those who need a little lesson on charity and basic social knowledge—and moved on with my life and duties.

When Bishop Sartain called to brief me on my new assignment, he told me to extend my ministry to the Hispanic community in Searcy. Armed with that summon and more, I went to Searcy hoping to offer the best pastoral care I could. So, despite the load of all the other pastoral duties in the three parishes, I made the decision to take up the Hispanic Mass every other week. Father Mark came twice in a month to help out because he had his hands full with the ministries in his own parish in Jonesboro. As the Sunday of my first Spanish Mass drew closer, I committed myself to learning rudimentary Spanish language and how to celebrate Mass in Spanish. Unfortunately for me, I was unaware there was a baptism at that Mass. It was going to be a huge test for my Spanish reading skills. I had prepared a short homily for the Hispanic community, which was translated by one of the members. The Mass went as well as could be expected under the circumstances—being my first in Spanish language. The ceremony, however, went into real slow motion after my homily, when I ventured into the baptismal ritual, in Spanish language. There were some unfamiliar words, and I believed I tripped on almost all. It was in the summer, the air conditioner in the church was not cooling well, and the church was unusually packed. The people in the congregation were sweating under the scorching heat and my punishing Spanish. When I thought it could not get any worse, it did. The little girl that was being baptized started crying. She would not stop, and her cries turned into screams. I did not blame her because she was probably hungry and also feeling the heat. At that point, we were one hour and ten minutes into the Mass. The air conditioner in the church, by all indications, had quit completely, and the big white linen dress the little girl wore may not have helped the situation. I had never so much prayed for the moment when water is poured on the child during baptism. Some kids giggle at that point, some cry, some just suck it up like grown kids and do not show any emotions. In that instance, I would bet any amount of money she would stop crying. I was right, and I was relieved to the extent that I could make a joke.

"I am sorry I made her cry," I announced to the congregation, and added, "She couldn't bear my poor Spanish anymore."

Those who understood English started laughing lightly. But when it was translated in Spanish, there was a louder outburst of laughter. The Mass lasted for almost two hours. The devout Catholics sat through it all, and those who only attended Mass on occasions like baptisms, *quinceaneras*, marriages, and more, were going out and coming into the church, I believe, for smoke breaks or to cool off. That experience strengthened my resolve to work harder on my Spanish language. Not only because of the humiliation I went through and the hell everyone endured at my hands, but also because of the hospitality and kindness of the Hispanic community. They were very gracious, and some actually told me they understood my Spanish and that I did much better than some priests they knew, which I believed was a stretch, but sweet nonetheless. It was a delight for me to note they were happy that I made an effort to say Mass in Spanish, and I was encouraged they expressed their wish for me to continue. And for that, I was grateful and determined not to disappoint them.

The Knights of Columbus hosted a Christmas party the year I became the pastor, and their band was going to play as part of the entertainment. That was an opportunity for me to sing and dance—hobbies I enjoyed a little bit—and to identify with more of the parishioners and know them better. In preparation for the party, I brought out my dancing shoes, which badly needed some polish, which they got. The last time I wore them and danced publicly was during one of the parish events organized in Saint Edward Parish, Texarkana the year before. While in Texarkana, I tried to make parish occasions special, interesting, and memorable for the parishioners in attendance. On one such parish event, I hopped on to the karaoke stage and sang "What a Wonderful World" by Louis Armstrong with Chris K. It was not boring at all. In fact, those who attended were under our entertaining spell. We even added our own personal special effects that made the crowd clap, cheer, and go wild. On another parish occasion, I believe a Valentine party, I decided to wear an exotic African outfit and loaned Big Brother Phillip one of my spare ones to wear. I also talked him into dancing an African song with me. The African song we danced required some level of flexibility to pay complement to every bit of the rhythm. Before we went to the Christmas party, Big Brother and I practiced a little. He did okay but was anything but flexible. My observation was that the job of getting him to loosen up would be painful and take time, and after that effort, only little improvement would be made. In fact, it would actually be more entertaining to let him dance the way he did. The African attire had pajama-looking pants and a long shirt that covered half of the pants; those hid his many dancing flaws and actually seemed to improve his moves. As we danced before the partying crowd, who were thrilled as they watched, I could tell he was trying very hard to sway his rigid body without success to the rhythm of the song—the only thing I saw flapping in every direction was the clothes he was wearing. Our captivated audience laughed, whistled, and clapped, and some came and danced with us. It was a one-of-a-kind parish party, fun-filled, and everyone enjoyed it in a fraternal Christian spirit that told the story of our great religious family. The benefits of the Christian family camaraderie that we fostered and the opportunity to know our parish family better, made me think that our playing the clowns by dancing was well worth it, and I would not mind doing it again if I had to.

A year later, at another Christmas party—this time in Saint James Church, Searcy—I entertained the people by singing "Love, Oh Love" by Lionel Richie and also danced to one of my African songs and by myself. As I danced to the music, everyone joined in to dance by themselves, perhaps, because the beauty of the song was irresistible—although I am quite certain they did not understand a word of the song. It appeared everyone had a good time until a few days later, when one of the parishioners asked me a question that changed my whole assumption. Her question was "Father, I was wondering about the other night at our Christmas party, if your dancing was lewd?"

As I listened to the question, I restrained myself and remained calm to reason with her, to be fair and not prejudge the question or cast doubt on her intention. I thought she was a distinct Catholic girl that wanted to set a good example or to aspire toward perfection. However, her question was shrouded in vagueness; at best, she seemed to be searching for clarification or, at worse, indicated a possibility of bad behavior. I was not really sure what direction she leaned. So I said in reply, "I do not believe anyone danced nor did something of that sort. I absolutely did not. I thought we were all dancing for the Lord and having fun." I would have stopped there and moved on to a different subject matter, but the look on her face appeared to suggest she was not convinced or was not satisfied with my answer, so I asked, "Do you really think the dancing was awkward?" I avoided the word *lewd*, which she used because it was too strong for me and instead used *awkward* for lack of better word. She was quiet and would not answer, and when she remained silent, I thought she said more by what she did not say. I was utterly stunned to imagine that her silence may have meant that I was lewd in my dancing; if she thought the opposite, which would have been complimentary, then she would have said so. In any case, I was willing to accommodate the fact that she was not sure, but even that did not offer any comfort. If she was in doubt that meant the possibility existed that she was scandalized, depending on which way she leaned. When she would not speak, I said, "I sincerely thought everyone was having fun and that we were all celebrating as a family. I certainly hope I did not scandalize you or anyone who attended."

Later at my private moment, when I reflected on the whole incident, I imagined what a terrible jester I may have been, dancing perhaps at the discomfort of at least one parish member while I thought everyone enjoyed the occasion.

I found the whole situation funny and confusing at the same time because the dancing she seemed to condemn could have passed for an offertory dance at Mass back in Africa. On Sunday Masses especially, everyone sang and danced as they brought their offering to the altar, in the spirit of what Saint Paul said that "God loves a cheerful giver" (2 Corinthians 9:7). To be fair to my friend in Christ who asked if my dancing was lewd, she has not been to Africa and has not seen such a dance and did not know what to make of it. Dancing in my part of Africa is a decent art, and that is why the offertory during Mass is graced with dancing as gifts are brought to the altar. Although we were not celebrating Mass, it would not be *lewd* to dance with joy while celebrating with a Christian family you are happy to be part of—Just like David and the House of Israel danced (2 Samuel 6:5). What was laughable and ironical was that, at the same Christmas party, there was a slow, soft song that was played by the band. At that time, I was sitting down to rest but watched others dance, and some of the couples who danced to the song had dancing partners who were neither their husbands nor wives. But I gave the dancers the benefit of the doubt because I believed they were dancing out of Christian love and in the spirit of our one big family, Saint James.

I had some thoughts, questions, and insight about all those moments: Why would everyone in Texarkana appear to have had fun and never saw what this friend of mine pointed out? Was it just one person that felt that way? Were there others who simply did not want to comment? The insight came from the intriguing lesson of human cultures, which are as varied as there are people. Obviously, there are subtle differences in African culture and American culture. Distinction also has to be made between the seeming relaxed culture in Texarkana and the tight religious culture in Searcy. Besides cultures, the mechanism that operates each individual's personal way of processing and interpreting things is unique to each person and should never be underestimated. There may, therefore, be tension created by diversity of cultures between people of different countries or different cultures across regions even of the same country. This possible tension is not limited to cultures; it may also be generated by different personal proclivities that distinguish one individual from another. We, however, can be comforted to know that the unconditional love of Christ, which Christians try to live by, cures possible friction between cultures and persons. That is, because this ultimate and therapeutic love has a way of soothing and uniting people, thereby neutralizing the conflicts that may come from discrepancies in cultures and individual inclinations.

I know this for a fact because the following year when I attended the Knights of Columbus's organized Christmas party I decided that I would not dance—the last thing I wanted to do was dance and scandalize someone. I sat at a corner like I was in a funeral home mourning the dead, while everyone else celebrated and had a good time. Mary, one of my old friends, danced by herself; she enjoyed dancing, and she danced very well. She was one of those feisty ones who, even at eighty, had not slowed down. When she saw me sitting in a corner, she came and dragged me off to the dance floor. Her poor husband, who could not cope with her energy, did nothing but laugh at both of us. At first, I hesitated to dance, but I knew I could not say no to Mary. Her husband had given an indirect approval by his laughter. In fact, a dance with Mary was a favor to him because if I did not dance with her, he would be out on the dance floor against his will. I finally gave in after I wondered how a dance with Mary would possibly cause scandal. I convinced myself to dance with her when I thought aloud, "Mary is eighty years old, for heaven's sake!" She really made my night; she danced so well that, at some point, I just had to compliment her. I leaned forward while dancing, smiled, and asked her, "Mary, how many young men did you get into trouble when you were younger?"

She flashed me a sweet smile back and said, "Too many to count and, I still do!"

We both laughed, and on that hearty note, the song ended.

That beautiful experience with my old friend, Mary, was evidence which proved that the intricate composite of the accidentals, like cultures and individual differences, surrounding and sometime propelling humans can, with a right understanding and approach, complete us instead of grind us down. Cultures and individual differences can truly engender friendship and love! Mary and I could not be any more apart when the configuration focuses on our varied age and culture, but she cut through all those barriers to be there for her priest who needed a smile. When that simple friendship and love we may seek because we perfect each other are immersed in Christ, there is a handsome transformation that takes place. That transformation breaks the shackles of selfishness emanating from fear and the unhelpful need to embrace only what we know and trust. After that happens, cultures and individuals are cleaned up or liberated—cultural differences and individual idiosyncrasies are harmonized, leaving us with true, pure Christian friendship marked with eternal love and a profound bond. That was exactly what Saint Paul was referring to when he said that Christ "holds all things in unity . . . because God wanted all perfection to be found in him and all things to be reconciled through him and for him, everything in heaven and everything on earth, when he made peace by his death on the cross" (Colossians 1:17-20).

Maria was one of the good Catholic girls I visited in one of the nursing homes. She was very witty, funny, and devout in her faith. She always picked my brain about religion, politics, and life in general. She loved hummingbirds and talked about them endlessly. The delightful way she spoke of them would get you hooked. If you came into her room in the middle of the story, you would think she was talking about her kids or relatives. They might as well be since she liked them a lot and spent most of her time with them. They always came to feed on the liquid sugar in the hummingbird feeder she kept outside her translucent glass door for them. One of the days I visited Maria, a nurse came to give her medicine. The nurse conversed with us for a few minutes before she left. As soon as she left, Maria said, "Father, that nurse likes you, and she was not discreet about it. She won't stop looking at you, and this is the longest she has ever stayed in my room." As she said that with a mischievous smile, I knew she was on to something harmlessly sneaky. She seemed to be enjoying the tease, and it would be cruel of me to dampen her joke and spirit by ignoring her ploy, so I played along. "You're very perceptive Maria. What's her name?"

Since that exchange, I never visited Maria without getting a message from the nurse, whose name I do not remember and who I am not sure I would recognize if I saw her again. Sometimes she would stretch it a little more by telling me that if I hung around for a few more minutes, it would be her medicine time and then rub it in by saying, "I know she'll be happy to see you." Then, I would say, "Tell your nurse I said she would be doing me a favor if she keeps taking good care of you." Most times I visited her, we would start with serious issues like religion, politics, or questions about something she needed clarification on. After that mental exercise, I would pray for her, give her communion, and anoint her. Then she would talk more about hummingbirds, which I dreaded, because that meant I would be late for my next pastoral appointment. I would not dare interrupt her as she was a very nice old lady. When she did not tell me the story of the hummingbird, she made sure I was updated on the nurse. The latter sometimes became a welcomed relief because it did not take as much time to discuss when compared to the hummingbirds' story. Moreover, I had an indirect control on how long she dwelt on the nurse; it was easier for me to change the subject whenever I thought it was time to move on to something more important.

On a particular day, I paid a pastoral visit to Maria; the door to her room was half open, and I knocked and went in. My arrival time was eleven in the morning. This was the time we agreed on and had kept to faithfully every last Friday of the month, and the parish secretary always called the home-bound senior citizens to be sure they wanted to be visited. Maria was called, and she asked for me to come, so I believed she was expecting me. She sat in her La-Z-Boy chair as she usually did and faced the sealed clear-glass door, through which she watched hummingbirds as they fed and fought. Everything appeared normal, except that, for the two minutes I had been there, she did not say a word to me. Not even to offer me to take a seat as she typically did. When I asked her if she was okay, she mumbled some incoherent words. Something else was unusual; she appeared to have made a fist with her right fingers and covered it with the left palm of her hand. It also seemed she was putting pressure on her clasped hands, and her face looked like she was in pain. With those abnormal behaviors, I began to think Maria was in some kind of trouble; I actually thought she was about to have a stroke. Then I said, "Maria, I don't know what is happening to you. I have a feeling you're in some kind of danger. If you don't talk to me, I'm going to call for help." What she did next was very dramatic, and I regretted that I made her try to talk. Because when she attempted to speak, she only mumbled something that sounded like "Mmmhuuu mmmhuuu!" At the same time, she opened her fist and showed me what she had been hiding from me; she had her dentures in the palm of her hand. She may have been cleaning them or trying to put them in before I knocked and entered her room. I believed she was embarrassed because she was so quiet, which was unlike her, and in my concern to make her feel better, I made a dumb statement. The words came out before I could stop myself. "You should have told me you needed privacy, and I would've gone out of the room to let you take care of things." She did not respond, and I thought of how dumb I was. I should have known no one can talk well without teeth in their mouth. I then left the room and gave her the privacy she could not ask for. When I came back to visit with Maria, she looked so downcast, and I felt responsible and tried to lift her up. I actually missed the old Maria who smiled and played pranks. I tried almost everything, but her lack of interest was obvious. I talked about hummingbirds, but the look on her face made me think I was reading the obituary from the newspaper to her. Then I played my last card, and it worked. "Maria," I said. "I think I like your nurse, you want to invite her over—" I barely finished when she laughed so hard. I was glad she was seated at that time. I did not want any more incidents. I laughed with her and thanked heavens the jester in me came out just in time and helped bring my old timid friend out of the gloom.

Being there for a family bereaved of a beloved one is a unique pastoral obligation. An obligation that makes a pastor feel fulfilled when the grieved members of the family are comforted. Sometimes, the circumstances of death seem so tragic and unfair that the pastor feels almost as though God has left him in an unfamiliar field with land mines to find his way out. The story I am about to write down exemplifies such a dark moment of abandonment.

I received a call that a baby boy was stillborn. His mom and dad had been married for nine years without a child. I had planned to be there for the family for whatever they would need, as any pastor would. The baby's father was not Catholic, and the information I received indicated that the funeral service would be officiated by his pastor, who would also preach. At the cemetery, on the day of the burial, shortly before the funeral service began, the bereaved couple pleaded with me to also preach after the Baptist pastor had done so. Because of the sudden change of program, there were some hurdles for me to jump. Each hurdle seemed higher and more insurmountable. First of all, what this poor couple had faced hardly left any room for words. What can anyone possibly say to such a grieved couple who had a stillborn baby after many years of yearning to have a child? My lecturer in pastoral care offered a good piece of advice: if you believe your words would make matters worse, do not say anything at all. Just your comforting presence would be more than enough. If you, however, feel the need, a few words and reassuring modest smile will do. Though it was my wish to preach, when I was told only the Baptist minister would preach, I was somewhat relieved because I believed no words could match the untold grief of that couple. But, I was willing to do anything the couple asked of me, so it was easy for me to accept their request that I preach after his church minister. I only hoped that anything I said would help them find solace. That led to the second hurdle: I did not have any prepared homily since I was under the impression only the Baptist pastor would preach. If a homily ever needed to be prepared, the one for this unprecedented funeral service certainly did. I wished I was well prepared so that my words would be consoling to the couple, which was my main concern. But it would also take care of the third hurdle, which was of less significance than the first and second, namely, religious rivalry.

Searcy was a city fraught with religious rivalry; the Baptist and Church of Christ denominations attempted to eclipse the other churches, especially the Catholic Church. As crazy as it might sound, I believed that since the Baptist pastor knew the Catholic Church members were going to be present at the funeral service, he would be extra good. Therefore, it would not surprise me if he gave the best homily not only to comfort the mourning couple but also to convert the Catholics he probably thought were spiritually impoverished. As expected, he gave one of the best sermons I had ever heard and left me with the burden of redeeming the Catholic Church under difficult circumstances.

With my lack of thorough preparation, I foresaw a scenario were my lackluster performance would be a shellacking for the Catholic Church and confirm the presumption of our separated brethren—that Catholics are shallow when it comes to the Bible and preaching.

I was not about to let that happen. When I realized the gravity of a seeming failure, all my survival instincts were activated. I first had to calm myself down so as not to be nervous, tight, or afraid. I then told myself not to try to replicate the sermon of the Baptist minister but to be myself and deliver the homily in my own terms and style. I wore a measured smile, which not only had a soothing effect for me, but also for the bereaved couple, their friends, and relatives. In my delivery, I avoided another long homily and quoted less biblical passages. With that approach, there was no appearance of sectoral competition with the Baptist pastor, which would have been grossly inappropriate for that tragic occasion, and I was also able to avert a repetitive homily, which would have made me come off as lame. The structure of my homily went like this: I complimented the pastor on the inspirational sermon he gave. I summarized his homily in three points, and then, linked it to the little boy who had died. My creativity came with my respectful and humanized impersonation of the deceased boy, and then addressed those gathered like he was speaking through me. Here is the summary of how I spoke on his behalf: "The soul of the just and innocent the Bible tells us, are in the hands of God (Wisdom 3:1). And I am innocent so you know where I am. I know how much pain you feel because I did not spend enough time with you. I have a complicated mission from God, and it required me to be incorrupt, and so I did not enter the world. Now that I am with God my creator, I assure you, I will always be your angel. I will pray for you, protect and care for you even from here. I will ask God to let my other siblings who will eventually be members of our family to live with you far longer than I did. I have so much work to do, and so do you. Stay well and know that I am united with you in spirit and can't wait to see you face-to-face after a ripe old age. Take heart, Mommy and Daddy, I love you both, and God bless you and comfort you." As a priest, there are times when you are more aware that God had worked through you; that was one of those times. God was obviously watching out for me; otherwise, I could not have pulled it off.

There was a funeral Mass in Heber Springs that almost bore the semblance of a circus. The woman who died was survived by her husband and five grown sons. She was about eighty-five years old when she died. As was customary, I met with the bereaved family, went through the funeral ceremony with them so they would know what to expect. At that meeting, I gave the family readings to choose from and listened to them share their family stories. Those stories were helpful as I was able to tailor my homily to be more personal than generic and to more effectively comfort the family. That meeting offered me an opportunity to find out which one of her sons would give a five-minute eulogy on behalf of the family. The family made a special request concerning the eulogy. They asked me to permit each of the deceased woman's five sons to speak for fifteen minutes, for a total of one hour fifteen minutes. They claimed that the request they made would have been the wish of their mom. I was sympathetic to the family and agreed to each son speaking for three minutes, fifteen minutes in all, which they agreed to. During Mass, before the final commendation, each son came up for the eulogy. The first son spoke for seven minutes. The second, ten minutes. The third, five minutes. The fourth, fifteen, and the last son, who was a lawyer, spoke for forty-five minutes. The first surge of inward reaction was a deep sense of betrayal. A betrayal that almost turned to regret when I knew the faithful would be kept in the church far longer than was necessary. I also realized that I would have to cancel a scheduled meeting in Searcy. I believed the last son to eulogize had planned his speech ahead of time and had no intention of honoring his agreement on behalf of the family. If each son took extra time and the last spoke for forty-five minutes—when each was supposed to speak for three—only heaven knows how much longer they would have held everyone in the church hostage if I had agreed to each son speaking for fifteen minutes. It was tough not to be upset watching that drama unfold, so I tried very hard to keep my mind on the Mass and the grace I would gain after I put up with that strange family. I could not believe that I even laughed when the lawyer said something funny. After he finished his forty-five minute eulogy and turned to go back to his seat, his dad got up from his pew and added some vinegar to the bad wine. He spoke to the hearing of everyone in the church, young and old: "When Martha was alive, she always reminded me to zip up my pants when I am going into town. I wonder who will help remind me now that she's gone." It was quite a show inside the church, but what could I do? It was important not to let my dissatisfaction show, so I laughed and remained somewhat in a good mood. After the Mass was over, I headed to the sacristy to remove my vestment. The son who spoke for forty-five minutes was close to the sacristy area. I said hello and then complimented him: "Don, you gave such a wonderful eulogy." His face lit up but quickly faded when I added, "I regret one thing though." After I said that, he went from being happy and proud to appearing curious, as if to ask, "What is it that he regrets?" Then I concluded, "I regret that I did not give you guys enough time." He was frozen; he did not know if it was a compliment or not, and he stood there, perhaps still confused, until I took off my vestments and left the church.

Someday I intend to give a full account of my attempt to build for God befitting houses of worship as a pastor of three parishes. Until then, I cannot resist to tell a few stories of events that took place in that process. It took two years after I became the pastor of Saint James, Searcy, to update the parish register. Before then, there were mass mailings that were sent out occasionally, and I would not be surprised if some of those mailings went to some dead members. The Development Committee and I had a strategy we adopted to ensure our new church building was on target; we believed the parishioners should be allowed to indicate which church design they wanted. We, therefore, sent cards with different designs of potential church buildings and their price tags to parish members, in addition to a letter from me and an instruction on how to fill out the card. A particular man in the nursing home, who only had a few months to live, also received the mail—or I should say, his daughters did on his behalf. One of the daughters wrote me a heartfelt letter and reminded me to update the parish register.

Her note reads,

> I am writing to inform you that my dad got the letter you sent him stating the dream of a new church project and request for money. The problem is that my sister and I received the letter on my dad's behalf because he has been in the nursing home for many years and now has only a few months to live. But all this time, he has been in the nursing home, none of the priests from Saint James, including you, has so much as gone to visit and pray with him. I am, therefore, not surprised you did not think twice about asking a dying man you have not cared for to give you money to build a new church. We already have a church, and you want a new one. And people wonder why my sister and I do not go to church anymore.

Her letter reflected one who had little or no information, or was simply misguided. Since I arrived in the parish, her father had been one of those I visited in the nursing home. Because her father was in pain most of the time, I believed the nurses gave him something to ease the pain he felt and that also made him sleep most of the time. Whenever I visited, and he was asleep; I did not wake him up but let him rest. In that case, I went at a later time to see him. There were some times when he was awake and we visited. Those times he told me about his family and other things. However, he was forgetful sometimes and told me the same stories over and over again. As his ailment got worse, he slept almost all the time.

So, I replied her letter:

Dear Ms. Boise,

Greetings of peace and love in the name of our Lord Jesus Christ!

I did receive your letter, and I am sympathetic to your frustration. I am truly sorry about your dad's deteriorating health, and I want to assure you that he is in my prayers always. I wish you knew I had visited your dad, George, since I have been in this parish—perhaps you would have been a lot nicer in your letter. My assignment here began on the twenty-fifth of June 2002. On the first day I celebrated Mass for the people, I told them that I would visit the seniors who are in the nursing homes or home-bound, every last Friday of the month, and I have done that ever since. I also announced on that day, and it was put in the bulletin, that if anyone is sick or knew someone—whether family or not—who needs a priest to visit, they should call and inform the parish office. Whenever I received a call to visit someone who was sick, I did so. I wonder why you never called to notify the parish office or me that your dad needed a visit from a priest, even when you knew he did. I did not only go to see the frail seniors on the last Friday of the month or visited any person who is sick when I received a call, but I also visited the two hospitals in town every other Tuesday to care for patients, mainly, Catholics.

George, your dad, was asleep most of the time I visited him, and it was not easy to wake him up. Sometimes I thought it was better to let him rest, and on such days, I just prayed over him. I had spoken to him some of the times he was awake, but I was not sure he remembered my previous visits. Find enclosed the list with which I visit the sick seniors. Your dad's name is the second on the list, and it was checked because I visited him on Friday, January 31, and anointed him. Since you are wrong about me not visiting your dad, I do not believe your allegation against my predecessors is true. I can vouch for how hard those fine priests worked to care for the flock entrusted to their charge.

The parishioners have been informed to provide us with names of parishioners who are no longer able to make it to church or wish to be taken off the parish list. I have taken note of your concern about sending your dad a letter from the parish. When more than two hundred letters are mailed out to the parishioners from the office of the secretary, it is possible to send some to the wrong people and to addresses that are not functional. Some people also get extremely upset when we do not send them or their loved ones letters from the parish. Their reason being that since everyone got the letter and they did not, that meant we had already declared them non-Catholics or dead, or that we did not appreciate their membership or contributions. Even when they are no longer as active as they used to be because of age or sickness, they still want to be informed about what is going on in the parish.

I am sure the letter I sent out and enclosed card with church designs did not say anything about donating money—we are not there yet. Nevertheless, you can be sure that your dad's name will be taken off the mailing list. I will continue to pray for him, you, and your sister.

Yours truly in Christ,
Fr. Udo

As I replied to Ms. Boise's letter, there were things I jotted down on my notepad that did not make it into the letter. Here are some of them: "Now that you know we care for your dad—and of course, you and your sister—would you consider coming back to the church with your sister? Maybe if you do, you will be better informed of what is going on; the least of which may be that having an accommodating church building is long overdue for Saint James. You might be surprised to find yourselves supporting and donating to the new church project." This perspective was an attempt to make light of her presumption and false accusations, and I even chuckled at the irony of life. I am glad my better angel took over and helped me stay above the fray. This is because when falsely accused, it hurts, and it is easy to react out of emotion, which leads to overcorrection or going overboard in seeking justice—a far less prudent thing to do. I never heard from Ms. Boise or her sister again, not even when their father died. Nor did I know if they came back to the church or not.

Some sort of drama also unfolded in my effort to build a new church in Saint Albert, Heber Springs. It was the penitential service for Lent, and I had invited one of the priests in a nearby parish to help out. That priest had been transferred to the area, and that was his first time to come to the parish. While I got things ready around the altar, he visited with some parishioners in the sacristy. When done, I walked to the sacristy, but through the confessional that was connected to the sacristy. I wanted to make sure chairs and everything needed were in place at the confessional. They were, and I made my way to the sacristy to put on my vestment. That was when I overheard the conversation of my priest friend and the two people who visited with him, even though I was just minding my own business. "I saw the design of your new church. It appears Father Udo is planning for you to build a new church," the priest surmised.

"Not just for Heber Springs, but Searcy, too. Actually, the project in Searcy has progressed more than ours," the first responder volunteered.

"To attempt building two new churches, he must be either over-ambitious or nuts," the priest concluded.

I was not sure he intended for me to hear that and whether or not it was a complement. It did not matter to me either way, except he looked shocked and remorseful when I suddenly walked in on him saying that. I quickly defused the awkward silence in the air around us. "You almost got it right, Father. The answer is, all of the above!" What I said and the way I said it made everyone laugh, and I did, too.

Saint Albert Heber Springs Catholic Community had a savings program in which a second collection was taken every Sunday, and the proceeds were put away in a building-fund account, with the hope to pay for repairs on the existing church building or other facilities if needed. You would think that this savings program was an indication that most of the faithful would be open to the idea of the money also going toward a new church building some day and even contributing to it, especially when studies and facts showed the community was due for a new space for sacred worship. When I decided to take on the challenge of considering the feasibility of building a new church, I quickly found out that the proposal required a lot of praying and believing God would send us a Messiah. That was because there were some oppositions and also fear that the active members or the registered members who mainly lived in Heber Springs could not afford it. Among the very first people who made me begin to think building a new church was remotely possible were Thad and Jeanie, his wife. They were the first to donate a huge sum of money when they visited their vacation home in Heber Springs, three months after I started the building campaign. The next time they came to visit, we already had the potential plan of the church we were to build. When they asked how the project had progressed, I was happy to tell them that we had the eighty percent of the cost in pledge and cash and, could now borrow from the diocese to start building, after the church design was approved by the diocesan building commission. I showed them the model of the church plan and the location where we planned to build. As I took them on a tour, and we arrived at the proposed site for the new church building, Thad asked me,

"Father Udo, what do you intend to do with these dogwood trees when you build here?" It was fall season, and the seven or more of the dogwood trees' leaves had turned red in color and were so beautiful. I also knew that in spring season, there would be spectacular white flowers on them. But at the time, I thought that if we raised enough money and were able to build on that site, then the dogwood trees becoming the casualties would be a small price to pay. I told Thad that when we build, we would remove the trees and did so without expressing any regrets or sympathy for the person who planted them.

Unknown to me, while I devised a plot to remove the dogwood trees and possibly build the new church in their place, I was, at the same time, removing the goose's nest that laid the golden eggs. Long after the dogwood-trees episode, I was invited by Thad and Jeanie for dinner on one of their trips to Heber Springs. After we had dinner and tried to catch up with family and church stories, I told Thad and Jeanie about the ceremonious groundbreaking we had a week before. His response was, "Does that mean I get to enjoy the beauty of my dogwood trees one more season before you kill them?"

Thad meant it to be funny and was laughing. I tried to join in the laughter because he was hilarious, but my brain was working too hard to take it all in, and I could not laugh even as much as I wanted to. I remembered how unsympathetic I was when I told him and Jeanie we would remove the trees. If I knew he had planted the dogwood trees and had enjoyed watching them grow, relished the flowers and colored leaves, my response would have been different. In fact it did not matter who planted them, I should have expressed some remorse or reluctance in removal of them or even pledged to replant them when we remove them to build. My laughter was brief, and I asked, "Thad, you planted those trees?"

To which he answered, "Yes, many years ago."

"Well, then," I said, "We'll be careful not to kill them if and when they are removed. We'll make sure they are transplanted, and if any die, I'll personally make sure new ones are planted."

I have never felt that beaten, and Thad was able to see through me and offered some comforting words, "Father, don't feel bad. Wait until you hear my confession, you'll actually feel better. The first time I heard you announce the idea of building a new church, I thought to myself what a dreamer you were. When we gave the initial donation, my belief was that the dream of such a project in Heber Springs wouldn't last, but we gave anyway. In giving, my concern was to make sure I was not among those who killed the project before it was conceived. You have exceeded all expectations and made me a believer."

Thad was right; I felt better after I heard his confession. Nevertheless, I could not but be amused at how, in the process of my counting my golden eggs before they hatched, I almost destroyed the nest built by the goose that laid the eggs. Unknown to Thad, however, I had my own confession, which I kept to myself: he was not the only one who thought I was a dreamer; I thought the same thing of myself, too. But the first donation he and Jeanie made toward the project turned me into a stronger believer. It was only after my friends supported the dream of a new church with their invaluable donation that I began to be a lot more convinced it could become a reality.

During a one-week retreat we had before my priestly ordination, my bishop (Bishop Lucius I. Ugorji), had a session with us on "Pastoral Responsibility". He talked about the seriousness of the commitment we were about to make with regard to our pastoral obligations. He mentioned that humor can be a useful tool in our future ministry. But warned, however, that we should be cautious on how, where and when to be funny. In other words, we should not turn into professional jesters or overplay the clown card. My bishop drove that point home when he told a story he gleaned from the book, "Introduction to Christianity" by Joseph Ratzinger (Pope Benedict XVI). The story was about a jester in a certain town who made everyone laugh by everything he did, even the way he dressed or talked elicited laughter. That town had an open market at its outskirts. There came a day when the town's market was on fire, and the joker was the only one who saw the market on fire. He ran to the town to inform people about the fire and possibly get help to put it out. But when he told those he met in town that the market was on fire, they all laughed and thought he was very funny. Even when he cried to show how grave the situation was and pleaded to be taken seriously, the people he addressed laughed all the louder. No one believed he was not faking the gravity of the event until the whole market burned down.

As I reflect on the life of a comedian, I am led to the fact that the greater part of what he does to entertain or have the attention of his audience is to not take himself and others seriously. That aspect of a jester can be useful to a priest and even those who are not, as we go through life, but only in a limited fashion. As my bishop taught, it was important for me in my ministry to strike the right balance by not overplaying a clown—playing one at all times and in all things. However, it mostly feels right when you choose freely to play a joker, than when it is forced on you or when you find out that you are playing one unintentionally. Consciously playing a clown and in a limited sense, can, therefore, be a good thing in life when used effectively to calm the storm and uplift people who are downcast.

As a cleric, the most challenging moments in my ministry were those times when I felt ambushed or in situations when I pinned myself to a corner. Those periods did put my humility, patience, prudence, intelligence, and fortitude to the test. I did not always succeed during those tough times, nor did I always go through them without bruises. I was edified, though, when with God's help, I was able to accomplish something good despite circumstances that made it harder. I always marveled at the irony that those discomforting events were helpful in preparing me for whatever would come next. What came next, I will be honest to say, was beyond any human preparedness.

Chapter 11

The Day I Lived

If there is anything a second chance at life teaches us, it is to count our blessings, which includes enjoying and being thankful for the times we spend with loved ones.
—Father Udo Ogbuji

The day I lived again was the seventh of January, 2007. It was a Sunday and not much different from any other Sunday. After five more months, I would have been celebrating my fifth year as pastor in Saint James Church, Searcy; Saint Albert Church, Heber Springs; and Saint Richard Church, Bald Knob, so I was used to the drill of what it took to serve in all those parishes. Even the five Masses on weekends, which at the beginning were tough, had, at that point, become easier. The only thing I could think that was different was that I had three days left before I went on vacation to Nigeria, and I was looking forward to it, especially after working so hard through Christmas.

As I left Heber Springs after the 11:00 AM Mass—and the final Mass for the weekend—my clean and freshly ironed clothes were hanging in the car. Since I was running out of time to get my things ready for my trip, I pleaded with Gracie, one of my old friends, to help me with my laundry, and she was happy to do it. I was thankful for Gracie's kindness in making it possible for me to have fresh-smelling clothes to wear on vacation and sparing my mom from dealing with any foul smell. Heaven knows she had smelled enough dirty laundry taking care of me as a boy. One of the parishioners had invited me for dinner. She was one of those who had supported the church in many ways and, if I might add, given generously to the new church project. It was not uncommon for her to make her valued contribution after such a dinner. Even if she did not, I thought she deserved a visit from her pastor. As I left her home after dinner and got to a curved part of the road, I applied the brake to slow the car and make the curve. I remember the brake being unusually stiff, and I could not get the car to slow down before it ran off the road. The off-road drive was rocky and noisy because the ground was so uneven, and with the car being unstable, I lost complete control. Instantly, I said a short prayer, "Lord Jesus, receive my soul!" since I believed it would end in death. With a violent sound, the car then flipped about three times as I helplessly listened to the loud roaring crash of mangling metal and felt every impact of the beating.

The car finally stopped itself in an upright position when it could no longer tumble. My first thought was, and it was said aloud, "I am still alive!" I was almost in doubt of my survival because it could be that I was dead and did not even know it. I was still in my seat, fastened by the safety belt. The car's engine was revved up to an excessive level, as my paralyzed right leg pushed down steadily on the accelerator. My left leg could not move, either and my lifeless hands were motionless as they rested on the car seat. My neck was bent westward, with my head almost resting on my left shoulder. My neck was the only part of my body hurting at the time, and the pain was superhuman. The unbearable neck ache confirmed I was alive and still here on earth, rather than an imaginary world. Once I realized the car's engine was being overworked as I involuntarily engaged the accelerator, my neck pain became a secondary concern since it was possible the car could catch on fire at any moment. It was the worst feeling to listen to the car's roaring engine and to watch the engine's meter show the marker staying on the end of the red zone! Every minute that passed reminded me of my mortality! As I continued to gaze at the engine's meter, I began to think of the imminence of the car catching on fire and what would happen. The thought grew scarier when it seemed I could survive the accident only to be burned alive shortly afterward. When I became aware of my condition—that is, that I was completely paralyzed and that my fate may be a possible painful death—I accepted it, and when I did, I suddenly became calm while I sat and waited to die. I believed that if I were lucky, I would die quickly, and if my angel was not too mad at me, I would be found and rescued. I still had hope of some sort, but not too much of it, and I will tell you why in a minute.

As I waited in the car, minutes felt like days, and every minute that went by made me think aloud, "The car has not caught on fire yet, and I am not dead, so it is going to be a very long, unpredictable night." My bent broken neck hurt more, and I wished for nothing but just to lie down with my neck straightened and the pressure taken off my possibly fractured bones. If I could do that, I believed my pain would be curtailed. While I tried to endure the pain on my neck, I also worked on not entertaining the fear of watching myself roast in my car because the probability of it catching on fire increased with every minute that passed. After about thirteen minutes, I began to hear voices of people, and that was a welcomed sign of hope. But since I did not know if they were coming for me and could not shout to get their attention, I was cautiously hopeful. The last thing I needed was the kind of despair that comes from being too hopeful and finding out that what was hoped for was a mirage. Now you know why I did not have too much hope about being found alive and perhaps rescued; if I had and no one came for me, then I would have been both disappointed and miserable as I died—and what a terrible way to die. If I were to die, I would want to do so happily, just like the happy person I have always tried to be. At some point, I began to hear the voices of the approaching group of about four men more clearly, and I could hear them saying things like "Yes, the noise we heard was definitely a car wreck." "Man, check out the car, could anyone have survived this?"

They were right; there was no way I could have survived! I agreed with them even more when I saw the image of a battered car that used to be mine in a picture. After I was discharged from the hospital and was well settled in my new family at Christ the King Parish, my friend Father Okey asked me if I wanted to see the picture of what was left of my car. He had already asked me when I was still in the hospital, but I told him to keep it until I was discharged. What I saw did not look like my car—a Toyota 4Runner—anymore. The car took a horrific beating! The roof of the car looked like King Kong had stepped on it. The only part of the roof that was not beaten down was the spot where I sat. That could be either because when the car flipped over, it did not hit the ground hard enough on that part of the car or my head became a wedge and kept that part from being knocked down. If the last part was true, then it would explain why my C3, C4 and C5 vertebrae were fractured and my spinal cord was badly bruised. One of my friends, a medical doctor, speculated that my workouts may have paid off, since it appeared the muscles on my neck were strong enough to keep my spinal cord from being severed—which if it had happened could have caused irreparable damage.

I believed my friend, but I also believed in the providence and mercy of God. God made it possible for the automobile accident to take place in an inhabited terrain around Heber Springs area, where I could be found. That it happened at a time and in a place where individuals in the neighborhood could take notice and find me within fifteen minutes increased my chances of survival. For instance, when my God-sent helpers came close enough to the car, I called out to them and told them I was alive. When one of them got to the driver's door, I told him my neck was hurting unbearably and pleaded with him to help me out of the car so I could lay on the grass to take the pressure off my bent neck. As much as I worried about my neck, I was as concerned with the inferno that was imminent if the car's engine kept running, and I pleaded with him also to help me turn off the car's ignition. I was surprised when he asked me, "Are you not able to turn it off yourself?"

Without replying, I tried to raise my hand to do so, but could not. "No, I am not able to," I answered.

He then confirmed what I already knew—that I was paralyzed. He also suggested and did what undoubtedly guaranteed my initial survival. "You may have a spinal cord injury and possibly paralyzed. If we try to get you out of the car, we may make things worse for you in the process. We have made calls, and the ambulance will be here in a few minutes." He turned off the car's engine and stood by the door at the driver's side. He gently raised my tilted head to a comfortable position and supported it with his shoulder until the ambulance arrived.

The paramedics first secured my injured neck with a neck-brace and slowly lowered me to the stretcher and carried me into the ambulance. I was driven to White County Hospital in Searcy, and by the time we got to the hospital, my dear friend David was already at the emergency section of the hospital where he worked. It was his day off, but he drove from Heber Springs to see me that night after he learned of my accident. Dr. David was a parishioner I came to know and love, together with his wife, Holly, and their two daughters, Fedora and Beatrice—both of whom I had the privilege of baptizing. David and Holly proved to be worthy friends; they were there for me whenever I was in need of anything. Dr. David ensured that an X-RAY and CT scan were done and quickly, and they revealed that my C3, C4, and C5 were fractured, leaving the spinal cord bruised and crushed. They immediately injected me with steroids to forestall further damage to my beaten-up spinal cord. As those procedures were being done, results began to emerge, but they did not look promising. The Diocesan Administrator, Monsignor Gaston, made arrangements for me to be transferred to Baptist Medical Center in Little Rock. He also made contact with Dr. Richard McCarthy (Dr. Mac) to see to it that I was well cared for.

About six months before my car accident, I was invited over by my very close friends, Dana and Julie, after the eleven o'clock Mass in Heber Springs. There was another guest who came on a fishing trip, whom I was blessed to meet. He was one of the nicest people I ever met in my life. He was a medical doctor, a neurosurgeon, but also a very humble man. It is not often that you use the word *medical doctor* and *humble* in the same sentence. He was quite engaging and very interested in people; at least, he was in me. He asked me questions about my country, Nigeria; the priesthood, and my ministry. Even though we met only once and for a few hours, we truly bonded. I looked forward to seeing him again, and unknown to me he also wanted so much to meet me again and even told Suzy, his wife, he had met a friend and priest he would like for her to meet. We did meet again, but under circumstances none of us would have predicted or wanted. When we met the second time, it was nothing like the first—perfectly grilled steak, good beer and wine, and great companions—but rather, decisions were being made on how to salvage my battered and trapped spinal cord, sandwiched in between my broken bones.

As soon as arrangements were concluded for me to be transferred to Baptist Medical Center in Little Rock, the paramedics, together with my friend David, accompanied me to a waiting helicopter, where I was carefully and securely tucked in. The last words of David as he gently touched my shoulder and said good-bye were, "Udo, I'll be driving down tonight to see you in Little Rock. However, before you go, I wanted to tell you this: wherever you are, whatever you do, whatever happens, don't panic—keep breathing!"

"Thank you, Dave, I will look forward to seeing you in Little Rock," I replied, and we flew to Baptist Medical Center.

The words of my friend Dr. David that I should not "panic," but "keep breathing," in the event of any danger, saved my life on multiple occasions in the hospital and at home after I was discharged. I remember one of the nights I was in great pain, restless, and could not sleep. I had been in the Baptist

Rehabilitation Hospital only a few days after I was discharged from the Surgical Intensive Care Unit. On that restless night, I called the nurses to come and help me lie on my belly, which always helped me sleep. At that point in my recovery, my arms barely moved, and my legs were lifeless. After the nurses turned me over and left, it became evident to me that I had made a deadly mistake. My nose was pushing against the pillow, and I was suffocating. Since I could not turn my neck and was not able to move my head or breathe, I pushed the emergency call button to get help. Help unfortunately did not come! The nurses may have been busy with other patients, so my pushing the call button a few more times as I waited for help was in vain. When my call went unanswered, my heart skipped when I thought that I might suffocate and die before the nurses showed up. My ordeal would not be serious if it were just a dream! But it was not, and I was practically suffocating and panicking. Unable to breathe in that situation, I felt myself slowly dying. I then remembered what Dr. David told me, that no matter what happens I should not panic but remain calm and find a way to keep breathing. It was almost impossible to breathe with my face buried in the pillow, but I calmed down and tried to draw in as much air that my nose would allow me to breathe in with the pillow pushing against me. My calmness kept me alive until help arrived two hours later.

The fifteen to twenty-minute flight in the helicopter to Baptist Health Medical Center, Little Rock, was smooth and I was not thinking of or worried about anything. I did not know whether to attribute my calm demeanor to the effective pain killer or the laid-back attitude I generally have about life, that things will always work out well, God willing, or all of the above. One thing I did do was to listen to the helicopter's blades make noise. It took my mind off the tragic event of the evening. After a few minutes, I adopted and enjoyed the unusual rhythm as if it were a soothing song. I did not know when we arrived at Baptist Health Medical Center because I was asleep.

When I opened my eyes, it was not the sound of the helicopter blades that woke me up, it was the soft tap from the nurse in the emergency room who wanted to know my medical history. There was nothing to tell. I could not recall the last time I was sick, which was maybe twenty years ago. The visit with the nurse and medical team were quick, and it consequently freed the night so that I was able to visit with many of my friends who swarmed the hospital. Someone in the group of those who came to visit was so kind as to volunteer to call and inform my sister Helena, in Kenya, of my automobile accident; she was hoping that my sister would, in turn, call and let my mom know. I thanked her for being so kind and thoughtful. However, I knew her calling my sister was not a very good idea. I am very close to my sister, and I knew the tragic news of my accident would be a lot more devastating and traumatic for her and my mom, especially if they did not know all the facts and circumstances. If I spoke to them myself, which I intended to do, that would bring great relief. If my friend Father Okey called them, it would be reassuring, too because they know him very well, and I trust him to choose his words more carefully, knowing how much information to give out so as to cushion the impact of the trauma. I regretted that I told my visitor to hold off calling my sister without explaining why to her, and so my reply seemed like a rejection of her kind offer. The circumstances made it difficult to explain things to her, and I may have left her wondering why I did not accept her offer.

All who came to visit me were in shock and awe, and they all prayed for me; they sympathized and expressed their wishes for me to recover soon. Among all who came to visit, only one summoned the courage to sit by my bed and lightly run her fingernails over my arm. At that point, it was clear that I was paralyzed from my neck to my feet, but I was unaware if my body had any form of feeling, and neither did anyone else. Meg's magical touch was the first proof, of some sort, that at least my arm had sensation. As she gave me that tender and kind treat, I laid there motionless, with closed eyes, enjoying every single stroke that had a healing and soothing effect, and I could not get enough. That I could not get enough was not surprising since there was nothing I needed more at that point in my life than care, calm, and healing, and Meg provided all. No wonder when she stopped, perhaps not knowing how much it meant for me, I gently protested, "Meg, whatever you were doing felt so good, please don't stop!" She did not stop until I fell asleep.

When I woke up, my friend Father Okey was with me, and we talked about my first surgery, which was scheduled to take place about eight o'clock in the morning. Dr. Mac, after reviewing my case overnight, decided to perform the surgery as early as possible. The benefits of that surgery were likely to impact my overall recovery. Since my spinal cord was bruised and perhaps caught in between my shattered bones, performing a surgery to free the spinal cord from that damaging union was a welcomed medical necessity. Father Okey and I also talked about one important mission, calling my mom, which had to be done in anticipation of the surgery and subsequent unknown possibilities. The unknown factors resulting from the surgery may be underscored by these questions: Would I survive the surgery? Assuming I don't survive the surgery, what would the consequences be? What if the surgery results in a debilitating impediment? What if my communicating skills are impaired?

In the light of the unknown outcome of the surgery, I thought it would be very helpful for me to talk to my Mom while I still could, especially since my plan to go home on vacation to see my family would be cancelled. If I did not talk to her, my unexplained absence would be most worrisome to my whole family, who would have been expecting my return.

It was always a delight to go home on a visit to see my mom. As much as I enjoyed it, she enjoyed it more although she tried not to make it too obvious that she did. Being home was beautiful, but the good-byes always left a big hole in our hearts. A year had passed since my last visit home to see my mom, and the good-bye drama during that particular visit was different from the previous ones. I spent the early part of the last day packing my belongings and purposely avoided my mom. She knew it was my last day and kept herself busy, too. We seemed to have silently agreed to leave each other alone, knowing what would happen if we started paying ourselves attention and conversing. For some strange reason, ignoring each other seemed to cure the pain we were feeling because of the pending separation. When I got my luggage packed and I was ready to head to the airport, I went to her living room to visit a little and say good-bye. We talked for about ten minutes—or I should say, I talked; my mom prefers to be silent and, if she has to speak, as I said before, only says a few words. So, while I talked and looked at her, she made every effort not to make any eye contact with me. Even as I stood up to go, she looked away, and at that point, I knew her not looking at me was deliberate. I then asked her, "Mom, are you going to look at me? Please look at me and give me a lovely good-bye hug!" She did not say a word but raised her eyes to look at me. The tears she was hiding began to flow more profusely, and she sobbed. When she looked at me again in the midst of her sobbing, which was now more forceful, her glance appeared to say, "Now you know what I was hiding from you. I might as well cry myself to sleep."

Since I was little boy and after my dad's death, my mom has always tried to put up a tough front. She may have done that to protect me or to teach me to be tough as a man or to keep me from worrying about her. Unknown to her, I liked those moments when she showed the soft feminine side of herself so I could jump into action and take care of her. Sometimes I let her get away with her facade of toughness only because I assumed it made her feel better. Perhaps I should have in that instance, so as to shield her from the embarrassment of feeling ill-equipped to cope in such moments. I hugged her and said, "Mom, it's not as if I am dying or going away and not coming back. Before you know it, I'll be home again to visit. Until then, you know

I will be calling to check on you and loving you even from a distance!" She stopped sobbing, remained silent, and did not look at me, but buried her head between my neck and shoulder until we were ready to part.

Back in the hospital, Father Okey and I, after we made a decision to call my mom, also had the daunting task of determining what to tell her when we called. Our decision, after deliberating the method of delivering the tragic message, was that it would hurt no matter how the news was broken. So, we decided I would deliver the news while being as sensitive and as natural as was helpful in order not to alarm her. Father Okey first called my sister Helena, in Kenya, and we spoke, and I thought it was an easy one and hoped talking to my mom would be fine, too. My mom's phone was dialed, and as soon as we exchanged greetings, I asked with as much of a clear and strong reassuring voice as I could summon, "Mom, do you know who's talking to you?"

"Yes, I do!" she replied. "You are my son, Udo!"

"One more question, Mom, how would it feel if you heard that I was dead?"

"I'll be sad, but hopefully, I'll also find peace in accepting the fact that I should not question God's choice," she replied.

"Well, then," I continued. "If I'm talking to you, Mom, then you know I'm alive and well. Mom, I was in a small motor accident. I was driving by myself, and I was slightly injured. I'm supposed to go in for surgery in the morning for a minor procedure. There may be another surgery, and with therapy, I will be on the road to full recovery. From now on my friend, Okey, will communicate my progress to you until I'm able to talk to you again. I'm telling you this so that you will pray for me and not worry, especially if you don't hear from me. Know that your favorite child is okay and will talk to you soon and see you in due time." She kind of chuckled at the last part where I rubbed in my being her favorite child.

As I reflect on the drama with my mom on our final moment together before I left home during my last vacation, I am inclined to believe she had a premonition that could be the last time she set her eyes on me. I guess that explains part of the reason for her refusal to look me in the eyes, besides the fact that she did not want me to see her crying. After the experience of my tragic automobile accident and my close encounter with the fragility and transience of life, I am glad that I persuaded my mom to look me in the eyes so I could communicate how much I love her.

In our lives as humans, it is not possible to know which moment will be the last with those we love. Therefore, it is worthwhile to spend each time we have with them finely like it would be the last. The seventh of January became a day I lived again by God's grace. It was a day I renewed my commitment to always spend every minute I have with my friends and family the best way that proves my love for them, because it could be the last. Since God spared my life, I believed he also may intend to mend and heal me. That prospect was soon set in motion by a great medical team, invaluable friends, and weary family members who were by my side and tirelessly offered support, prayers, and healing throughout my hospital saga, which lasted for more than two months.

Picture with my mom during my last visit home

Chapter 12

Hospital Saga

It takes a village to raise a child and a medical team that has a soul to raise the dead.

—Father Udo Ogbuji

When I arrived in Baptist Health Medical Center on the night of my accident, a thorough medical examination at the emergency room was conducted. The report reads as follows:

HEAD AND NECK: There is no obvious head trauma. He is mobilized on a spine board with a cervical collar. There is a small amount of blood above the left ear. There is some tenderness on palpation in the mid cervical region on the right. There are no other traumatic signs about the head or neck other than some conjunctival hemorrhage in the left eye. The tongue is in the midline. There is no trauma to the clavicular area. Shoulders have a full range of motion. The patient is quite muscular.

NEUROLOGIC: The upper extremities reveal intact biceps bilaterally. Both triceps are weakened, more on the right than the left. This is a grade 0-1/5. Wrist on the left has 2/5 both flexion and extension. The finger flexors are weak 0-1 bilaterally and the biceps is 3/5 bilaterally. There is a sensory level at approximately T3. There is no motor function below this level. There is light touch sensation with accurate determination of sides, across the soles of both of his feet.

RECTAL: No rectal tone. The patient reports he can feel some sensation during the examination. There is a negative bulbocavernous reflex, that is, there is no response.

ORTHOPEDIC: Otherwise shows no areas of crepitus, no areas of tenderness.

ABDOMEN: Soft, non-tender. There are no masses. Foley is in place with some hemorrhage around the Foley.

HEART: Heart sounds are normal.

LABORATORY AND X-RAY DATA: The radiographic studies that are examined include CAT scans and the cervical area reveals lateral element fractures at C3 on the right, essentially non-displaced. The inferior process on the right side of C4 is fractured with disruption of the facet on the right side at 4/5. The facet on the opposite side is intact. The rest of the examination shows no vertebral column fractures. No injuries to the abdominal structures, and no parenchymal damage to the lung. There was a small benign, calcific nodule in the lower lobe on the right.

IMPRESSION: Quadriparesis secondary to spinal cord trauma.

After going through my medical report, Dr. Mac made the decision to perform surgery on me first thing in the morning. The surgery was scheduled to start by 8:00 AM. Before the anesthesiologist put me to sleep, Dr. Mac came in and tried to explain the procedure to me. "Father Udo, what I am intending to do is to operate on your anterior spine, and that will entail a decompression of C4 to 5 with a disk excision, realignment . . . ."

I did not let him continue. It sounded like I was back in classic Greek class in the seminary, so I politely protested with a smile, "Doc, please, may I have the layman's version."

He smiled back and said, "This first surgery is around the front area of your neck, and my objective is to make sure your spinal cord is freed from any fractured bone pushing down on it."

I then understood clearly what he was about to do and was thankful that he was so kind as to describe the surgery in simple language I could follow. "Doc, let us get on with it then," I suggested.

"Before we do," he said hesitantly, "is there any other thing you would like me to do for you?"

"Doc, I don't want you to give me special treatment because I am a priest. Treat me like any of your patients!" I requested.

"I won't treat you like you are special," he reassured me, but shocked me in a nice way with the next thing he said, which was underscored by pure love and kindness. "I will treat you like my own brother!"

Before he said that, I already loved him and had no reservations entrusting him with my life. But, after he said that, my only hope was to be able to recover and have the opportunity to return the love and favor someday. Then, with a smile and all the nice things said, anesthesia was induced, and I went to sleep.

My neck was stabilized during the endotracheal intubation, and I had a minor aspiration. I was then placed in five pounds of Halter traction with a roll beneath my shoulders and a silastic pad beneath my occiput, and then I was carefully aligned with the cervical Halter traction. Following that, the cervical collar on my neck was removed. The left side of my neck was prepped and draped in the usual fashion, and a linear incision was made in a transverse fashion in the skin crease along the left side of my neck. The anterior approach to my cervical spine was carried out by splitting the platysma in line with the incision and a preservation of all the surrounding structures, a digital dissection anterior to the vessels, and just lateral to the endotracheal tube in the trachea and lateral to my esophagus. My vertebral column was palpated, and smooth retractors were inserted with careful retraction of my esophagus and trachea. The longus colli was cleaned to a slight degree from the anterior margins of my vertebral bodies. A bayonet spinal needle was inserted, and the C4 to C5 levels were identified. Electrocautery was used to incise my anterior longitudinal ligament, and then curettes and pituitary rongeurs were used to remove my disk. Some of my disk fragments came out as large loose fragments, and my doctor thought that they were some of the fragments coming from the spinal canal. Those fragments were pulled out with the pituitary rongeur. Following the cleaning of the disk, the Kerrison rongeurs were used to undercut the posterior margin of my vertebral bodies sufficiently enough to allow for the insertion of both short and then long nerve hooks to palpate the posterior margin of my vertebral bodies anterior to the dura. Any loose fragments found were palpated and pulled out. No further large fragments were identified. There was clear visibility of the anterior margin of my dura, and there was no violation of my dura or any obvious trauma to it. There was no cerebrospinal fluid leak. There was small to moderate amount of blood, and the endplates were then decorticated, and Gelfoam was placed posterior to the posterior margin of my vertebral body to prevent any DBX from going into my canal. A moderate amount of DBX was then placed into my disk space, and the measured allograft Synthes bone was filled with DBX, and a 6 mm graft was placed into my disk space, and it was checked with a C-Arm to be sure it was properly aligned, and then a titanium plate was used to fix my vertebral bodies 4 and 5 together. Some 16 mm-long screws were directed into my vertebral bodies. The alignment was checked in both the AP and lateral views, and the locking nuts were then placed into the head of the screws. The fixation was secured. The wound was irrigated. A drain was left deep using a one-eighth-inch Hemovac, and this exited through a distal site. The platysma was closed with a running Vicryl suture. Interrupted sutures were placed into the subcutaneous dermal layer, and then Monocryl was used to close my skin in a subcuticular fashion. Dermabond was applied. A Steri-Strip was applied and then a dry sterile dressing. The drain was taped in place. The cervical halter was carefully removed. The cervical collar was put back on my neck and intubation continued. I was then carefully moved onto my bed and then taken to the Surgical Intensive Care Unit (SICU) in stable condition. The blood I lost was less than 100 cc, and I was in stable condition. The final x-rays showed the desired correction.

After the first surgery, I remained sedated in Surgical Intensive Care Unit, and four days afterward, on the twelfth of January, I underwent another surgery for posterior cervical stabilization. Here is the description of what took place, according to my doctor:

After satisfactory general endotracheal anesthesia, I was carefully placed into a Mayfield Tong, or head holder. Then I was carefully rolled onto the operating table with the chest rolls and my neck was stabilized. While that occurred, there was a placement of the Mayfield head holder into the attachment, which was secured in place. The locking device was taped in place. The back of my neck was then prepped and draped in the usual fashion as was the right posterior iliac crest area. The transverse incision over the right posterior iliac crest occurred with a subperiosteal dissection of the outer wall of the ileum. The retractors were inserted. Cortical cancellous strips of my bone were taken with gouges, osteotomes, and curettes. The area was back-filled with tricalcium phosphate crystals and then anatomically closed with absorbable suture throughout. The midline approach to the cervical spine was accomplished with a midline incision, dissection of my muscles from the midline, and then the self-retaining retractors were inserted. The Cobb periosteal elevators were used along with electrocautery to dissect my muscles off the side of the posterior elements. These areas were tagged with a towel clip, and an X-RAY was taken to identify the levels, and the soft tissues were cleaned from the posterior elements of my C3, C4, and C5 bilaterally, with the fracture noted at C4 on the right as well as C3. The articular surface at my C4, where the dislocation of the facet had occurred, was decorticated. The drill was used to start the holes in the middle of the lateral mass on the left and then in the lateral masses on the right of my C3 and C5. A hand drill was utilized to drill out the lateral mass, and then a 14 mm screw was placed anatomically into the center of the lateral mass, directing the screws superiorly and laterally so as to provide good purchase. Each of the holes was probed with a depth gauge, and then the polyaxial head 3.5-diameter Synthes-type titanium screws were placed into the lateral masses on the left side of my C3, C4, and C5, the right side of my C3 and C5. The 4 mm rods were chosen, bent into a slight amount of lordosis, and decortication with a bur was accomplished over the posterior elements on both sides. Copious amounts of cancellous and then cortical cancellous bone was placed on both surfaces. The rod was placed deeply into the screws and tightened in place with the torque/countertorque wrench utilized for the final tightening. X-Rays were taken, but it was very difficult to visualize the lower portion of the instrumentation due to my large size and shoulders. My wound was irrigated with saline multiple times, and then the closure was accomplished with interrupted sutures through the cervical spine (and then interrupted and running in the more superficial layers). Monocryl was used to close my skin in the subcuticular fashion. Dermabond was used to seal the skin, and the cervical collar was replaced. I was then turned supine. The Mayfield head holder was removed, and I was placed on the Trimedyne bed, intubated and taken back for recovery in the Surgical Intensive Care Unit. The amount of blood I lost during this second surgery was 400 cc.

Since I got into the habit of chewing on and trying to fight off the ventilator and feeding tubes that were lodged down my throat, because it was very uncomfortable, a tracheostomy was done. That took a lot of strain off of my mouth, throat, and neck. Any tug on my neck was the last thing my doctors and other medical caregivers wanted. At best, it would prolong the healing process around the surgical area, and at worst, I would disassemble the unique, skillful and successful work of Dr. Mac—who pieced together my fractured neck bones and bruised spinal cord. Also, at that point, my medical team had no choice but to put me into an induced coma with the medicine, Propofol. That kept me from moving my neck but, in turn, raised another possible issue. There was a chance that if I stayed on the same spot for a considerable period of time as I healed, I would eventually develop pressure ulcers. A special bed was ordered that helped prevent that. My being strapped securely to that rotating bed allowed my body to move at a safe timing and in different postures to keep me from putting pressure on any particular area for a long period of time, thereby reducing chances of skin breakdown.

Even though I was in a state of induced coma, there were times when I believed I was conscious, and during those periods, I heard and visualized what people said or did around me. I frequently hallucinated perhaps because of the morphine or other narcotics I was given to alleviate the pain I felt. The things that happened in my hallucinations became the only world, life, and reality I knew and lived. How real things seemed in my hallucination made me realize that the line between hallucination and reality was very thin and almost impossible to distinguish, especially while I was under the influence. Some of the hallucinations were most horrifying; you only have to recall the narrative in chapter 1 about "The day I died", to get an idea. That was just one among many others. I am going to share some more of my hallucinations because they formed a major part of my experience as I was hospitalized until a few days before I was transferred to the rehabilitation unit for therapy.

One of the most bizarre hallucinations I had was the death of my sister Helena and her funeral. In that hallucination, she was in the convent in Kenya, east Africa, and during that period there was a tribal conflict. One of the tribes—Ujanja, as I recall—broke into the convent after an informant told them the nuns were hiding and caring for people from the other tribe they passionately hated. The nuns did indeed take in some women and children who fled from the massacre that befell their husbands and fathers. The Ujanja militants slaughtered everyone they found in the convent. My sister was among the dead, and the brutality that each of them faced is too graphic for me to describe here. I wept and wept, but only when I was by myself. My mom cried, too and would try to hide her pain for my sake, but did not succeed in doing so all the time.

My mom was at the hospital every day; she was the first to come in the morning and the last to leave to make sure she said good night. One of the mornings she showed up, I had had a bad night. I was clumsy, and getting out of the bed was like pulling your own rotten tooth with bare fingers. I had struggled to get out of bed a few times before I looked up and saw her watching me. "Udo, you've always been brave! Don't give up!" she said. "You know that a lion does not father a cowardly cub!" After I heard the last part of her statement, I smiled and was able to get out of bed. I smiled first to reassure her that I was not going to give up on her or myself. I also smiled to acknowledge her being so witty; the last part of her statement was a proverb my dad used when he wanted to rouse me into embracing resilience and succeeding. She knew how much I respected my dad and obeyed his command. So, she was aware that her borrowing his "words of summon", had the potential of literally raising me up from the dead. I got up, and I walked around, and that made her smile too.

Because my mom came to the United States in winter season—which she was not used to—she became sick. She was admitted in the hospital, got an infection while in the hospital, and ended up having her right leg amputated. It was most painful to watch my mom walking with one leg and crutches because she left her home in Africa and came to the United States to care for me. Despite her condition, she still came to see me in the morning and at night. Sometimes she talked to me, and sometimes she only looked at me and smiled. Whenever

I saw her, I would either smile or tease her. Once I told her, "Mom, you walk so fast with those crutches like they were your real legs, you may have to teach me your skill. You never know, it may come handy someday." She laughed, and I did too.

My sister's funeral was scheduled ten days after she was murdered. My mom and I flew back home for the funeral accompanied by Father Okey and my other friends. There were many nuns and priests in attendance in addition to villagers, parishioners, and many of our friends. Those who knew my sister had wonderful things to say about her, which was comforting. The eulogy was given by my brother, Henry, who did a great job of highlighting what a fine woman she was and was able to hold himself together till almost the ending part of his delivery when he broke down and cried. I did not speak, but sat through the whole funeral Mass and ceremony in pure mental agony, wondering why God took her instead of me. I finally found solace in the thought that God took her because she was a living saint, unlike me. Twice, I was out of breath and blacked out during the ceremony because I was extremely sick and should not have attended the funeral in the first place, but I went although my doctors advised me not to go. Fortunately, the medical team who went with me rose to the challenge and resuscitated and helped me with the oxygen mask. I was taken to a hospital in Nigeria where I got well enough to be flown back to the United States.

My hallucinations were not all horrifying; some were about me getting out of my bed when the nurse was not in my room and doing push-ups like I used to do before my motor accident. Sometimes, instead of push-ups, I would run around the neighborhood. The events were so real that I felt well and active when I did the push-ups or ran. On the contrary, I felt so heavy and sluggish when I did not. One of the many days Father Okey came into my room to know how I was doing, I told him I was able to get off my bed and exercise. He then asked me what I did, and I told him I did push-ups and ran around the neighborhood. "Where was the nurse while you were doing push-ups and running?" he asked, and I told him the nurse was busy with other things. Even though he knew that what I told him was unbelievable and not anywhere near the reality, he said nothing to indicate he doubted me, but rather told me he was very proud of me.

I knew I was being given something for pain, and I believed it was Morphine because I overheard that word many times. I did not know how it was administered but thought it was released in the air in my room and that it lingered in a powdery form for about fifteen minutes before it dissipated. While everyone was out of my room, I breathed the air filled with the medicine, and it had such feel-good-power, it made me feel really fine and pain free—my miserable world became momentarily too perfect to be real. The perfect, good feeling effect was very disturbing to me because I knew my life and the world was not as perfect as the medicine made it seem. I should have been feeling some form of pain because I was hurt, and the lack of pain did not appear right or normal. As strange as it was, I got upset that what I felt did not reflect my real-life situation. I actually had to tell my doctor that I did not like whatever medicine they gave me for pain. I am not sure he understood why I wanted it changed, but he did change it to one that did not catapult me into a wonderland.

I wish I had known my hallucinations only seemed real but were far from being so, and if I could have spoken, I would have asked much earlier if I could be exempt from the pain medication that gave rise to them because those unpleasant hallucinations were pure horror. For instance, one day I entered the unreal world of nightmares and, my little brother, Henry, visited me in the hospital and accidentally came into my room when the powdery Morphine was in the air and breathed it. Upon inhaling it, my brother, who showed great strength and courage went crazy and, started moaning loudly in anguish—grieving uncontrollably in the hospital because of my tragic state. I was worried when he wept so indiscriminately because I did not want him to disturb the peace of the hospital, and I was also heartbroken to see him in such pain and crying hysterically for my sake. I was also concerned for him, hoping the Morphine he inhaled did not damage his brain, causing him to lose his mind.

I anticipate that, at this point, you may want to know when and how I found out that my hallucinations, both terrifying and delightful, were mere dreams. When I found out, I was still in the Surgical Intensive Care Unit and had recovered to the extent that the doctors were encouraged to remove the ventilator, and I was able to communicate by speaking a few words. On that day, Father Okey told me my sister Helena would be coming from Kenya to visit. I was not very happy with him because I thought he said something about my sister visiting as an attempt to keep from me the news that my sister was "dead". I then said to him, "I know my sister is dead, why are you trying to hide that from me? You can be open and frank with me. After what happened to me, I believe I can handle anything."

"I'm not hiding anything from you!" he protested. "Helena didn't die, she's flying in tomorrow."

My friend was right, my sister did come to visit, and that revelation and experience challenged all I thought was real since the day of my surgery. I was relieved to find out my horrific hallucinations were all in my imagination and had nothing to do with reality. I was, however, regretful of the fact that my pleasant ones, like running and doing push-ups were not factual, either. It hurt even more to realize that my first shower, which felt like heaven, never took place—which meant that, for almost a month, I had not had any real shower.

Hallucinations were arguably the least of my problems while I was in the Surgical Intensive Care Unit. After my surgery, I contracted a staph infection and was put on a strong antibiotic. As I was recovering from that, I contracted pneumonia. I was given antibiotics again, and because I was not able to cough up the mucus from my lungs caused by pneumonia, the pulmonologist was called in to perform a bronchoscopy in order to provide me with needed relief. That procedure was done several times before I improved. After I recovered from pneumonia and healed from my surgery, an attempt was made to wean me from the ventilator and feeding tubes. As I noted in the first chapter, attempts to wean me failed. A stress test was performed on my heart by a cardiologist, and my heart was declared healthy. The third attempt to get me to breathe on my own succeeded. I used the oxygen mask for a couple of days, and the amount of oxygen was gradually reduced until I was able to breathe on my own. From that point on, I was fully awake and aware of what was happening around me.

I was in that induced coma state for almost a month, and as I improved, arrangements were made to transfer me to the rehabilitation hospital within the Baptist Health Institute. The talk of transferring me to another hospital and my doctors trying to wean me off the ventilator and feeding tubes may have been what I overheard and experienced when the hallucination I talked about in Chapter One took place. The success of removing the feeding tubes launched me into another phase of health care that had to do with Occupational and Physical Therapy. I had not eaten anything in weeks except for the liquid protein food fed to me through the tube, which I hated but could not do anything about. I was hungry for some real food, like a juicy grilled steak, fish, baked potato, some hot soup, or even tea—just something cooked. The opportunity came to eat something other than liquid protein when the Nutritionist brought crackers and Jell-O for me to eat. I was to consume them while a technician observed with a camera positioned in my throat, in order for her to have pictorial or visual image of where the crackers and Jell-O would end up. It was a very uncomfortable procedure, and eating for the first time in weeks was not exactly pleasurable. After two failed attempts, I asked the technician, "How many more times are we going to do this?"

She answered, "One more time."

I thanked her, indicating I did not think I could take much more. I ate the crackers and Jell-O one more time—which felt more like punishment than dining—and swallowed while she observed on her monitor to be sure the food travelled through the desired route. Again, for an unexplained reason, her observation was inconclusive. "Can we do it one more time?" she pleaded, but because it was so strenuous and I could not endure any more of it, I declined her request.

It had been two or three days since I ate the crackers and Jell-O. But, because the observation of the technician was undetermined, and no one wanted to feed me more solid food when it was not clear where it would end up, I was put back on a liquid protein bag. While I could not get a shower, I got bed baths, and on a certain day while I was being cleaned up, the nurse ventured around my buttocks area where she made an interesting discovery; she found some feces. As soon as she made that discovery, she was delighted and left me almost unclad. She went to the nursing station where she celebrated with the other nurses. I was confused as to the reason for the celebration and was not impressed. It was uncomfortable to be left in that state while she announced her discovery to her comrades, and all, surprisingly, had a mutual festive parade at my expense.

When she came back to my room, I made my concern known to her, "Jane, I can't believe you left me here almost naked while you announced to your friends that you found fecal matter on me."

She was truly apologetic and explained to me the implications of what she found. "Father Udo, I am very sorry I got overly excited. I was happy for you and had to announce the good news to my colleagues. Until now, we did not know what works and what does not work after your spinal cord injury. However, what I found on you means that your intestines may not have been affected. If they were, that might cause your doctor to recommend a special surgery to help you empty your bowel, which would require a colostomy."

What she said did not make that much sense at the time, but the joy and great sense of excitement in her eyes and voice made me think that whatever she was excited and happy about must be something worth celebrating.

I did celebrate later with the nurse, but only after two years had gone by. I had been discharged from the hospital but still went to Baptist Health Rehabilitation Hospital as an out-patient for my therapy. On one of the days I was there, I had completed my therapy and was ready to go, but I decided to use the bathroom first. Someone was using the bathroom, and I queued in the line with others. While I sat in my wheelchair, waiting, someone arrived and joined in the line—a very tall black man that appeared to be in his early sixties, and on him hung a strange bag. What got my attention was the foul odor that came from his direction, a stench that made a public statement that was difficult to ignore. I did not know why he smelled and refused to look his way because I did not want him to be embarrassed. I could not leave, even if I wanted to, despite the torturous smell because I did not want him to think I did so because of the smell. I remained there but thought to myself, *Good Lord, I hope that was not what the nurse was talking about two years ago when she was singing and dancing because she thought my intestines were working well.* I later asked my aide whether she had perceived the smell from the man and what she thought it was. She confirmed what I feared it was! I was so shook up when I got home that I could not eat, but spent a good part of my day in the chapel thanking God.

The day before I was discharged from the Surgical Intensive Care Unit was one of my happiest days. It started with my having a cooked breakfast and getting a haircut and a shave, followed by a bed bath. Later, during the day, one Occupational Therapist and two Physical Therapists helped me to the edge of the hospital bed in a sitting position and supported me while I did so. That was the first time I sat down since my accident, with or without support. As they gave me support, I did well, but found myself dizzy and slumped over when left to sit up by myself. It was only then that it became even clearer to me that all my running around the neighborhood, doing push-ups in the middle of the night, and the many trips I took to Nigeria were only hallucinations. A few hours after the therapists tried to help me to sit, I was told I had an important visitor, and that visitor was Helena, my sister. Until I set my eyes on her, I thought there was still a chance she was dead, and everyone was hiding it from me. It made me very happy to see her, and I was relieved to know she was alive, even though she would not stop shedding tears because of the condition she found me. My friend, Father Okey, was indeed right that my sister was alive. That concrete evidence made me wonder why he did not challenge my claims about my adventures of running and doing push-ups. He probably liked the fact that I was hopeful and happy in my harmless fantasies and did not want to kill the only thing I had left, and I loved him more for it.

Not being able to move any part of my body except my neck probably made my doctors apprehensive as I headed for the rehabilitation hospital. When I asked my rehabilitation doctor, Dr. Kiser, if I would walk again, he said I had a fifty-fifty chance of doing so. I knew he was being very careful not to give me any false hope or kill my hope completely. But unknown to him, I was grateful for the 50 percent chance because it could have been much worse. He was actually generous when you contrast his measured appraisal with the assessment of one student doctor who told me that I was paralyzed—that I would not be able to walk again, and there was no need for me to have therapy. I did not think she was well-informed or prudent in her assessment and choice of words. Instead of being discouraged by her misguided and insensitive evaluation, I was more determined to get well and possibly walk.

As soon as I got to the Baptist Health Rehabilitation Hospital, Dr. Kiser, the nurses, and my therapists were eager to put me to work. The first indication that I would like my new hospital was that, on my second night, one of my sweetest dreams was realized; I had my first shower in a little more than a month. Simply put, it felt like heaven, and I did not want it to end. I savored every splash of the warm water that touched my body. I will never see having a shower the same way again! It will no longer just be a cleaning venture, but an adventure to be enjoyed. The aide informed me that my showers would be every other day, for which I was thankful—Man, I would have been as grateful if it were once a week after not having any for a month! Many of the patients had roommates, but I had a room to myself, and the privacy it offered was priceless. I would say that was another reason to like that place, but many people would disagree since the reason for giving me my own room was to have me quarantined because of the staph infection and pneumonia I contracted while I was in the Surgical Intensive Care Unit. It was a terrible disease no one wanted, but a gift the hospital gave me, which oddly became rewarding. I accepted and cherished the advantage of staying in the room by myself although it came with a stigma. As a precaution not to transfer the disease to others in case I still had it, everyone who came into my room—the nurses, doctors, and visitors—wore a yellow gown and gloves like those venturing into a compromised nuclear plant and needed to avoid radiation. I wanted them to have as much protection as possible since the protection would work both ways; they were protected from me as much as I was from them. I had no doubt the staph infection and pneumonia slowed down my recovery after my surgery, and being infected again with any disease was the last thing I needed. So, the precaution and protection was a welcomed idea as it was entertaining. The doctors, nurses, therapists, and visitors did not know how funny they looked in their yellow suit and gloves.

One part of my therapy consisted of doing physical exercises. The very first thing my therapists tried to teach me was how to transfer from my wheelchair to the bed with a piece of wood. I learned the techniques, but since I had no strength in my arms, and my abdominal muscles felt like overcooked noodles, I could not do it. The second day my therapists made me sit at the edge of my chair. I really thought I was going to fall over with my forehead hitting the floor first, but I was assured I would not, and they were right. They encouraged me to always try and sit in an upright position to help me strengthen my core muscles. When my therapists thought it was due, they took me to the next level. They helped put me on the equipment called Easy Stand, and after I got securely fastened, my therapists warned, "If your vision starts fading, say something, okay?"

I nodded in agreement. They raised the Easy Stand, and in a few seconds, I found myself in a squatting position. They inquired if I was doing well, and I smiled and responded, "Yes". They continued until my vision began to get blurry; they stopped and let me stay in that position until I got fatigued. I was not exactly standing straight and tall, but my therapists said I did well considering that it was my first time. It was encouraging to hear from them that I would hopefully get better with time. I did improve, although in small increments. That my therapists were very kind and able to take a little teasing and also capable of giving it back made therapy more fun.

One of the days I went to therapy, I was quite upset. Before I left for therapy, I had gone to the bathroom and, for some reason, took off my shirt for the first time since my car accident. What I saw was horrifying. My right shoulder looked shriveled, with bones clearly exposed except for the thin flesh that covered them. It was obviously smaller than the left shoulder, which looked fuller and healthier although far from being normal. I hurried and put my shirt back on and went for therapy. I tried to keep my mind off what I saw in the mirror, but the harder I tried, the clearer the picture presented itself stubbornly in my mind. What I saw did not seem to be the effect of my accident, but something far more deadly; I thought that maybe I had cancer and that the doctors did not even know it.

I had thought about cancer because of a parishioner whom I met at the first Sunday Mass I celebrated in Saint Edward Parish when I first came to the United States. Martha had come to say hello after the Mass and welcomed me to the parish. She also told me that if I ever needed help with the Spanish language, that she would help to teach me. I had been in the parish about three months when she had come to Mass again and afterward came to extend her greetings. She asked if she could have a word with me, and I told her she could. She had some very bad news for me: "Father, I have been diagnosed with cancer, and the doctor gave me six months to live." Though the news she gave me about herself was devastating, she appeared calm and strong, regardless. I thought she was a very kind and gentle person and did not deserve the catastrophe that befell her. Physically, she looked well and healthy, and unless she told you, you would never guess what fate unfortunately had in stock for her. I saw her again after four months, on a day I went to anoint and pray with her. I could not believe how fast she had been devoured by that fatal disease. She looked so thin that it took me some time to process in my head and accept that it was Martha whom I met on my first Sunday in the parish, seven months earlier. I felt for her and wondered how hard it would be to live through your own mortality, counting down your final days, until you breathe your last breath. I did not look bewildered and sad for her sake; instead, I tried to cheer her up. "Martha, I have not stopped praying to God to heal you since the day you gave me the news of your cancer. Each time I pray, I tell him to heal my Spanish teacher so I won't have an excuse not to learn the language." I was smiling as I said it, and she smiled back and tried to say "Thank you, Father," but choked and managed a weak cough in the process. She died the following week.

The image of that beautiful and graceful woman reduced to mere bones had been stored somewhere in my subconscious all those years. After seeing my bony self in the mirror, the thin, weak, and dying Martha kept flashing through my mind as I tried to do my therapy. My therapist noticed because she asked with a smile, "What is wrong with you today, Father Udo?"

"You don't want to know," I answered, smiling back, and then added, "If you're nice to me, I will tell you after the therapy."

"I will be nice to you. Now sit for ten minutes on that ball." She was sarcastic when she said that, acknowledging that she gave up nothing.

"Is your working someone like a rented mule your idea of being nice?" I asked, and we both laughed.

"Okay, sit for six minutes," she bargained.

"You got a deal," I quickly accepted, still laughing. I ended up sitting on that ball for eight minutes and called for help when I could not take it anymore. "Do you have a private room here?" I asked.

She thought for a minute and said, "Yes."

"Take me there. I have got something to show you," I said. When we were in the private room, I requested for something I was surprised did not shock her. "Take off my shirt!"

She laughed, and I wondered why. The expression on my face may have given away what I was thinking, because she told me why she was laughing without my asking, when she said, "I bet you want to show off your muscles to me."

I smiled and asked, "Are you a mind reader? Take off my shirt, and I will show you."

She quietly came forward and helped me remove my shirt, perhaps apprehensive that it was something more serious. After she took off my shirt, I politely made another request for her to stay close to the door, which was six feet away, and look at me. She looked but was not alarmed, and even her voice was reassuring. "I don't see anything."

"You don't see anything?" I asked, confused that she thought I looked alright. I then felt obliged to point out to her my area of concern. "Look at my right and left shoulder, don't you see any difference?"

"Oh, I see what you mean," she confirmed. "That is from your spinal cord injury and not being able to use those muscles since your car accident. Your right side is the most affected area."

I was truly relieved to know what was wrong and even more alleviated to find out it was not cancer.

Another area of my therapy had to do with emotional well-being. On one sunny afternoon, a petite middle-aged woman came into my room and introduced herself. "I am Dr. Reed, and I head the Rehabilitation and Neuropsychology Department of the hospital. My task will be to evaluate and help you adjust emotionally as you heal from your spinal cord injury. If you will accept my services on behalf of the hospital, fill out this form. After you fill out the form, I will have a few questions for you if you don't mind."

I filled out the form, and she proceeded to ask me some questions. Her questions were directed toward determining if my cognitive abilities were still intact, and she seemed to be impressed with my answers. Dr. Reed asked if I could recall the details of my accident, and I told her I could. She pressed to know if my tragic accident caused me sadness, anxiety, stress, or depression. Dr. Reed was not convinced when I told her I did not feel any of the above. She scheduled to come again after a week, and I was surprised when she asked me the same questions again. I patiently answered them even though I wondered why my previous answers were evidently not satisfactory to her. She scheduled to visit me again in a week. On that third visit, I thought she would have new questions or business, but she asked the same questions. As she asked those questions all over again, some thoughts ran through my mind: Why does she not believe me? Do I not sound convincing enough? Does she think I will change or change my mind? Whatever her reason was for the repetition, I hoped to sound convincing enough for us to move on to the next level.

"Do you want to know the truth?" I asked her. She lit up, and her eyes seemed to say "Now I am happy he's about to open up and be more forthcoming."

The word that came from her lips was simply *yes.*

"Dr. Reed, I want you to know that the last things that will die in me are my peace of mind and happiness."

She then left me in peace only after she asked, "Father Udo, what happened to you was quite tragic, tell me what helps you to cope with your situation."

My answer was short, "My faith, family, and friends."

I believed she was truly convinced that day because she never asked me again.

My other sources of therapy and healing were my faith, family, and friends, as I had told Dr. Reed. I tried to silently say my prayers, mainly short ones, when I woke up in the morning and before I went to sleep at night. The bulk of prayers on my behalf came from family, friends, parishioners I had worked for and even people whom I did not know from all over the world. Eucharistic Ministers from Christ the King Parish brought me Communion, which was truly and spiritually refreshing. The sustaining power of prayer, together with its healing effects, cannot be underestimated. The love and support from friends and family were phenomenally therapeutic. My friends never let a day pass without a visit. Even when they could not see me, they still came to the hospital and spent the time praying in the hospital's chapel for me. Their love and prayerful presence were powerful, and I felt it even when I was in a coma. Their companionship, words of encouragement, doing my laundry, and even the food they brought were invaluable in expediting my recovery. My friend, Father Okey, for all practical purposes, almost lived in the hospital. Dr. Mac—who not only was my surgeon, but became my brother and friend—came every day to see me unless he was out of town. We would talk about different things; it was so delightful to visit with him, and I always looked forward to his coming. Once he asked me, "Father Udo, will you still keep your promise to me about teaching in Catholic High School?"

"Doc, when did I promise you that?" I asked, smiling.

"You did when you were in the Surgical Intensive Care Unit," he answered.

"I barely remembered my name while I was there, Doc, because of the strong medicine I was given for pain, and so I hardly recall making you that promise. For all I know, it could have been the Morphine talking. Now that I am clear-minded, ask me again because I was under the influence when you asked me the first time." At that point, he was laughing so hard, and so was I.

About the second or third week I was in the rehabilitation hospital, my sister Helena had returned to Kenya. Most of my friends were beginning to visit less because I was doing better, and it had been a long, emotional, and traumatic undertaking caring for me, and they needed to recuperate before they come back to visit again. During that time, Kevin became my very close friend. He was an African American and one of my nurses. When he was done with his duties and had a minute, we would visit, enjoyed some fruits, and talked about different things. One of the times he came to visit, I was by myself, so he asked me, "Do you have a wife?"

I answered, "No!"

He did not stop with just that question. Kevin followed up with another question. "Do you have a girlfriend, a mistress, or a concubine?"

I again answered, "No!"

He looked so puzzled at first and then appeared downcast after he thought about my reply for a few more seconds. The next question he asked me brought to light a unique perspective I was not expecting or had thought of. His question was, "Why then do you want to be alive?"

I started laughing because I thought that his disappointment and the obvious frustration in his voice were very honest and funny at the same time. He did not laugh with me but rather looked very serious. Kevin could not understand why I was happy or why I worked hard on my therapy to get well if I did not have a pretty girl to make me smile or color up my seemingly boring life. It was difficult to know what was going on in his head, but I could tell by his countenance that he wished he could drag me off and get me married, so I had to do something. I asked him a few questions. "Kevin, you have a wife you love very dearly, don't you?"

His answer was "Mmm-hmm!"

"You also may have a mistress on the side?"

To that implicating question, he answered, "I take the Fifth! I will remain silent on this matter."

I smiled and continued, "Don't worry, I won't tell your wife. Seriously, you would do anything to make your wife happy, like take her to a fancy restaurant for dinner, buy her something she likes, and more?"

"You're damned right," he responded, drawing the "damned right" as he spoke for maximum emphasis, a sign that those were his best moments.

Then, I asked him the final test question after a preamble. "Now answer this last question as honestly as you can. I know you love your wife very much, but are there times when you would rather be anywhere but around her?"

Kevin pondered for a few seconds, I believe, wondering if that was a trick question. When he did not see any potential trap, he truthfully plunged right in. "Yes, sometimes she makes me so mad I almost want to kill her!"

He gave me all the materials I needed to drive the lesson home. "Kevin, to the extent that your peace and happiness depends solely on her, to that degree you will be miserable, especially those times she makes you mad. My peace of mind and happiness depend on God and won't dry up because with God, they are always sustained. I always pray and hope that my ties with God will not only define but influence my relationship with family and friends because it makes it stronger and lasting. If your joy depended on God, then even when your wife tries to get under your skin, your joy will not evaporate because it comes from God—it comes from within and not from her. With the abundant joy that flows from you, you might even turn her into an angel of sweetness at those awkward moments."

A few days after that incident, I had many friends who visited me, and some came bearing gifts: chocolate, fruits, food, and more. I was unaware my friend Kevin had been taking notice. When things had calmed down and I was by myself, he came for a visit. He was always upbeat whenever he came for a visit, but on that occasion, he looked upset and defeated. I almost asked him if he fought with his wife, just to tease him, but his question stopped me short. "You told me some days ago you didn't have a wife, girlfriend, mistress, or concubine. Who were those beautiful white girls who visited you today?"

I could not help but laugh so hard and loud at his emphasis on *white* and *beautiful*, which could not be missed. "Kevin, are you jealous?" I asked him, still laughing, and I did not wait for an answer but taunted him some more. "You have all the black girls, so I am stuck with the white ones." I was surprised he did not see any humor in what I said and did not laugh, so I continued, "Those beautiful white girls really got your attention, did they not? Your perception is selective. You didn't say anything about the guys who also came to visit. Those are the people I serve as a Catholic priest. I am their pastor. I pray for them and with them, rejoice with them when they have reason to celebrate, and I also comfort and support them when tragedy strikes. What you don't know is that they come to visit and care for me because I was there for them when they needed a priest and a friend. The other day you thought I was miserable, bored and had no reason to be alive, and today you are so jealous and think I am getting a better deal out of life—how ironic. If you think I am, then, become a pastor in your church at best or, at least, serve the Lord and let your joy depend on God, and you will enjoy even greater privileges than I do."

After about five weeks, Dr. Kiser recommended that I be discharged. I was not thrilled about being discharged because I did not know what would follow or what his decision was based on. However, when he explained to me that my discharge from the hospital would begin a new phase of my being reintroduced to my former life, which would include therapy at home, it made sense, and I was happy with his decision. When it was clear that I would leave in a few days, my doctor gave me some helpful survival tips. He also informed me that most of those who had been through enormous trauma and were hospitalized like I was and then discharged were likely to suffer depression. He recommended a temporary depression medication I could take to help me adjust to my new environment. I was not in favor of an antidepressant, in fact, medicine in general, and my doctor knew it. He tried to persuade me one more last time. "Father Udo, the antidepressant I'll prescribe for you will be temporary and helpful."

"Doc, I don't doubt you," I replied. "But, you know I laugh and smile a lot, like I am high on something anyway. So, taking an antidepressant may put me over the edge. Doc, know that I am not shy about what I need, so if I feel the need for the medicine after I go home, I will call and let you know."

We were both laughing even before I finished talking. "Father Udo, call if you need anything. I will come tomorrow to discharge you and say good-bye." I thanked him and expressed my wish to see him the following day when I would say a proper good-bye.

The day I was discharged started like a normal day, and I was happy to be going to my new home, Christ the King Church in Little Rock, where I would continue my priestly ministry and, of course, my therapy. My breakfast went well, but slowly, and would have been slower if the hospital aide had not helped me. After breakfast, two nurses, together with the aide, put me in a plastic chair for my shower. Before then, the aide used the overhead hanging lift to get me on a plastic bedlike platform for a shower. But, because I was going home and would not have access to that sophisticated and costly hospital equipment, the plastic shower chair was used to help me experience what my new reality would offer. When the shower was over, I had expected the aide to invite the nurses to help him take me from the bathroom to my bed since it took three of them to move me from my bed to the bathroom. When the aide attempted to take me by himself, I declined and encouraged him to get help, but he told me not to worry, that he could handle it by himself. I trusted him and waited to see how it would work. He grabbed me by the legs and, raised them while I was in a sitting position facing him, and he gave me a gentle push. Using the weight of my body, he was able to move the plastic shower chair, which had four wheels, but only the two back ones were on the floor because the chair and I were tilting backward. When I saw how dangerous it was, I tried unsuccessfully one last time to talk him out of it. I let him continue when he reassured me he knew what he was doing. As we got to the bathroom door, the two wheels bumped into the raised floor which prevented water from getting into the room. Not having any trunk muscles, the jolt made me put all my body weight on the back of the chair, which made it crumble. I fell, and it was a colossal fall! I actually heard the sound of the impact the moment my head hit the concrete floor. The aide was in shock, thinking he had killed me. He tried to lift me off the floor, but I knew it was going to be a futile effort and that he may hurt himself in the process. I asked him to get help, and that time, he listened. I was supposed to be discharged about 10:00 AM, but the doctor recommended X-Rays and an MRI to make sure there was no concussion and that the hardware in my neck was still intact. Everything checked out fine. When Dr. Mac came to see me, I could tell he was worried about me. Anyone would have been, but I tried to convince him I was fine when he said, "I heard you fell, and I had to come to make sure you're alright!"

"Doc, I'm alright," I confirmed, and then joked, "You didn't have to come. We thought that before I left the hospital, it would be helpful to conduct a controlled fall test to make sure your handiwork is fall-proof. Well, our test just proved one thing—that you're the best surgeon." We both heartily laughed.

It was two in the afternoon before I left the hospital to go to my new home, Christ the King Parish.

CHAPTER 13

Homecoming

A home is a place the young go to grow, the sick go to recover and everyone else goes to rest.
                                    —Father Udo Ogbuji

Two weeks before I was discharged from the hospital, I had a visitor, my old boss, Monsignor Malone. Earlier I had told the story about him picking me up from the airport the day I arrived in the United States, and I had stayed with him before I became the associate pastor in Saint Edward Church, Texarkana. We still kept in touch, more so when I was assigned as the pastor of Saint James Church, Searcy; Saint Albert Church, Heber Springs; and Saint Richard Church, Bald Knob. Being a new pastor, I sometimes needed help and clarification with some pastoral matters. I would call Monsignor with questions or problems, and he always gracefully provided me with helpful answers and solutions. Monsignor was a good sport; he could take a joke, and he knew how to give it back, too. Since he was so good at teasing me, I did not spare him either but, once in a while, took a swipe at him to get a good laugh. I remember that at the send off party for Bishop Sartain, Monsignor came and whispered in my ear so no one would hear him, "The bishop told me you're leaving the diocese and going back to school."

"Yes, I told him that," I acknowledged, but quickly added just to taunt Monsignor, "But I also told him that in confidence, not expecting he would tell you."

To which he responded, "He tells me everything."

"Monsignor, it's quite a scary thing to imagine the bishop tells you 'everything.'" I knew he was kidding, and I laughed, and so did he.

He stopped laughing and looked serious for a moment and said, "I hope that you will reconsider your plan to leave. Your parishes are doing well and are enthusiastic about the new church buildings you talked them into."

I made him an offer: "Monsignor, you know how much I covet your big parish, Christ the King Church. I'll stay and work in the Diocese of Little Rock for a few more years, if you agree to switch places with me for just three months—you will minister in my parishes, and I, in yours." The look in his eyes told me there was something that worried him about my offer. So, I added, "Don't worry, Monsignor, I won't hurt a thing! I just want to have the joyful feeling being in a parish as big as yours brings."

"No!" he said. "Not even for one day will I let you set foot in my parish."

"Well, then," I said, making him a different offer. "Let me be your associate pastor then."

"I would not, that's a ploy for you to take over my parish!" he replied, and we both had a good, long laughter.

As I sat across from Monsignor Malone a few years later in my hospital room while he informed me that I would be his associate pastor, I could not but wonder how we had come full circle. I obviously took his advice to hang around until the new church buildings were completed before I considered going back to school. During that period, we tried to raise the funds needed for the new church projects and worked with the Diocesan Building Commission to have the tentative church plans approved. Then, I had the car accident and was hospitalized, and here was Monsignor visiting me in the hospital and announcing that he was granting me my wish to be his associate pastor—a wish which was a joke at the time I made it known. I was ecstatic, but I still had to milk it some more. So, I jokingly asked, "Monsignor, what made you change your mind and accept my offer?" I did not wait for an answer. I had him cornered, so why waste a rare opportunity. I therefore continued, "Is it because I am incapable of taking over your parish now?" I laughed so hard at his displeasure and I doubt that he enjoyed the tease as much I did.

He grinned, perhaps thinking of how to stop me from having too much fun at his expense. "You're laughing now, but I will have the last laugh when I work you so hard and you beg for mercy," he threatened as his grin evolved into a broad smile. I sensed that he wished I could stop and be serious for a minute, so, I honored the unspoken truce while I laughed and said, "Monsignor, you know I am not intimidated by work."

"We'll find out in two weeks! Udo, the parishioners are looking forward to welcoming you into the parish," he interjected.

"Thank you, Monsignor. I look forward to being your associate and ministering to the faithful in Christ the King Parish as best as I can."

Monsignor was right; the parishioners made a lot of sacrifices in preparation for my coming. That was evident as I approached the parish premises the day I was discharged from the hospital. On the fence of the church and school hung colorful posters with inscriptions that read "Father Udo, welcome home!" "Father Udo, we love you!" and more! I was told the school kids made the beautiful posters, and their thoughtfulness melted my heart. The refurbished rectory was spectacular and had newly built handicapped ramps in the front and back of the house. At the back of the rectory was an asphalt pathway that led to the church. The rectory used to be a house the parish rented out to a family, but after the decision was made that I would stay in Christ the King Parish, Monsignor and the faithful renovated the rectory to suit my needs. Those who had the task of getting the rectory ready anticipated my needs. I had a chapel, a big parlor for my exercise equipment, a nice roomy kitchen, a beautiful den, a walk-in bathroom, and more. I had more than I could have asked for, and when told it took thirteen days to give the rectory such a magnificent makeover, I was speechless while filled with gratitude.

Arrangements were made for the aides to take care of me for twenty-four hours and the therapists to have two-hour therapy sessions with me at the rectory on weekdays until I was strong enough to return to the hospital for more therapies. My ministry as an associate pastor was designed to run concurrently with my therapies. Dr. Kiser believed that continuing my ministry in some capacity, among other things, provided some form of therapy for me. Dr. Kiser was so kind to let me take home one of his research bikes. He explained that the bike was an experimental bike that had the possibility of improving the knowledge of how to rehabilitate a patient with a spinal cord injury. Doc explained that studies had shown that the spinal cord tissues may have the potential for regeneration. The bike was built in such a way that one's feet were fastened to the pedals, and when turned on, it moves the legs as if you were riding a real bike. In using the bike, the specimen (which, in that case, was me) was passive—only sat and enjoyed the ride. The hope was that, with an incomplete spinal cord injury, at least the tissues of the damaged spinal cord could be tricked into awakening, reconnecting, rewiring, or healing themselves through enhanced sensory and motor stimulation. Dr. Kiser knew how devoted I was with my therapies, and he trusted me to take his bike home and become one of his guinea pigs, and I was more than happy to be selected in that study although his theory and expectations sounded like science fiction.

I was dedicated to riding that bike in the hospital and at home after I was discharged. Three months after I returned home, I was able to sit for a few minutes and also transfer myself from the bed to the wheelchair with the help of the wooden transfer board I had been given in the hospital. Since my legs did not move, Dr. Kiser's bike became my only means of exercise even though I just sat and let it ride my legs. I needed assistance to get onto the bike, and that help was provided by Lindie, the aide who worked with me during the day. She would lift my right leg and place it on the bike's pedal, and do the same with the left leg. On a certain day, when she was helping me get onto the bike as usual, she lifted my left leg, and as she did so, my left ankle moved. I saw it, and Lindie did too, but neither of us said anything. If it did actually move, it would have been the first time since the night of my accident. I was not convinced my ankle moved, and my doubt was more out of abundance of caution than fact. It would be devastating to rush to the conclusion that I witnessed a miracle when, in fact, I did not. Lindie was perhaps thinking the same thing and therefore kept quiet about what she observed. Since I did not know if the movement on my leg was reflexive, I consciously moved my left ankle, and it obeyed me. I was overjoyed! Lindie then confirmed that she saw it move the first time but did not tell me because she wanted to be sure first. Anyone could guess what I did next; I kept moving that left ankle until it got so fatigued that it was not able to move anymore. With that improvement came a stronger resolve to take the whole program of my rehabilitation even more seriously. I worked my left ankle every single day afterward until it wished it were not mine. Sometimes, I tried to move my right ankle, but it was lifeless, and after about a month of trying, I gave up. I did not realize that the right ankle had its own plan and schedule. Approximately three months after the left ankle moved, the right toes also showed signs of movement. That was also discovered by chance exactly the way the movement of the left ankle was. On that blessed day, Lindie was again putting my feet into the pedals of Dr. Kiser's bike when she noticed my right toes move slightly, and she asked me, "Father Udo, did you see that?"

"I did!" I replied. We were more hopeful and forthcoming that time because we had experienced the movement of my left ankle. "I am somewhat excited, but let me willfully move them before we start celebrating," I added. I did, and those toes moved. I deliberately moved them so many times until they got weak and could not take more. It was a joyful experience that called for great celebration and thankfulness.

Since my left ankle and right toes were coming alive my therapies became more daring and aggressive. My therapist tried to help me stand up, first with the equipment called Easy Stand, then manually. There were three therapists at the time, two worked for Baptist Home Health and one volunteered. After two years, Dr. Kiser determined that my medical record and level of improvement supported the recommendation that I was permanently disabled because he thought that continued recovery for me would be at an insignificant rate. What followed was the insurance company withdrawing their payment for my therapies. However, God sent me four angels in the persons of therapists who took care of me. The names of my therapists who volunteered had M as their initials: Mary Jane, Mary Margaret, Maria, and Monica. I was definitely in good hands; three named after Mary, the mother of Jesus. Mary, being Jesus' mother, was there for him and, later, for the apostles. She does not fail to be there for priests who dedicate their lives to the service of her son. Monica, the mother of Saint Augustine, never gave up on her son, even when he strayed. I did not have any doubt that the four M's would be there for me just like the two beautiful women from whom they took their names, making sure I did not talk myself out of my therapy.

All my therapists—volunteer or non-volunteer—made my therapy interesting and, that made it easier for me to work even harder. Unknown to them, I worked some more with my aide on the exercises we did during my therapy sessions. Although my therapists made the exercises as much fun as possible, sometimes, part of my therapy felt like a tedious chore I wished to avoid. I remembered the first day my three therapists took me to the movie theater. We had previously cancelled going to the movies three times mainly because I had one excuse or another. With their determination and my running out of excuses, they dragged me to the theater while I was silently screaming. I did enjoy going to the movie theater in spite of the fact that I had to slip out three times to take care of private business and so missed parts of the movie.

After the bathroom visits that ruined my movie, it was not my wish to go out any time soon, especially if my bladder was going to be leaking like a basket with big holes in it, but my therapists had other plans. They were fantasizing about taking me to the grocery store for shopping since, for them—and I guess for me in some way—going to the movie theater was a huge success. That lovely conspiracy of taking me to shop had been deliberated in secret, agreed on, fully planned, and ready for execution. After we ended therapy on a certain day, my therapists: Georgia and Mary Margaret, whom Baptist Hospital sent to work with me, left me with a proposal, a plot I thought they had abandoned after I indicated a lack of interest. "Father Udo, wouldn't it be nice if we go to the Fresh Market tomorrow?" Georgia suggested, leading the charge, with Mary Margaret nodding in agreement.

I knew she was being polite and, that behind that sweet suggestion was a band of therapists' wellness decree that would possibly be carried out to the letter. I had known them for some time, and I understood they could not wait to accomplish that mission, which, I should point out, was for my own good. My reluctance was based on my conclusion that the movie-theater experience was not a great one. The therapists, on the other hand, had a different perspective; they believed my going to the movie was a success and wanted to build on that momentum and, hopefully, break me free from the shackles of whatever kept me in my cocoon. "That would be interesting," I replied to her request of going to Fresh Market while suppressing the fact that I wanted to decline accepting her offer. I pretended to be open to the trip to the grocery store because I loved and respected my therapists, and it was for my own good. I also thoroughly enjoyed the unsurpassed care they provided for me in addition to their genuine interest to see that I get well.

The next day, when my therapists came, I was hoping they would forget their Fresh Market-trip proposal the day before or that they would come up with a different therapy for the day. The Fresh Market was within walking distance; in fact, the rectory shared a boundary with that grocery store. They were going to walk while I rode in my wheelchair. When I became aware of that plan, I suddenly wished for heavy rain to pour down to keep the therapy within the confines of the rectory. It did not rain, and I was brought back to reality when Georgia said, "Father Udo, are you ready to go to Fresh Market?"

I thought to myself, *Boy, how naive I was to think the therapists would forget. I better come up with something good and fast enough or I am going grocery shopping!* I finally came up with a grandiose offer the therapists could not resist, which momentarily put the shopping trip on hold. I was not sure I could deliver the bargaining chip I promised them, but I knew an attempt to deliver it would buy me more time and maybe save me from grocery shopping with the girls. If I did succeed in following through with my proposal, it would be a big win and reward for them and for me.

My therapists could not believe their ears when they heard what I intended to give them in exchange for them to postpone the trip to Fresh Market. That revelation came when I humbly asked, "I know you planned to take me grocery shopping, what if I stood up for you without any help, would you spare me the trip?" My offer sounded incredible and was certainly irresistible! I believed they thought that if all this time I relied on them and others to stand up, then, my standing without help would be a miracle worth witnessing. My therapists, Georgia and Mary Margaret jumped at the offer I put on the table, and hoping I would not change my mind quickly responded together with an unintended synchronicity, "Yes, we will!" The response came with some shade of apprehension. The look on their faces indicated confusion and wonder, which suggested they were thinking, *Is he really serious or pulling a prank on us?* I did not blame them for thinking it was a prank since I had pulled off a few harmless ones at their expense before. I could not guarantee that my promise to stand up unaided was completely made without any intention to tease. They probably thought that I could not possibly stand up on my own and was bluffing, but I also believed they did not want to live with the possibility that they could have witnessed a miracle but missed the opportunity. When they could not bear the suspense anymore, Mary Margaret earnestly requested, "Come on over, and show us what you've got!" as she motioned me to come around the sink in the kitchen.

As I approached the sink, my aide sarcastically joked, "We need this one on the video!"

With that announcement, she left to fetch my digital camera so she could get video clips. When I got to the right spot approved by my therapists, they fastened me with the guard belt in order to keep me from hitting the floor in case I could not hold myself up. By that time, my aide arrived with the camera ready to shoot. With my feet on the floor, I held on to the edge of the sink and tried to pull myself up. I did get up to some degree, just to know how I would feel if I stood up and if I could do it. I sat down after ascertaining what it felt like and was somewhat convinced I could do it. But my therapists, witnessing me sit down, became more apprehensive and perhaps nervous. After sitting for a few seconds, I held as firmly as I could to the edge of the sink and began to pull myself up. When I was almost up and on my feet, I staggered, and the therapists' safety instinct kicked in immediately; they both jumped to my side to keep me from falling. I adjusted my balance before they could help and stood tall, and believing I was safe, my therapists became less guarded and more relaxed. As if the whole incident was not riveting enough, I suddenly freed my hands from the edge of the sink and started dancing. That caused my therapists to be on guard again, but only after they escaped a mild heart attack I almost cost them.

While still on guard, they cheered. Just as I was full of pranks, so were my therapists; they always found new ways of torturing me. One of them volunteered, "Now that we know you can stand, we should start working on you putting on your pants."

I did not respond, but my aide, who was still shooting the video, found it amusing and started laughing so hard. In between her laughter, she added, "You don't want that in the video!" And we all joined in the laughter.

I was happy to have been spared of going grocery shopping with the girls, and thankfully, none of them brought it up again. I was even happier that I discovered, for the first time since my accident, that I could stand up again without help. That was simply sweet!

My therapists and aides were everything to me: greatest fans, family, friends—you name it. They were the first to notice that I had gained a few pounds or that I had more strength or worked up a tiny muscle. I remembered when I quit working with the weights because I did not think my muscles grew fast enough or could improve at all. Two weeks after I stopped, and unaware to me, I lost the tiny muscles on my arm. One of my therapists, who usually did a full range of motion on my arms, noticed after she came back from a two-week vacation. "Father Udo, it appears you did not exercise enough while I was gone."

"How did you know?" I asked.

"I have got a way to keep track of you, and I'm not telling," she said, smiling.

It was kind of puzzling to think that she knew me that well, and I did not know how she gained her knowledge. I believed she was indirectly challenging me to solve that intricate mystery if I could. I could sense the challenge, and once I did, my brain swung into action, and I inquired, "The other therapists told you?"

"Nope, I just got back last night and have not talked to any of them," she replied.

I looked bewildered, and she laughed as loud as she could. I believed my therapists enjoyed it when they made me sweat or squirm, either physically or mentally. I was usually the one who tried to have fun at their expense, so whenever the table was turned, they did not hide their great pleasure. Their laughter told me that they enjoyed it a little too much. When they first started working with me, their laughter was subdued while mine could blow off a rooftop. A few months later, they started laughing almost as loud. On those occasions, when I was at their mercy, I almost wished they did not learn from me to have that much entertainment when they laughed. In the midst of her laughter, she asked, "You want me to tell you how I found out?"

"Yes, please!" I replied, acknowledging I had suffered a miserable defeat.

"It was easy to find out. I looked at your arm and saw that you lost those muscles you've been building up for months now, and there is no other way to explain it than the fact that you stopped exercising."

The look in her eyes was like that of my mom when I neglected what I should have been doing. That incident made me realize how obvious missing some of my exercises was, and I promised myself that I would, going forward, take even the least of my therapy very seriously.

As reliable friends, my therapists never gave up on me; they always made me believe I could do things even when they seemed insurmountable. They helped set goals for me and guided me toward meeting them. Whenever I expressed a wish to meet a certain goal, they worked judiciously until it was realized. Never did I hear "Father Udo, you're not able to do it." What I always heard was "Let us see how we can help you do it." Even when unsuccessful, words of encouragement flowed like a fountain, and I often heard "We know you can do it. We will try again in a month or two!" My being able to use the elliptical trainer again was a clear example and one out of many benefits their encouraging nudges provided.

The elliptical trainer was a piece of exercise equipment I owned and used before my accident. I tried to exercise with it every night because, apart from staying in shape, riding it increased my chances of sleeping like a dead man. After one hour of intense beating on the elliptical trainer, my body did not have any other choice than to sleep the entire night. Whenever I missed a workout, I doubled my exercise time and effort the next night. There was a night I rode the elliptical trainer for two and a half hours because I missed the night before. The sweat was profuse, and my muscles burned as I peddled up and down, and I increased the resistance to punish my muscles for the utmost results. To make it fun, I had my favorite movie on and covered the monitor of my exercise equipment since looking at the monitor made time drag as slowly as it was painful. When the movie was over, and I finally looked at the monitor, two hours had passed, and since I still had energy left in me, I decided to continue for an extra thirty minutes. When I was done, I slowly got down and lay on the carpet, which felt fine and soothing. I intended to lie on the carpet until my body temperature cooled down before I took a hot shower, but I fell asleep and woke up the next morning, wondering what I was doing on the carpet until I saw the elliptical trainer in the middle of the room, which reminded me of my nocturnal activity.

What started as a lofty dream spoken out loud, and at the time seemed unrealizable, became a mission statement and a mission. During one of my therapy sessions, I said to my therapists, "I used to enjoy exercising with that fine machine!" My therapists followed my pointed finger and glanced at the elliptical trainer. It was a sobering moment, and they silently took it all in. I continued, "Any day I am able to ride it again; I will know that I am on the way to recovery." Unaware to me, they consulted one another and decided to help me get on it and possibly help me ride it. At that stage of my therapy, I was able to stand and walk at least thirty-five feet with the walker. On the set date, I was very excited about the prospect of being able to ride the elliptical trainer or, at least, find means of getting on it. It took several unsuccessful efforts and an excruciating ninety minutes before I was able to finally mount it with plenty of help. Having expended my energy trying to get on the elliptical trainer, my muscles weakened, and I was unable to move the pedals. I was delighted, and I declared victory after my therapists confirmed that finding a way to get on that equipment was a great accomplishment. We all silently pledged to do it again soon.

The next time my therapists gave me the pleasure of attempting to ride the elliptical trainer was after seven months.

On that day, we expected a better outcome because a lot had happened that could boost my chances of success. During that waiting period, I had time to recover a little more and to undergo another surgery where a Baclofen medication pump was put in my abdomen and a catheter with valves directed the medicine in the pump from my abdomen to my spinal cord. That surgery was performed because I was having frequent spasms, and my joints were very tight. As a result, I could hardly do anything. Ordinary tablets of Baclofen medication did little to bring me relief, and I went for nights without sleeping. After Dr. Kiser recommended the pump and my inquiries led me to believe it would be beneficial, I signed on for it. I still had other questions that the neurosurgeon helped me answer. The least question I had was, "Doc, how are you going to pass the catheter from the left side of my abdomen to my vertebrae and spinal cord?" I was smiling when I asked the question.

He smiled back and answered, "Are you sure you want to know?"

His answer made me laugh. He was not only funny but also right; I did not really want to know. But I was happy to know that before my surgery the last nurse I saw and talked to was from Christ the King Parish where I was the associate pastor. Before she gave me the dose of anesthesia to put me to sleep, she introduced herself as a Catholic and told me she belonged to my parish, and then added, "Father, I have this last injection for you. After I give it to you, you won't remember anything that happened from here on. After this injection, there will be many of us lining up to go to Confession." She was laughing as she said it. I remember laughing with her, but I did not remember who she was or whether or not she confessed her sins afterward with her friends, which was a good thing.

With my spasms reduced through that medical miracle and lots of exercise that helped strengthen my muscles, I was ready to conquer the elliptical trainer. After many months of noticeable improvement, my therapists decided to give me another opportunity to prove myself on that exercise machine.

On that day, my two volunteer therapists had help from my aide and Father Mike, who lived with me at the time. The elliptical trainer was kept closer to the wall, which kept me from capsizing. The open right side had my aide and Father Mike on guard, ready to keep me from hitting the floor. Climbing on it was easy; my practice paid off. I raised my wheelchair, put my legs on the pedals, and got help while I pulled myself to an upright position. One of my therapists was in front, helping to pull the long metal bar that enables one of the pedals to go down, which happened simultaneously with another therapist at my back, trying to help me move the other pedal down. Still remaining in an upright position, I moved my legs in the direction of the pedals for about three minutes before I got fatigued and had to sit down. It was not clear how much effort came from me; however, I was grateful that I was able to do it even with lots of help, and I lived to fight another day.

Unknown to me, my therapists had a surprise for me and were more determined to carry it out when they learned that I had been assigned to be a Chaplain for the Benedictine nuns in Jonesboro. In the few days before my departure, they kept talking about a gift they would have for me on my last day of therapy. They would not tell me what the gift was except that it was a surprise, and they could not wait for me to have it because they knew I would love it. It was obvious they were very much excited about their surprise for me, and I wished I knew what their unknown gift was so I could be as joyful as they were. I kept wondering what the gift could be, but gave up doing so because I do not deal well with suspense. When they finally revealed their surprise, I was happier and more animated than they were! They hoped to help me ride the elliptical trainer almost without help before we went our separate ways; what a way to wrap up our therapeutic journey. I should have thought about it because my therapists were good at pulling stunts like that, but it had been almost a year since the last time they got me on it. One of them remembered my desperate wish of being able to ride it. I actually got on it without help and was able to ride it for about a minute and half before I got fatigued. It was a beautiful surprise, and their thoughtfulness was truly inspiring. That long awaited victory led me to understand that I could succeed in life even when the situation seemed uneventful and hopeless—especially when I persevere and put in my best effort and keep believing.

The Baclofen medication that was injected into my spinal cord through the pump relieved the spasms and muscle tightness I had to endure but created another problem. The medicine weakened me to the extent I was no longer able to walk or stand longer than I used to do. That was in part due to the fact that my doctor was increasing the dosage every time I went for a visit in the hope that the spasms I felt could be completely eradicated with a larger dose of Baclofen. The most disturbing part of that adversity was that the medicine made me so drowsy and I began to doze off in church during Sunday Mass when the Deacon was delivering the homily. That discomforting experience made me realize I had to do something although it was unclear what I was going to do. The weakness I felt made me realize how difficult it would be to build up my strength and stamina, and to help me accomplish that, Dr. Kiser recommended that I go to Saint Vincent Rehabilitation Hospital to use their state-of-the-art AutoAmbulator. That machine aided me as I walked, thereby improving my motor skills and helped me get stronger. At first, it did little for me until Ashley, my Physical Therapist—in Saint Vincent Rehabilitation Hospital—encouraged me to mention my concern to Dr. Kiser, who then started reducing the dose of Baclofen that I was receiving instead of increasing it. As I got stronger, I returned to Baptist Rehabilitation Hospital for more therapy. The therapies that I was engaged in paid off, and that was evident in my noticeable improvement.

One of the days I went to therapy, my therapist asked me to work with a particular piece of exercise equipment. At that stage, I had mastered the use of it and was able to exercise for ten minutes. One of the patients, a woman, went to use it after me, thinking it was easy because she observed me do it. But she quickly found out that it was not easy at all and only lasted a few seconds. At the end of my therapy session, I was heading home and got into the elevator with the same woman who had used the exercise equipment after me. She asked me, "How long were you on that exercise equipment?"

I answered, "Ten minutes."

She looked me in the eyes and exclaimed, "I hate you!"

We both started laughing at the same time. In between the laughter, I told her, "I couldn't do it three months ago!" I also told her not to worry, to keep trying and never give up, that she would be surprised how much she would be able to do after a few months.

The next time I was at the hospital for therapy, I encountered a very young man who was in his twenties. I was exercising with a piece of equipment while he was on the one I had used the week before. Unlike the woman, that young man appeared not to be motivated at all. He just sat on the workout equipment like someone had forced him to get on it. As I exercised and looked toward his direction, we made eye contact, and I smiled at him and said "Is using that equipment hard for you?" He nodded, and I continued, "The first day I got on it, I thought I would never be able to use it for exercise!"

"Do you mind if I ask you what happened to you?" he asked.

"No, I don't. I was in an automobile accident, and you?" I said.

He replied, "I dove into a shallow swimming pool! I'm an incomplete quadriplegic."

Then I inquired, "Did they tell you, you will not walk again?"

He nodded.

"I was told the same thing too! One of the intern doctors did, but I am able to walk a little bit now. Don't give up on yourself. You are much younger than I am, and I believe you will heal faster, too. Keep exercising even when it appears there is nothing to hope or work for, okay?"

At that time, he smiled, nodded, and thanked me. He also started pedaling a piece of exercise equipment he was initially reluctant to use, even as he struggled to keep up.

After I was discharged from the hospital, it was about six months before my public appearance and ministry in Christ the King Church began. That intermittent period gave me time to settle in and recover a little more. During that waiting time, I had Monsignor, the aides, nurses, therapists, members on the parish staff, some parish members who volunteered, and many friends who cared for me. They were charged with catering to my different needs ranging from medical and therapy to cleaning the rectory, grocery shopping, and simple visits. To say the least, I was well cared for, and the excellent care I received translated into a faster recovery.

The warm welcome and superb care I received in every respect could not be more evident than the very first Sunday I celebrated the Eucharist with my new parish family. It was Palm Sunday of 2007, and Dr. Mac, my brother, came early that morning to visit and to help me get ready for the eight o'clock morning Mass. My aide was busy with other things, and Dr. Mac went to the kitchen and made me scrambled eggs for breakfast. Shortly before the scrambled eggs were ready, we found out there was no coffee in the rectory. Doc drove to Starbucks and bought me a rich, delicious cup of coffee to go with the eggs and toast. After breakfast, he accompanied me to the church. I have never stopped bragging about the extra special treat I got from my surgeon and brother. It was not just bragging; it was a testimony of how blessed I truly am! I do not know many people who are so privileged as to have their surgeons come to their homes, cook breakfast for them, and accompany them to the church.

With the blessing of Monsignor, I made the choice of Palm Sunday to be the day I would meet my new family. My choice of that day was easy to make; I was drawn to the rich symbolism, meaning, and implications ingrained in the celebration of Christ as the universal King. The kingship of Christ is inextricably intertwined with his service and suffering. Even as he rode in triumph into Jerusalem, he knew he was about to face unbearable humiliation, torture, and death. His acceptance of that reality deepens our knowledge of his kingship, saturates our hearts with his unconditional love, and marvels us as we behold the victorious power of his sacrificial love and glorious resurrection. Since the name of my new family parish is Christ the King, I could think of no better day to identify with them and have the opportunity to thank our members for their unconditional love and hospitality. Another reason I picked that day was because of the personal lesson and implication the celebration of the kingship of Christ has for me. Namely, that we all share in the kingship of Christ (Revelation 1:5-6), and as kings with Christ, our sufferings and services in love are inseparable parts of and glory of that kingship. In light of that fact, the pain I felt and the service I may be able to give in my unique circumstance would become my union with Christ, and united with Christ, I was able to draw strength and grace. That was part of the message I wanted to share with my new family until I became aware of how far they had come in their service of God. Their worship of God and charity humbled me and made me speechless; they had more to share and more to give me than I had for them!

Doc and I, as we approached the church building, went through an automatic door and onto a ramp leading to the altar. I later learned those were constructed to help me get around. I was truly touched by all the sacrifice and preparation that were made to make me feel at home. I was even moved to tears and smiles when Monsignor introduced me to the gathered congregation, and the introduction was received with a long, sweet standing ovation. My heart melted with joy as I was overcome by the welcoming love that filled the air. I thought to myself, *My new family is a lovely one, and I am truly blessed!* I enjoyed that moment so much, and I just sat in my wheelchair before the congregation and smiled.

When they stopped applauding and settled down, I started my speech with an acknowledgement as I smiled. "Thank you for the dull welcome!" Those who got the humor and sarcasm chuckled loud at different spots in the audience. That was followed by more laughter when the rest caught on. Then I continued, "With this much welcome, you have really made it too hard for me to ever leave you!" More laughter followed. After I lightened the audience up and had their full attention, I went ahead to drive home the message. "Today is a special day for you since you took your name after Christ the King, who rode triumphantly into Jerusalem. He did not go into Jerusalem for a picnic but to die for us—a unique proof of his eternal kingship. Today is special for me, too! I bet since it is a special day for me, you will be wondering why I did not make the occasion more fun by riding into the church on a donkey like Jesus did. I got my donkey with me, my wheelchair!" I said, pointing to my wheelchair. The laughter and cheer was explosive. When the laughter stopped, I continued, "Today is special to me because I have the opportunity to see you, to be with you, and to thank you for adopting me into this royal family. You exceeded my every expectation! Jesus went to Jerusalem so that we might have the fullness of life. As kings with Christ, you mirrored him to help me live again. On the thirteenth of March, when I arrived home from the hospital, there were signs and the smell of love and hospitality everywhere. There were signs on the church and school fences with inscriptions—'Father Udo, we love you!' 'Welcome home, Father Udo!' 'Our prayers and wishes are for you to get well soon!' and more. Then, I went into the rectory and saw all the unspoken words of love and care. When told it took thirteen days to complete the renovation of the rectory, I had goose bumps and marveled at your sacrifice. You couldn't do that if you weren't kings with Christ and living out his loving service. I thank God for the gift of you! I thank Monsignor, whom I respect very much and who has been my mentor since I arrived in the United States, for his great leadership. I owe a debt of gratitude to Monsignor Gaston the Diocesan Administrator and your former pastor, for his care while I was in the hospital and for granting Monsignor Malone's request that I stay with him. For you, my family, I cannot thank you enough. But I promise you that, while remaining ever grateful to you for your goodness to me, I will spend each day praying for you. To justify your sacrifices, I will take my therapy more seriously so we can witness more miracles. You may not know it, but all your prayers for me have yielded miracles. Right now, no one can mess with me because I can kick like an ostrich!" As I said that, I kicked up my left leg from under my vestments. The rejoicing and jubilation could be heard from the heavens. I then concluded, "I feel every prayer you say for me, so if you stop, I'll know. Please continue to pray for me! You have my word; I will always pray for you and never stop until you tell me to. I hope you don't mind if I sing for you? 'Count in your joy, even when things seems so hard to you! God will never give you more than you can handle!' Thank you, thank you, and God bless you!"

All stood up and clapped and clapped! The applause was even louder and longer than the one before my speech. I was truly humbled and, at the same time, overjoyed. I waited after the final blessing at the altar and shook hands and visited with all who came up to say hello.

That ceremonious event began a three-year journey of ministering in a limited capacity as an associate pastor. I have always known that being compassionate goes with the priestly territory, and I have tried to exercise it. But my condition as a quadriplegic somewhat predisposed me to be extra merciful. Perhaps it has to do with the compassion and help I receive from God, friends, and strangers, more so now that I have some physical limitations. I truly know what a joy it is to be helped by someone in a time of need and how joyful others feel when they benefit from kind acts and love. I feel much more joyful and fulfilled when I reach out to any one in charity. As Saint Paul said, quoting Christ, "It is more blessed to give than to receive" (Acts 20:35). Any form of compassion I show or love that I give brings me a good measure of a sense of accomplishment.

A time to show kindness came during one of the Masses I celebrated in my new parish and family. One of the Eucharistic ministers had spilled the consecrated hosts by mistake behind the altar. She had picked all of them up, but to make sure there was no tiny piece left on the carpet, she proceeded to pick up small particles of anything that looked white and put them in her mouth. She was frantic and remorseful as anyone in her situation would have been. The reverence and piety she expressed in searching for any piece that had broken off and on the floor was commendable. It spoke eloquently to the seriousness with which she attended to her duties as a Eucharistic Minister. While she still searched, I was also looking around the same spot too, hoping to find any she missed. After about two or three minutes of thorough search, I was convinced there was not any piece of consecrated host left on the floor, but she was still bent down, looking and beating herself up and throwing things in her mouth I was sure were not pieces of host. I knew if I did not do something, she was not going to forgive herself and would keep eating things that may make her sick. I leaned forward, close enough for her to hear me, and said, "Stop eating dirt!" She turned around to look at me and saw I was smiling at her; she smiled back and stood up.

As expected, my physical limitations made my pastoral duties challenging and sometimes left me in some embarrassing or distressing experiences. During the earliest days when my bladder was leaking like a sieve, I wore a catheter with a bag around the lower part of my leg as I went to Sunday Mass or other activities. The standby bag strapped to my leg collected and prevented any possible leak. At different times, I wondered, with a smile, how wonderfully discreet and convenient it was to be able to take care of my business without calling attention to myself. I also wondered what a mishap or any malfunction would mean. But since the bag seemed accident proof, I did not worry about it. However, I found out what it was like to have a leaking bag on a Sunday Mass, 11:00 AM to be exact—the family Mass that was always fully packed even in the summer.

The Mass was going well until my homily when my bladder began to spasm, which was a sign that it was full and could only hang on for a few more minutes. I managed to conclude my homily while ignoring the imminent threat. Although I wore a concealed leg bag that offered convenience and privacy, I still felt like I was out in the open and that everyone knew exactly what I was doing. When in public, I tried to hold the line of fire until the heat and pressure were humanly impossible to contain. On that day, it became unbearable as the deacon prepared the bread and wine for consecration. Usually, the urine goes into the bag quietly, but during that episode, there was a faint whistling sound. The sound was a warning sign. Meanwhile, I waited for the two altar servers to bring me water and a towel to wash my fingers and wipe them dry as part of the Mass ritual. From the corner of my eye, I could see one of the altar servers who brought me water staring in horror at the carpet on the floor. It was then that it dawned on me that I just peed on God's holy sanctuary. However, I did not look down because I was sure I would draw more attention to whatever was on the floor. I washed and wiped my fingers, and continued with Mass like everything was normal. After the Mass, I told the Deacon, whom I am sure was the only one that knew with certainty what happened, to see to it that all the evidence was erased. I said with a smile. "Deacon Dick, you know I will need your help to get the janitor to take care of that mess I made. Please make sure no DNA of mine is left at the crime scene!"

"Yes, Father, I will!" Deacon Dick, replied in his baritone voice and started laughing, and I laughed too.

Evidently, my aide, when she strapped the bag to my leg, did not check to see if its valve was shut. It was not, and an honest mistake turned into a disaster. As I drove back to the rectory with my shoe drenched in my own urine, I could not but reflect on the mishap and thank God for his kindness. It disturbed me to think it could have happened while I was preaching, in which case, the fountain, as embarrassing as it could be, would have been flowing toward the congregation. It was scary to think everyone could have watched that ugly drama unfold. I then, said to myself, "My Goodness! God just saved me from an immortal humiliation—thank you, Lord!"

One of the scariest moments as I performed my pastoral duties was when repairs were taking place in the parish church. While the repairs were being done, we celebrated weekday Masses in one of the parish buildings. Since the venue was a good distance from the rectory, my aide drove me there in my van. My van has a ramp that comes out with a push of a button, to enable me to drive out of the van in my wheelchair. Unfortunately, the spot my aide parked the van was elevated, so that the ramp was steeper than usual. As I drove out of the van in my wheelchair, I flipped. I had a premonition that I could not make it safely, so I drove down slowly, holding on to the door frame. When my wheelchair tipped over, what kept me from hitting my face on the asphalt paved road was that I had held on to the car door frames. The safety belt on the wheelchair held me back too as I hung peering at the paved road. Strangely, I was not scared, but on the contrary, I laughed quietly even as I stared at my own possible death. As my aide came over to help get me and my wheelchair back on the floor of the car, a parishioner, Angela, who was attending Mass, came over to help, too. As it turned out, my aide needed help. My wheelchair weighed three hundred and sixty pounds, and at the time, I weighed two hundred and fifteen pounds. Five hundred and seventy-five pounds total weight of me and my wheelchair would need a lot of force to get back in balance. It turned out that, with one push from my aide and Angela, the back tires got back on the car floorboard, and I was in a sitting position again. Unknown to me and my helpers, Jim, who would later become my friend, watched from the second-story building. It took about six months—when Jim and his wife, Monica, invited me to their home—for Jim to recount how he watched that dangerous incident unfold from the window as he arrived early for the Mass. As he concluded the story, he said, "Father, I couldn't believe you were laughing in the face of an imminent violent death! Do you mind if I ask you why you were laughing and didn't seem to be bothered?"

"I don't mind, Jim!" I told him. "It's simple. I didn't want to make those ladies helping me nervous or get them scared or too alarmed. If I had, they might be confused on how to help me or, at worst, hurt themselves." I gave him the short answer and one of the reasons for my behavior. I had another reason, and I will make it known before I conclude this book.

Though my circumstance made it a lot more difficult to minister to the parishioners as I would love to, my limited ministry was nonetheless very rewarding. What I consider my greatest reward was the acceptance I got from the kids, which, in turn, enabled me to minister to them in the best way that I could. An experience I had in the hospital made me wonder if my being in a wheelchair as a priest would undermine or compromise the traditional posture and appearance of a priest. As far as I can remember, I have never met an active priest in a wheelchair. There was a time when a family from one of my former parishes visited me in the hospital. The family came with one of my little friends. My little friend hung to the door and was too frightened to come into the room after she saw me in a wheelchair. I pleaded with her as calmly as I could. "It's me, Father Udo, don't worry about the wheelchair. I had to use it after my accident and will get rid of it very soon!" What I said helped just a little, enough for her to take her hands off the door post. Then her mom tried to calm her fears by coming forward to hug me and said to my little friend, "You see, Father Udo is okay, come and say hello!" My little friend, I believe in my heart, wanted to come to say hello, but she may have been traumatized by the news of my accident. That would have been one way of explaining it. But then again, hearing such a scary story was one thing for a little girl who was about seven years old, but another to behold a friend who used to look healthy and strong now appearing so weak and confined in a wheelchair. I can see how such an experience may be terrifying for a child. Her older sister came and said hello and was not rattled at all. As I lay in my bed and reflected about that incident, I felt so much for my little friend! I knew her parents had the best intention and could not have predicted how she would have reacted. I wished she was not so scared and prayed for her. I knew she always prayed for me because she told me she did before my accident, and I did not believe she stopped. If anything, I was convinced that after she saw me in that condition, she would pray for me much more to get well.

When Monsignor announced to me that I was going to be his associate, a major concern I had was how the kids would react to a priest in a wheelchair. So my greatest joy and sense of accomplishment came from ministering to the kids in Christ the King. Their acceptance of me was whole and without reservation. I would say that Monsignor and the kids' parents did a great job in preparing them before my coming. It also helped that almost all of them never met me and did not know what I looked like before my accident. It was, therefore, much easier and simpler to accept me in the only condition they knew me. As opposed to the unfortunate comparison my little friend had to grapple with. Actually, those who were much smaller thought my wheelchair was cool and could fly. They probably got the idea from the times when I raised my wheelchair up to nine inches during Mass when I was behind the altar. In fact, instead of being repelled, they were fascinated by my wheelchair and coveted it. They always asked me if I would let them drive it, and I always told them I would, but only if they keep praying for me until I was able to walk, then I would let them. They kept praying and hoping I could someday walk out of my wheelchair and let them drive it. I had to reward them with something sometimes to keep their interest alive; I wanted them to keep their prayers coming, so I let them play with the horn sometimes. They would always gather around me in the parking lot during their recreation, and it became an opportunity to teach them about the church, life, politics, and more. They did not ever run out of questions to ask. The little ones were happy to run to me to show me their lost tooth and tell me how much the tooth fairy paid for it. After one of the Sunday Masses, one of the little boys ran to me to show me the hole in his gum. He opened his mouth, pointed eagerly to the location of the lost tooth. His mom also came to say hello. I asked my friend how much he got from the tooth fairy, and he said, "Twenty dollars!" He was proud of his bargaining power. Then I responded, "You did well, but certainly you can do better than that—far better than twenty dollars!" I laughed while saying it, rubbing it in as the mom listened. I was, of course, kidding. When she could not bear it anymore, she said, "Thanks, Father Udo!" She was being sarcastic and probably wished she could hit me on the head with a baseball bat. When going to or from Mass, I would see the kids, who would always come to say hello, and I never let them go without showing interest in their well being, teaching and blessing them.

Part of the ministry and joy of a priest in the parish is to baptize, witness marriages, bless homes, conduct funeral services, and more. During those occasions, and other times, the priest may be invited to the homes of the families to share in their joy or grief. I knew that part of my ministry would be close to impossible because the parishioners would have to renovate their homes to be handicap-accessible to make it easier for me to come into their homes. It was a great joy and honor to experience some families who—out of their own initiative—went through the trouble of building ramps or working out unconventional ways of getting me into their homes. The first family that insisted I come to their home was Dr. Mac, my brother, and his lovely wife, Suzy. I was very apprehensive since that was my first time of visiting any family, and Doc had told me there was a part of their house that was a little elevated, and that it would not be a problem. It was! The elevation was too high for my wheelchair to ride over. Doc then employed the services of his sons and their friends. The plan was for them to lift my wheelchair, with me in it, over the hump. I was a little worried about that arrangement. Not just because the wheelchair and I weighed about five hundred and seventy-five pounds and may be too much for these four men to handle but also because a little bit of drinking, I could tell, had been going on, and none of the young men hid the evidence. I thought of another plan, in which case I would transfer to another chair and let them carry my wheelchair over, and then I would get back on my wheelchair. But before I could say, "Wait!" I was already high in the air and put inside the house. While in the air, I started laughing boisterously. No one knew what I was laughing about, but whatever it was, my laughter gave a clue it would be interesting. When they asked me why I was laughing, I laughed even louder, and that made them more curious.

The reason I was laughing was that the Irish missionaries who brought Christianity to my country worked under difficult situations. They travelled on foot with some helpers, including the catechist, who also interpreted their sermons and instructions to the local people. To get from one small Christian community to another, some of the priests had to pass through a river. The cassock worn by the priest did not make the crossing easy. Even if it did, the people so much respected the white priests that they did not let their feet touch the water, so the priests were carried over the water in a chair by four strong young men. When in the air in my wheelchair, carried by four young white men, I could not help but think of the striking similarities of how my ancestors anticipated the needs of the Irish priests and provided for them and how these young white men were returning the favor. Doc, and everyone around, thought my story was funny and laughed more than I did myself. I would be right to deduce that such stories, experiences, and blessings—even the ones in disguise all though my life—have helped to shape me into the man I have become.

CHAPTER 14

The Man I Have Become

To become the person we love, we must use our past to improve our present, and feed a hopeful future in the present in order to make the present relevant.

—Father Udo Ogbuji

This chapter is going to be the most difficult to write, and that is because I will have the task of exploring and writing an analytical summary of my life, which spreads through a span of more than forty years. It is not going to be an easy endeavor or narrative describing who I am, especially when the person I am is still in a state of flux. There is also the aspect of the inherent temptation for me to embellish my positives, tilting the balance so I will look good. Part of my struggle will entail working against the natural instinct that may make me more inclined to judge myself more favorably. Furthermore, this chapter is not just about a phase of my life or parts different people have played and how the parts I played at different moments unfolded; it is more of an elevated tale of my intellectual interpretations of events in my life and how I applied those interpretations in livable moments that brought about such a cohesive peace to the person I see and have totally embraced.

Who is the man I have become? There is no question that many people who know me have perspectives of the man they think I am. I will lay out a few testimonies from my respected superiors. It had been a few months since I was discharged from the hospital, and Monsignor Malone called and told me that Bishop Sartain was coming to pay me a visit. I could hardly contain my excitement. He had, at the time, just been transferred by the Vatican to be the bishop of Joliet. To make the trip from the state of Illinois to Arkansas to see me made me feel like I had just been given the whole world. We visited for about an hour and twenty minutes, but it felt like ten minutes because I enjoyed every moment of it, asking the bishop about his new assignment and showing off my newfound movement of my left foot. I believed he had a good time too, recounting the highlights of my working under him as the Bishop of the Diocese of Little Rock. When it was time for him to leave, and we headed for the door, I knew it was time to ask for the best favors. "My Lord," I said, "May I have your blessing?"

"Sure, Udo!" he replied in his endearing deep voice and then proceeded to give me the best blessings I ever received. As he opened the door to leave, he turned around, making me think he forgot something important. As I looked at him, trying to know what it was, he looked me in the eyes and said, "Udo, if anyone can survive this, it is you!" His words were as powerful as they were inspirational, but they also left me with a vague description of who he thought I was. The vagueness came from my not knowing why he thought I was best suited to survive an ordeal of such magnitude. I was obviously lost in that profound moment and, unlike me, did not think to ask him why he thought I was someone who could survive such a tragic accident. Now that I think of it, I should have asked him, and since I did not, I am left to fill in the blank. He probably meant that I seemed to have a delightful outlook toward life, and I could persevere in hardship.

My bishop, Most Rev. Lucius I. Ugorji, was in the United States around the same period that Bishop Sartain paid me a visit. He called and told me he was coming to spend a few days with me. I had no doubt he saw the pending visit as an opportunity to condole with me on my ghastly accident, assess my situation, and know if he could personally be of help in any way. He arrived about 10:30 AM, and we spent the rest of the morning and afternoon visiting, catching up with everything ranging from my health to his pastoral leadership and people back home. We were both exhausted after the long visit but were happy to have engaged on matters of interest. Sometimes we were lost in deep theological dialogue; at other times, we tried to solve the world's problems and also made jokes and laughed. At about 4:00 PM, he announced he was going to take a nap. I understood how much he needed it after the fatigue of flying for fifteen hours from Nigeria in addition to the hours of waiting for his flight at the airport. He was also grappling with jet lag, which made me appreciate his spending hours with me and being gracious the whole time. As he stood up to go to the guest room, I responded to his announcement of taking a nap, "My Lord, get a good nap and rest because you will be cooking the dinner for tonight."

He was shocked, and I could see it in his eyes. If he was not, I would have been surprised because as I narrated earlier men generally do not know how to cook in Nigeria. Mothers or sisters pitch in, and they actually appreciate it when men stay away from the kitchen. Men's presence in the kitchen is considered a distraction. To make matters worse, priests—and more so the bishop—have chefs back home, and so I understood every detail of the shock in his eyes, which, at that point, was turning into horror. I was not about to torture my bishop any more than was necessary; it was a joke, and I did not want to fall from his grace, so I started laughing. It was only then he knew I was taunting him, and he laughed with me. I believed he was relieved to know it was a prank after all. I had a wonderful visit with my bishop, and at my request, he blessed me before he left. I knew he was sympathetic of my situation even though he did not say so; he did not have to say a word—I just knew. Apart from the feeling of sympathy and the great company of each other that we enjoyed, I did not know what he thought of me, my situation, or our visit; but thanks to him confiding in Father Kevin, who also works in the Little Rock Diocese, I was able to find out.

All the Nigerian priests who worked in the Diocese of Little Rock planned an annual meeting, which I was going to host. The news of my being the host was a welcomed one, in fact, a great honor. That was because of the bond of love we shared and the invaluable camaraderie we have when we meet, which altogether was edifying and therapeutic. As I expected, the meeting was exciting, with lots of teasing, laughter, eating, drinking, and catching up. It was also productive because extensive deliberations were held on the best ways to minister to the faithful entrusted to our care. There was not a dull moment; I teased and laughed even more than I did before my accident. Unknown to me, Father Kevin had observed my demeanor since he arrived for the meeting. I was unaware that he had taken my joyful appearance and easy-going attitude each time we met with a grain of salt. He could not understand how anyone who seemed, from every indication, to have lost everything would behave like he had gained the best of everything he wanted out of life. He thought there was no way that could be real, that I must have been faking it. But, on that day of the meeting, he was ready to unveil the secrets he had kept from me. He did so either because of the celebrative mood, or to encourage me, or other unknown factors, or all of the above. Nevertheless, I was happy he let me into his deepest thoughts and secrets.

"Udo, I have something to tell you," he said.

"I am all ears," I replied, unaware of where he was going, hoping it would not be a sermon similar to that of a puritan of the sixteenth century. Being a former spiritual director in the seminary, it would not be an exaggeration to imagine he might drag me into a long dry spiritual lecture when my only desire was to be in the festive spirit of the moment. Thankfully, it was not a sermon!

"Udo, first, I have to say I am sorry about your accident," he said. "But, I must note that your cheerfulness and strength has been an inspiration for me and many people. For a while, I thought you were putting up a front or faking your happiness. But after this long period of time has passed, I don't believe you are. Even if you are, you're doing a great job at it. After your bishop visited you, he gave me a call and said something that sealed my admiration for you. He said, 'I went to see Udo to comfort him, but I went away being the one comforted.' I have to tell you that you have been an inspiration for us all."

I listened in amazement and was humbled and speechless!

My limited ministry in Christ the King Parish ended with farewell Masses on the weekend of March 13th and 14th, 2010. After each Mass, Monsignor addressed the parishioners. He recounted how we first met, the hospitality of the faithful and family of Christ the King, my recovery so far, and my transition to be a Chaplain and minister to the nuns in Holy Angel Convent in Jonesboro. After thanking God for the grace of continued healing granted me, he expressed his gratitude to the people for the sacrifices they made to ensure I received excellent care. He thanked me for the ministry and inspiration my being his associate pastor brought to the parish. As he thanked me, he said something that was apparently obvious to me and to those who knew me well enough, but only he could say it as bluntly as he did: "I am glad you are the stubborn person you are. That has helped you to diligently keep up with your therapies and exercises. Even when the doctors were doubtful of your continued recovery, you did not waver, and we have seen the fine results of your resolve!"

Those testimonies, if true (and I do not doubt they are), leave me to determine other aspects of myself—good or bad—that only I can see. To have that knowledge leads me closer to the quest of exploring the man I have become. This exploration, as far as I can tell, will be a more meaningful adventure if it also includes sorting through the complex twists and turns of my life to identify the whys and the hows of becoming the man I am.

The first time, as a young man, I knew I was quick-tempered—and that it caused ugly pain to those I love and, by extension, restlessness to myself—was during an incident between my sister Helena and me. I was in high school and a big boy. My mom had let me have the luxury of inheriting one extra room in the family house that I could use as my study or living room. I quickly bought pieces of furniture to get my new empty room to look handsome. For the sake of details that may not matter so much here, I painted my rooms pink just because I liked the color, and it reminded me of being an Umuahian. That was the color of the school uniform we wore at Government College, Umuahia. It was actually when I came to the United States that I found out that pink is a color for girls and blue for guys. However, I once wore a light-pink shirt, and one of the nuns complimented me, saying, "Father Udo, you know what they say: 'Real men wear pink!'" I accepted her compliment without pressing her to explain more what she meant. My understanding was that by "real men," she meant gentlemen. Wearing a pink shirt to school and painting my rooms pink may have launched me into the ranks of real men like my dad. But my ugly behavior to my sister, who was helping me haul in my new pieces of furniture, was far from what real gentlemen do. As my sister dragged in one of the long wooden attachments to my bookshelf—which was evidently too heavy for her frail frame and small size—and raised it a little higher, she knocked off the electric bulb hanging low from the ceiling. I jumped on her and scolded her. "Have you no brains as to know to keep that away from the electric bulb?" She recoiled; her enthusiasm, excitement, and joy were gone! You could tell before then how happy she was for me, but all that evaporated, and the only thing left was sadness. I may have said this before—if I have, please excuse my repetition, but it is a truth worth emphasizing: that Helena, my sister, cares for everyone, tries to do everything right, and unlike me, avoids getting into trouble. As proof of that fact, as soon as she could let go of the part of furniture that caused her to be beaten up unfairly, she went to the store and bought an electric bulb to replace the one she accidently broke with part of her allowance money, which she had been saving for several months. I deserved to be kicked in the gut for my anger and outburst. After the initial embarrassment and disgust at my behavior gave way to reason, I resolved that I would turn that quick-tempered, sharp-tongued young man to one that is gentle and kindhearted.

As I made a paradigm shift from soul-lashing to rational soul-searching, the mission of reinventing myself was launched. I have to note at this point that it is not helpful to replace something bad with nothing. That is because a vacuum in life leaves an emptiness that begs to be filled—and when that emptiness remains without being mended with something good, it is a matter of time and opportunity before it gets occupied with something less desirable. That may have been what Jesus was talking about when he warned that when an unclean spirit goes out of a man, it wanders, and not finding a place of rest, it comes back. If it finds the place empty, swept and ready, it goes off and brings seven other spirits more wicked than itself to live in him; and the man becomes worse (Luke 11:24-26). So, the elimination of the part of me that was not useful, left a space that not only required to be filled up, but needed to be revamped with a portrait that is good, existentially real, and alive—a remedy that would enhance my life and growth. The story of Jesus is one of great faith which offers hope that does not disappoint. However, when it moves from a narrative to a personal and practical experience of his love and goodness in our day-to-day life, that experience reinforces our faith, elevates all the more what we can accomplish, and increases the possibility of achieving our goal. In other words, the love and grace of God we experience in that process brings life—in its spiritual aspect—out of the realm of hope and dream to a lived reality. In my own case, the concrete real-life experience of love and kindness which I needed in order to patch up the hole in me was supplied by what I knew of my dad and what he taught me.

Even before I thought of the exemplary legacies my dad left behind, I reflected on something closely linked to my identity: my name. My soul-searching led me to appreciate the link between a name and the person who bears it. When a person is identified or called by their name, it invokes a certain sense of self-awareness as a rational, existing entity. Conversely, when someone's name is maligned, it not only appears that he is under attack, but he also experiences the assault in actuality. As I considered that social reality, I convinced myself that one of the best ways to show full appreciation for my name, which is essentially woven with my identity and personality, was to live out its meaning. My first name is Udochukwu, which means "the peace of God." But everyone who knows me calls me Udo, a shortened form of my name, which means "peace." My first name seems to be at odds with my middle name, Vincent, which is Latin for "he/she/it is conquering." Putting the two together, I tried to bridge the tension by rearranging things a little bit: "He is conquering with the peace of God," or better still, "I will be conquering with the peace of God." If I should live by my name, then my victory should only be defined or assessed by my being able to work for the peace of God wherever I am and in whatever I am doing.

Let us, for the moment, leave my name out of the discussion and talk about the universal belief of Christians that the peace we have and share as individuals and in the society comes from God. Our peace, being derived from God, means that his peace has to be present in order for us to know a life of peace that endures as we struggle through life's journey. Without God's peace, there is no life for us, no existence, and we cease to be. So, if the song "Let there be peace and let it begin with me" is a dream worth realizing, because of my name, I should have it written all over my body like a billboard, and I should spend my whole life working toward it.

My dad was the meekest, gentlest, and kindest man I knew. When I reflected on how much peace he appeared to feel and know, which was in total contrast to my outburst toward my sister and the turmoil I felt afterward, I resolved to emulate my dad. I failed many times at first to be a man who feels that abiding peace and gives it. However, after many years of practice, I can say that, although I am far from perfectly knowing peace all the time, I know that by seeking it through kindness of heart, in word and deed, I feel it much more. One of the things I had to learn was to keep quiet and not say a word when I am upset or cannot find something nice to say, and to defer my comment until I have had some time to think before speaking on the issue. I try to anticipate the needs of others and to care as best as I can; those things bring me contentment, and contentment predisposes me to receive the peace of God and facilitates my sharing of it.

Since my accident, aches and pain of twisted muscles eaten up by atrophy have become the norm. From questions people ask me, I know they have an idea that I am in pain. Sometimes, I candidly admitted that I was when asked, and at other times, I simply laughed without answering the question. But since I appear to be in a good mood most of the time, even though physically hurting, those aware of my situation are baffled and often wonder why and how I am able to hold up such a genuine joy in spite of my plight. I remembered very well the first day my sufferable pain was very obvious.

It was on a particular Saturday, when the pain I felt increased to a nagging degree after my breakfast, and I was unaware of what caused the heightening of the severity. Since I had Mass that evening, and the pain would not give me any relief, I took some over-the-counter pain medicine. I hardly take those, and I would have gladly taken prescription medicine, which I disliked, but only if I could get a desired break. The only reason I stayed away from stronger medicine was because it would make me sleepy or disoriented during Mass. The over-the-counter medicine seemed to have actually made matters worse. Forty-five minutes before the Mass, I was dressed up ready to go, but my physical self was fighting me. I thought about how disappointing the Mass was going to be. I knew it was not a good day to hold up a genuine smile long enough, even though I wanted to, as I always did. I contemplated faking my smiles, but I had never done so before and doubted it would work. I had tried smiling at my aide a few times to keep her from noticing how much pain I was feeling, but my smiles fell flat; she would never smile back. Somehow, she knew I was hurting. When she could not bear my weak camouflaging smile any more, she nicely accosted me, "Father Udo, you don't seem to be doing well today."

"Do I look like I am not?" I asked her, hoping she would not probe further.

She knew me better than I realized. "Yes, you do!" she said. "I know I might not be able to help you with whatever it is, but maybe by telling me, instead of bearing it alone, you will feel better! You don't have to tell me if you think otherwise."

My aide was genuinely concerned, being the wise and good person she was. She had observed me all day and knew something was wrong but exercised restraint in not asking. But at the moment, when she asked, she knew I was getting ready for Mass and wanted to help if she could to avert a possible imminent disaster. In delaying her wish to know what was wrong, she practiced an age-old wisdom I learned from my older friend, Brother Nwali, whom I talked about in Chapter Five. When I was about sixteen years old, I asked Brother Nwali for certain information, and he declined to give it. When I inquired why, he used that as an opportunity to teach me a life lesson. The lesson was that I was not old enough to have such information. He taught me that whenever someone possesses information, he or she becomes responsible for it. That, he explained, was true not only for the recipient but also for the person disseminating the message. He was of the opinion that sometimes it was better not to possess knowledge of something or volunteer to be made aware of it, especially when it is odious. That is because when you are not privy to the information about something, then you would not have to either manage it or be protected from the shock, shame, fear, or scandalizing effect it could unleash. He also opined that some kind of information should be given only to those who have a right to them and only when it would not cause grave harm.

In the light of that knowledge, I proceeded to tell my aide the torture I had been through all day; she was, after all, my caregiver and may, in some way, be helpful. She did more than I expected; she was of great assistance. Among other things, I told her that "this would be the very first day I celebrated the Mass without a smile on my face because I don't think I am able to smile, even if I tried. If I attempt to smile in the condition I am, I will be like an actor on a stage. If you were able to know that I am in pain, then I have reason to believe everyone in the church will notice. In that case, I will either receive an overwhelming condolence or disappoint a few who may think the priest is not human but a deity and, therefore, is not capable of showing physical weakness."

What my aide did next was unexpected, and it surprisingly cured the pain. Even though the pain was present the overpowering gesture of love she showed magically eased it to a bearable level. I was looking down when I talked to her because it was a painful admission and a tough act to make that revelation. When I raised my eyes to see her face to know what she thought about my confession, she was right there in front of me. Before I could say another word, she leaned over and hugged me, and as she stood upright, she kissed my cheek and said, "I am sorry about what you have been going through all day. Evidently, I can't help you, but I will pray for you, Father Udo!"

"Thank you, you just helped!" I replied with heartfelt laughter, and she started laughing, too. "Seriously," I continued, "I can't feel that much pain anymore!" I then told her that there was no better place and time to pray for me than during Mass. I invited her to go to Mass with me, and she did, and that Mass turned out to be one of the unforgettable ones. I was glad I did not have to fake a smile because it flowed naturally and plentifully, thanks to my aide.

That night, I reflected on the incident that took place earlier; how God used my aide to bring about a miracle. Before then, I had tried different things that did not work. I even tried the technique I used when I was an adolescent to block my physical pain. It worked when my uncle undeservedly spanked me, and I did not feel a thing. It was like a mind game that focused intensely on other parts of the body, and I would imagine the area that received the spanking did not belong to me. That pain was at a certain part of the body, but this one was all over the body and could not be targeted. Again, the other pain was inflicted by someone I could walk away from. The pain from the accident comes from within me, like my body was attacking me, and trying to block the pain through that method on that day was not successful. That night, I thought of how noble and gracious my fine aide was and how priceless the healing that followed was. Nevertheless, I knew that since I am celibate and living alone, such hugs and kisses are scarce especially when you need them most, and for me to depend on them would be unrealistic. I also was aware that even if I were not a priest and was married, that would not guarantee having hugs and kisses when needed. Assuming I was married, my wife could be sick, at work, dead, on tour, in the nursing home, et cetera; there can be a whole set of scenarios that could prohibit the provision of that soothing remedy. What then was the profound lesson of love and healing that God intended to teach me through my aide? Digging deeper led me to this helpful insight: the hug and kiss I received from my aide are the accidentals, not the essence of love. They were only the remote cause of the relief from pain. The direct cause of the healing was the love she showed through those gestures, which I also felt. The fruits of that love were the genuine laughter, the sustained smiles, the calming effect it had, and the joy of all who benefited from my recovery.

Having enjoyed that privilege, I wondered how I could possibly experience love in my circumstance so that my smile, strength, and serenity would endure especially during a traumatic time. To live out that unique aspect of life and love, there is need for me to have a better understanding of them. I will attempt a description of love that reflects my personal conception of it mainly in that context. I would simply say that a definition of love must have the important element of *giving*. Those who wait to receive love instead of giving it are often frustrated because it is in the giving of it that we receive it. On the day of my great pain, there was a hesitation on my part to give love because of a sense of inadequacy I entertained or my attempt to spare others of the grief they might feel because of my ordeal. Since then, I have learned through experience that in giving even the least my condition allowed, my sacrifices are multiplied, and the love I received in return remained abounding. There were many other times I had excruciating pain, which I accepted, and gave the gift of me just as I was, and the reward was such overwhelming joy, more complete than any I had known at other times. At those periods, the faithful did not have to feel sad for my pain because there was none; the joy and love that filled the air helped me smile more, and smiles helped my hurt to disappear. Even when they shared in my pain or felt sad for my cross, it was still helpful and enlightening because it was within the context of Christian love and care.

At this point, I will write about the other reason I smiled while I was falling out of my van, which Jim, my friend, witnessed as I narrated in the previous chapter. Apart from smiling to calm the fears of those who came to help me, which was an act of love, the second reason, which is the reward of the first, was to find relief from the pain I felt as I was hanging precariously on the wheelchair safety belt. Furthermore, if I were to die in that horrific incident, I would rather be smiling as I journey to heaven than to do so crying. My concluding opinion on this subject is that loving and feeling loved brings about healing, and the genuine smile that may result from it soothes the soul and pain. Discovering this love leads me to adopt another aspect of giving, that may be material in nature but bears some spiritual significance. I try to express that love when I have the opportunity and means by giving gifts and nice surprises to friends or giving alms and showing kindness to strangers. These gestures bring me joy as I see a reflection of love in the eyes of the recipients. But even as wonderful as doing those things feels, the giving that completely fulfils me and perfects the love inside of me is the one that is totally rid of self.

The most fulfilling experience of love that I will ever remember and cherish, occurred on Good Friday of 2008. On that day, there was confession before the Stations of the Cross, which started at 11:00 AM. It had been barely a year since I was discharged from the hospital. I was weak, could hardly stop anything flowing from me, and had to wear a diaper. The confession lasted for almost two and a half hours, and diarrhea chose the worst moment to pay me a visit. I had many accidents that caused a stench and I believe peeing twice did not help matters, so, I refused to imagine the extent of the mess. But since the penitents kept coming and did not mind, I did not either. Monsignor came after he was done with the Stations of the Cross and pleaded with me to discontinue with the confession because I had been there for almost two hours and he did not want me to be in any danger. "Monsignor, are there still people lined up for confession?" I asked.

"Yes!" he answered. "And it is a long line!"

"Well, then, Monsignor, I won't stop until the last person who wants to go to confession does so," I replied. Unlike me—as I am very particular about my hygiene—on that day, I did not mind smelling like an unclean overflowing toilet. Rather than feeling embarrassed or pity for myself, I felt at peace. I felt joyful and fulfilled; I felt the LOVE! As I looked at the crucifix hanging on the wall in front of me, I thought to myself, *How fortunate I am to share in the cross of Christ whose love and sacrifice is beyond human imagination!*

The picture of the man I have become will be incomplete without a reference to my car accident and how it has helped to shape me. It is inadequate and unhelpful to approach my mishap only from the perspective of what I seemed to have lost. That is because what appeared to be a loss may be a precursory event, a preceding sign that divine bliss is about to rain down, perhaps in an unidentifiable capacity. Our physical self is our visible part, and we use it to perform most functions in this life, and since it tends to get most of our attention, it is not difficult to see how we may sometimes want to define ourselves by it or let it define who we are. When we do, any ailment or disfigurement of our physical body would mean losing our identity, or parts of it, because that by which we defined who we are no longer held together. There is no doubt that to live in this world, we need the physical part of us; however, our spiritual self is far superior because it does not die; it is the image of God in us. It gives meaning, purpose, life, strength, as well as sustains the physical. When the spiritual part of us is well and sound, any attack—aging or defaming of the physical body—does not make us cease to live or be, feel fulfilled, peaceful, or happy. I have always been aware of the above fact, that is, the importance of our spiritual self, since my philosophy study days. That knowledge before my motor accident more or less existed in theory or as an article of faith. My being paralyzed after my accident moved that knowledge further to the level of a life lived. I was, therefore, able to tap in, to some degree, to the life and strength of the Spirit in order to have sustained peace that satisfies and even helps me in coping with any physical trial or loss.

When mishaps happen in life and shake things out of shape, we may wish it did not happen. We also tend to bemoan the fact that our lives appeared normal or even perfect, and now it is a mess. Was it really normal and perfect, or did our imagination tell us it was? Since our knowledge is limited, how can we ever know with certainty that it was? Some strong approach or mind-set I adopted made my accident seem far less a tragedy and more like a challenge that leads to blessings. The human story is one that is punctuated with events I would characterize as trying and fun at the same time. It is part of human experience to try, at times, to avoid the challenging events. Unnecessary and avoidable suffering does not deserve our attention or time. However, if we have to live with it or deal with it because we do not have any recourse, then we should do it with joy since challenges make us tougher and wiser and teach us patience and humility. Just like our Lord Jesus, in undergoing our suffering with grace, we become a source of inspiration, strength, and salvation to all we meet (Hebrews 5:8). It was so gratifying and enlightening for me to not only wish that my spiritual strength and smile inspired someone but also to actually have a testimony that it did. Here is a beautiful letter from Joshua, one of my little friends, who wrote me after I left Christ the King Parish to become a chaplain for the nuns:

Dear Father Udo,

You are the best priest ever. You are amazing and funny. I wish I were as talented as you and as ansome as you. I wish I were you. How are you? Why did you have to leave? I birst in to tears when you left.

Love,
Joshua Hester, 3A

This letter will live forever in my mind. I will remember to consult it if I ever entertain the thought of giving up facing my challenges with grace and loving with a glowing smile.

The knowledge that being human and Christian has an attached expectation of undergoing some form of trial at different points in our lives leads me to kneel in prayer. I not only pray that God prevents the pending ordeal if he may, but also, in the event he wants me to go through it, that he will give me the understanding and strength to persevere. I furthermore pray that if there is any blessing from carrying my cross with fortitude, grace, and loveliness, that I may be made aware of it. The acceptance of that human and Christian condition keeps me from wishing things were different or wishing to be the person I am not. Such wishes amount to a waste of time and resources. The result of wishing my life away in that context is not difficult to predict; it likely could lead to lack of focus or even failure. On the contrast, accepting my challenges and trials as a Christian affords me contentment and happiness.

When I say I have contentment and happiness even in my seemingly tragic condition, it may be difficult for many who have not felt peace in the midst of adversity to comprehend. As I accept my trial, I try to search for and embrace the good embedded therein—a blessing, a silver lining, which makes the concurrent excruciating experience I might face more tolerable. That process also helps me to stay positive and remain optimistic, even as it accords me a profound understanding of life. When it appears there is no notable blessing, I still presume there is one, and that it is spiritual and therefore invisible. After having baked that concept into my consciousness through repeated reminders, that mind-set has become a way of life for me. It feeds my thinking, decisions, and actions in almost everything. For instance, when my new assignment to become the chaplain for the nuns was made public, some of my friends and parishioners knew exactly where they believed my ministry would be more beneficial; the convent was the last place on their minds. A few months after I started my new assignment, one of the nuns thanked me for accepting to be their chaplain, but added, "It was nice of you to accept to be our chaplain. I believe that Bishop Taylor will probably take you from us as soon as you get well!"

"Why do you think he will?" I asked.

To which she replied, "I happen to believe your being sent to us is a waste of resources."

I have to be honest or perhaps modest to say that my friends, parishioners, and that graceful nun gave me more credit than I deserved. Assuming that I possessed a special talent as they claimed, I would agree to the truth and benefits of reaching out to many in my ministry. However, I disagree with the conclusion that ministering to the nuns circumvents my ministry and does not achieve the same result as ministering to many souls like in the parish where many attend Mass. Serving the nuns as a priest amounts to serving numerous faithful by extension. My summation, which I made known to my friends, parishioners, and the nun, is that ministering to one nun is, in some way, like ministering to a priest. When you minister to one nun, you are, by extension, ministering to hundreds, if not thousands, of people the nun will have the opportunity to touch. When a priest provides the spiritual needs of the nuns, he contributes in some way to the dream of keeping in existence the ministries the nuns have managed to keep alive in the church. One such ministry is managing Catholic schools and hospitals. When the nuns are ministered to and they are happy, there are more prospects of young women being drawn to the religious life. When they are unhappy, vocations are likely to dry up. I do not believe a young woman wants to come into a religious community where members are in perpetual mourning. In the light of the above assessment, I can rightly argue that if I minister to a small community of nuns, I am indirectly ministering to all the people the nuns will inspire.

I have come to know that if it were not for challenges, I would not only be bored out of my mind, I would also get into trouble more frequently or just simply exist or perhaps go through life without living it. Some of my challenges were self-made, some were dealt to me by life, and some by others or priestly duties. The way I approached the challenges vary. When I created the challenges myself, I did so with the hope that they would help me become a better person or produce finer results. During the period we were considering building a new church in Saint Albert Church, Heber Springs, I made the choice of those who would make up the Development Committee. Among the five members, I purposely chose two whom I knew did not agree with the project.

The very first meeting almost became the only one. Thomas, whom I knew did not agree with the reason we gathered in the first place, did something no one, not even me, anticipated. He went to the blackboard, wrote down some numbers, and began lecturing everyone on how impossible it was for the parish to undertake the project of building a new church. That happened before I even said the opening prayer for the meeting. I would admit he knew his math, had all the figures right, and sounded very convincing. Thomas first assumed a realistic cost for the new church, which he wrote on the blackboard. He also had an accurate figure of the number of parishioners who were financially active. Next, he wrote down the average amount of our monthly collections. He then divided the cost of the new church project among the financially active members. Each portion was frightening! Even when he divided it to be paid weekly, what each would have to give for that project paled in comparison to their contributions to the Sunday collection. The financially active members would donate about five times the amount they gave each week for offertory. That revelation was saddening. The room was so quiet; everyone looked depressed and felt defeated. If there was any one who felt vindicated or relieved, it was Thomas. All looked at me for a response. His argument was so sound and logical that I almost said the first and final prayer for the committee and let everyone go. I believed in the people and had faith in God; however, faith is a spiritual phenomenon you cannot mathematically demonstrate. There are always many unknowns when relying on the providence of God, and I did the best I could to explain my position. After all, that challenge was part of the reason I picked Thomas and his friend, who disagreed with the need and feasibility of the project, to be on the committee. The only unexpected thing was that I did not anticipate the tension that soon began and not in the form it came. Thomas' presentation appeared to have the fingerprints of a plot all over it. Moments like that, I admitted, could make or mar my leadership, depending on how I rose to the occasion.

My response was, "Thomas, I have to thank you for opening our eyes to the enormous task before us. I agree with part of the conclusion you reached, namely, that undertaking this project will not be easy and will require a lot of sacrifice. If it were easy, it would have been done a long time ago. That it will be difficult is the reason we are meeting to deliberate and examine all options and possibilities. Your math and logic may be accurate in the sense you applied them, but I wish you took some other important variables into consideration. The variables you excluded should not be overlooked if our reason for meeting is to build a new church where God will be worshipped. One of such variables is that the parish is made up of many members who have vacation homes here in town, and they contribute financially to the parish but are not officially registered. The other variable is one I will refer to as the faith factor. Faith, unfortunately, does not follow the rules of math and logic but is important and makes an enormous difference. If we have the blessing of God to build, he will provide us with the means. Do not ask me how because I do not know—that is where faith comes in. If we all throw in the towel because the task appears impossible, then we would accept to have been defeated even before we tried. We would also indirectly have given up believing and hoping in God's providence in this matter."

As I spoke, the room was dead silent, and I could tell the members of the Development Committee were reassured. I did not know what Thomas's intentions were. However, if he meant to put a damper on the fire, he brought some dry wood and fed the fire himself. With him feeding the fire, we had enough heat needed to launch our rocket of deliberation and possible accomplishment.

There were many times when the challenges dealt to me, by life or circumstances of life, were awkward. Being a Catholic priest and unmarried, there are some shelves or aisles at the stores that I did not have to visit. After my accident, I used certain products in those aisles. When in Little Rock, a big city, all my supplies were mailed, and I did not have to buy them myself. In Jonesboro, I had to go to the store to purchase some of those products. On one occasion, I went to the store to buy groceries and other supplies. One of the things on the list to buy was K-Y Jelly, which helps me lubricate the catheter. To save time, my aide went to buy a few other things while I went to the personal convenience area. I knew exactly where to get what I wanted, but it seemed things were rearranged. I needed help to locate the product, and I was fortunate to find someone to help. At one of the aisles, a worker was restocking empty shelves. I asked her, "Please, I need help, where can I find the K-Y Jelly?"

The look on her face told me she did not understand the product I was trying to locate. Maybe my deep accent threw her off a little bit. Then she asked, "What is it used for?"

Well, there is only one popular use for it that I would not say, and telling her it is for the catheter would probably throw her off the course some more. Besides, it would have been too much private information. I replied, "You don't really want to know!" I said that while smiling and that clarified what the mystery product was.

Then, she smiled back and said, "Go the opposite direction and turn right, it will be on the right."

At that instant my aide arrived and asked, "Have you found it?"

I would have to admit that my aide was really cute and would pass for my girlfriend or wife. The look on the face of the girl who helped me revealed that her imagination was running wild. So, I told my aide, "Take a few more steps, it will be on your right!"

As I drove in my wheelchair toward her direction, my aide said, "Found it, how many should I bring?" She said it loud enough that the restocking girl heard it, and I could only imagine what she was thinking and what she would think of my response or lack of response. For me, it was already too awkward and embarrassing, so I had to resort to one of my best weapons—humor. "Bring four. You know we need a lot of it!"

As we left the store, my aide could not contain her laughter anymore. In the midst of her laughter, she asked, "Father Udo, did you see the face of that girl? I don't think she was happy I showed up."

I could tell my aide was milking the situation a little too much, rubbing it in a lot stronger and having fun, making up a few more facts to get the story juicier. I answered, "I don't think she paid any attention to us, and even if she did, she deserved a little break from the burden of the day's toil." I smiled at the whole comedy but did not tell my aide how awkward the whole situation was to me, but my throwing in some colorful humor helped very much.

So far, I have addressed some of my approaches to challenges I gave myself or life made possible for me; the next would be how I tried to perform the tasks I was given. But, before I do so, let me note that I have always respected and valued every individual person in their uniqueness—my parents taught me well. I am also grateful for the contributions each person brings to the table of humanity and the sacrifice and struggle it takes to do so. The reality of being human, demands that we work together in order to succeed and survive. In being a priest, I am faced each day with how important each person is, the role and vitality of the Christian community and the vast potential embedded in the human community. However, just as priestly duties can heighten our knowledge and importance of the individual person and community, being a priest can somehow, if one is not careful, diminish the awareness of the daily difficulties of others. The spiritual bubble we live in can give us an edge in surviving with ease and may make us oblivious or unsympathetic to the struggles of the rest of humanity. I was used to demanding nothing but excellence or even perfection from myself and tried to bring it out of everyone around me or that worked with me. In some instances, I not only tried to fit myself and others into that perfect mold and standard I created in my mind, I also wanted the result to come fast. I remember one of the meetings we had in Heber Springs as we prepared to celebrate as a family and mark the end of the Year of the Eucharist in October 2005. We were hoping to have a one-week retreat in addition to a seminar on the Eucharist and conclude with a grand outdoor Mass. When everyone at the meeting had included what was on their wish-list and the cost was added up, it was more than we could afford. There was an outcry about the financial burden by some who even blamed me for planning a big celebration. The grumbling and despair that filled the room got under my skin, and I told the Parish Life Committee that the extensive plan for the Year of the Eucharist was no longer under consideration—we would have a simple ceremony instead. Deacon Bob, in his usual graceful way, asked me to forgive some members for their harsh complaints. He thought they were unwarranted, since all that we were doing were deliberations. Deacon Bob, pleaded with me to continue with the planning, which I did. I scrapped all the unnecessary things some members on the committee piled up as items they wanted during the festivities, like a canopy with an air conditioner, catered meal, and more. We were able to have a spiritually enriching ceremony I wanted for the people without breaking the bank.

After that heated meeting, Deacon Bob came to me and apologized on behalf of the small group who caused the trouble. He also used that opportunity to open me up to myself. He began with a story of when he was in the air force and there was one of the radical aeronautic engineers who came up with an idea of building a cargo aircraft. The aircraft would be so massive, which made other engineers think there was no way it could fly and that he was nuts. It took several years for everyone to realize that that novelty plane could fly—that the engineer was right and far ahead his time. "Father," Deacon Bob said, "You're kind of like that engineer in some way. Your ideas are sometimes out of the ordinary, and it takes us time to catch on. Please, Father, don't give up on us. If you're patient with us, I promise you, that we will catch on."

I listened to Deacon Bob's words of wisdom and thanked him for helping me learn something about myself that I needed to work on. The attitude of wanting it perfect and fast had led me to indirectly define those who work with me by what they do or accomplish. And I say *indirectly* because it was not intended and should be understood in the sense that I am trying to describe. No one should be defined or identified by what they do, except the priest, to an extent (I hope to elaborate on this if I write another book someday). It is unfair to define or identify people by what they do or the result they produce because everyone is not gifted in the same way or with the same things. Also, on another level, it chips something away from their humanity. When people get old or impaired and cannot do things, do they cease to be? No, they do not! The indirect way I fell victim to that aberration was when I insisted on a very high standard in such a way that may have pressured some people, maybe against their will, to fit into my straightjacket of perfection. Stretching it further, I will argue that I may have been thinking for them, which may constitute my temporally rendering their intellect inactive. I, at the same time, may have bent their will to accept my proposition, which also momentarily may have taken away their will. If the intellect and will are stripped from a person, even in that sense, it amounts to treating them as subhuman. The victims somewhat ceased at those moments, in that perfect world I tried to create to be human. In my passion, therefore, to help create a perfect world, I overlooked what makes a person an existential being: the image of God, the intellect to help a person know, and the will to enable an individual to choose.

Deacon Bob pointed that out before my accident, and I was aware of it and worked on it. Since my accident, my awareness of it has been more acute and my approach to address it has been more effective. The man I have become still believes in the importance of excellence and perfection. However, I have tried not to make perfection the enemy of kindness, patience, humility, and gentleness. Especially since I know that I have failed miserably in attaining that perfection in many ways and instances myself. I am now more aware of the burden people carry every day and how hard they work to keep humanity and each individual that makes up the human family in one piece and at peace. The lesson I have learned is that punishing people, in whatever form, for their failure or falling short of a perfect standard is less effective if you intend to improve output. On the contrast, encouraging them by appreciating the good in them and the good they have done increases and perfects the fruits of their labor. It is the best to let individual persons think for themselves and to do things because they have understanding of the importance. Their involvement in that instance would be very fulfilling.

It is fascinating to experience the unfading kindness of God to me since my automobile accident; God continues to heal me. I do believe Dr. Kiser when he said that I am a miracle patient because I have recovered and improved beyond what anyone would have expected. Whenever it seemed my recovery was coming to a standstill and that there was no need for me to keep exercising more, I would see or feel something new that motivated me and helped me to find new energy and encouragement. My situation has really left me more in awe of the complexity of the human body and necessity of divine assistance when all human skill and technology have reached their limits. Sometimes, I felt or believed my nerves were growing back, and at other times, I thought they hit dead ends. They do not give up; they try to rewire through other channels. Sometimes, too, I believed they had rewired but were weak and waiting to be used, and whenever I worked the muscle around them, they seemed to tell me, "Boy, where have you been? You kept us waiting!" This is only my unconventional summation, but it has helped me learn in my physical exercise not to give up just like my "Nerves" which persevered and invented different ways of continuing on the path of recovery. I would say that listening to my body, heart, and soul has been a major source of help on my path to recovery.

The credit for my miraculous recovery I give to God, and any leftover credit, I give to my families, relatives, friends, parishioners, and medical team, whose lovely, gentle, and reassuring care and words reinforced my resolve to not give up. All these wonderful people and some divinely granted circumstances have helped in shaping the man I have become. However, the crystallization of the man that I have become came from my intellectual assessment, personal discernment, and my strong will to not quit until I have molded myself into the person God wants me to be. I believe that the person God wants me to be must see and accept my seemingly tragic situation as transformational and rewarding—a way to triumph in him and live in his peace.

CHAPTER 15

Finding Peace That Endures

It is only when we quit believing in self, others or God, it is only at the point when we stop embracing our blessings—even the ones disguised as pain—that our quest for peace becomes a chase after a mirage.

—Father Udo Ogbuji

We all desire peace that remains even in the midst of tragedy; therefore, a great and true triumph in life should include finding peace of mind in spite of the everyday storm that we face. As I journey through life and grapple with challenges as everyone else, my experiences have led me to regard tragic incidents as facts of life that have the potential to perfect me. I have gleaned from my reflection that those challenges, and the trials that come with them, linger through life in different shapes and forms. Since trials will always be part of the human condition, the best we can do is to exercise hope in dealing with them and learning through the experience. Hope comes from the knowledge that there is always a message, a lesson, or a blessing in our challenges. Trusting in God while having the right approach and attitude opens up the fountain of bliss embedded in trials. Although every challenge has its own reward, such blessings may not be revealed until much later. For the many years I have reflected on my life's ordeals, it has been fascinating to note that they are not pleasant experiences, but nonetheless satisfying when I connect the dots leading to the reasons for which God allowed them to happen. After a thorough contemplation, I see how my whole person has been shaped, among other things, by catastrophes and how my triumph in life is partly defined by blessings from those tribulations.

My parents were married in the midst of a civil war in my country, which was a sign that they were hopeful and lived their lives to the fullest, not letting anything, not even war, get in the way. The fact that my parents brought me into the world at a time of great hardship and uncertainty is remarkable. The name they chose for me—Udochukwu Vincent, which means "You will be conquering with the peace of God"—is a sign, that in spite of calamities and ruin, they joyfully planted the seed of hope in me. They did not spare anything when they taught me that I could overcome all things, just as they had done, if I plant the seed of love and peace on my journey through life. My parents did the best they could to prepare me on what to expect out of life, even in the things that appeared inconsequential or skills that other people would rather avoid. For instance, I have often wondered what I would have done if I came to the United States unprepared with regard to cooking and had no one to help me. If my mom had not defiled my native culture that barred men from the kitchen and dragged me there against my will, I would have died from hunger or from eating unhealthy food long before now. I thought she was so cruel when she insisted I wash dishes or made me observe her while she cooked and forced me to cook sometimes. At the time, I believed it was a meaningless and unusual punishment as I seemed to have been denied my freedom while my friends played and did what they pleased. However, those cooking skills came in handy when I arrived in the United States and had to cook for myself and for my friends. I have my mom to thank whenever I enjoy a delicious meal I have prepared and when my friends compliment me on my culinary skills. Someday, I hope to buy my mom flowers for her "meanness," stubbornness, and ability to think into the future and beyond the culture. She prepared me to adapt to life in all circumstances, in different things, and in every place. The cooking skills my mom taught me were only a rudimentary foundation; there were other challenges that led to my learning more about cooking and caring for my guests. Those later challenging moments had to do with the intricate balance of knowing what to cook and being a fine host. It also involved learning that the compliments I may receive should not lead to pride or be the only reason to cook. I learned to always cook and entertain my guests with love, remembering that such moments with friends should be a thanksgiving to God for putting fine people on my path and an opportunity to improve on my relationships.

The gulf created by differences in culture, food, and personal taste made cooking more complicated and taught me humility and other subtle facts about life. I got it right sometimes and wrong at other times. The lessons I learned were good ones although there were times when the outcome of the occasion made me disappointed in myself because I only found out after the fact that my guest may not have enjoyed my cooking but was gracious through it all. Personal preferences differed—some liked it spicy and many did not, few liked strong-smelling fish and some preferred very mild ones while some were completely opposed to any type of seafood. I remember a day I was cooking a native soup and rice in the rectory, and Father Mike had just moved in to live with me in the second rectory at Christ the King Church. I knew my dry codfish and ground dry shrimp, which were part of the recipe for that delicacy, had a strong smell to it, but I did not know it would be beyond what Father Mike could endure. As he approached the kitchen and put his head through the door, the expression on his face changed. He twitched his nose as if he had inhaled something unbearably pungent, which, of course, he did!

"Udo, what are you cooking?" he asked, almost alarmed. "Some dry codfish, ground shrimp, and more. You want some when I am done? Come and see."

I observed his reaction when I asked "You want some?" His face looked like he was in pain, like I was already stuffing it down his throat. However, he was willing at my invitation to make a second attempt to come into the kitchen, but was overcome by the smell. "No, Udo, I can't!" he cried out and hurried outside to get some fresh air.

As he tried to escape, I laughed and shouted, "If you can get pass the smell, it's very delicious!"

I did not give up on him, and on another day, I set out to prove that Father Mike would enjoy my native recipes and perhaps thank me for not letting him miss out. I believed that if he did not know what went into the cooking of the rice, he might like it. I put some of the ground dry shrimp in one of the rice dishes and skipped the other. When it was time for us to eat, I brought out the two different dishes of rice and asked him to taste and tell me which one he liked, hoping to prove him wrong.

"Udo, I like this one!" he said, pointing to the rice with no ground shrimp, "The other rice would have been more delicious, but you ruined it with your smelly ground shrimp!"

Needless to say, I learned a lot from that experience and have come out a better cook and host. But none of those experiences would have happened without my mom's effort—although unappreciated at the time—and my learning more and perfecting the art of cooking and hosting. Even though I am a better cook and host for those efforts, there is still room for more improvement.

Challenges in life can be likened to a cook's training. All good training brings a cook closer to being efficient and able to pleasantly feed the hungry in a satisfactory manner. Good training for a cook may involve many things, but I wish to highlight a few basic experiences that make the best cook. For a cook to be trained well enough to become excellent, that cook should experience the good, the bad, the unexpected and what constitutes failure and success. To be the finest, a cook must also learn and grasp the fundamental reason why he/she wants to cook or become a cook. Each experience or hurdle a cook faces in the kitchen, while being a host and in everyday life, better prepares him or her to lift up those being fed and deal well with the next unforeseen problem. Just like the cook in training, our experiences and challenges prepare us for fullness of life. Each ordeal in life, in some way, lays a foundation for strength, courage, and wisdom, thereby facilitating the efficiency we exercise in dealing with the next trial while preserving peace. It is important to mention that learning and recalling why we have life and the reason we seek peace help to keep the search for peace and the discovery of peace in perspective.

The trying moments in my life helped me develop a tough mental attitude, thick skin, broadened knowledge, and a positive way of interpreting and dealing with things before I had my car accident. If not, it would have been much more difficult to accept the pain of the accident and happily deal with it. To attain inner peace that endures, we have to embrace our tribulations, or crosses, in life. You may think I am out of my mind to link abiding peace of mind with things in life that get under our skin. Jesus, the Prince of Peace—one who could teach us everything we need to know about peace—may have hinted that having and preserving the perfect peace he gives requires accepting the crosses that come our way in life. When Jesus resurrected from the dead, he came into the room where the disciples were for the fear of the Jews, stood in their midst, and said "Peace be with you." After he said that, he showed them his hands and his side. (John 20:19-20). In reading that passage, the first interpretation that comes to mind is that Jesus was reassuring his disciples that he was indeed the one that appeared to them. A deeper reflection would also lead to the conclusion that he may have been associating his suffering and cross to his eternal peace by pointing to his nail marks and pierced side. It was not uncommon for Jesus to use images or gestures to drive home his message; for instance, when he asked those who accosted him for the money with which they paid tax to Caesar (Matthew 22:15-22). There was also the occasion when Jesus was writing on the ground with his fingers, as the Jewish religious leaders persisted with their questioning and intention to stone a woman caught in adultery (John 8:6-10). During that particular occasion, when Jesus gave the disciples the gift of his abiding peace, his words were immediately followed by his focusing their attention to one of the ways they could sustain that peace. That is, their willingness to accept their crosses just like he did. In the next verse, Jesus reaffirmed his intention to give the gift of eternal bliss and, soon after, instructed the disciples, "As the Father has sent me, so am I sending you" (John 20:21). That summon to his disciples to go and share his peace with the world is the next way of retaining and perfecting his peace in us and the world. Peace, like love and joy, does not grow and is not perfected until it is shared. Before Jesus concluded, he left the disciples with the third and most important means of maintaining peace in our lives and society, namely, accepting forgiveness from God and others for our shortcomings and forgiving those who offended us. If you have ever borne grudges against someone and experienced the restlessness it brings, you will be quick to acknowledge the necessity of forgiveness if peace is to be restored.

When we aspire to find peace through the spiritual act of forgiveness, it helps to keep in mind that the past events or experiences in our lives are only important and useful to the extent that they help us prepare for fullness of life and have a better understanding of it, as to live happily in the present while looking forward to a future that is bright. In this endeavor, we should work toward remembering with gratitude the good things and blessings we have received, including the forgiveness we were shown and the opportunities we had to forgive others. An attitude of gratefulness lays a solid spiritual foundation that enables us to give up past experiences or events that leave a bitter taste in our mouth. Forgiveness is a spiritual process; therefore, to truly forgive those who trespassed against us and even forget the sad events that occurred, we have to pray for the grace of forgetfulness—a prayer that finds favor in God's sight. I should also remark that the litmus test or indicator that forgiveness has taken hold and produced fruit is when our minds are rid of rancor, reprisal, bitterness, betrayal, envy, and sadness. To those, we can add every other similar sentiment that impedes the peace we can know. Harboring any of those ill feelings keeps us imprisoned and living in the past, which undermines our peace of mind. One of the ways living in the past corrodes our peace is that we spend our energy in regrets or wishing for what could have been instead of taking charge and living gladly in the present—living for what is and could be. There is no question that it is better to live in the present, and in true serenity, while keeping a hopeful and peaceful future in view. We can achieve this by praying for and pursuing whatever leads to peace; accepting the gift of peace from Jesus, embracing our crosses, sharing the gift of peace with others, accepting forgiveness, being ever ready to forgive others and every day counting our blessings in thankfulness.

In writing this, I am not by any means conveying that searching for and finding peace is easy, but it can seem easy and actually get easier as we persistently look for it and perfect it. It is not uncommon to find peace elusive at the early stage of the search or later, although we worked hard to do everything right. We should still be comforted when that happens, because, in seeking peace, our success must be measured not only by the attainment of the goal, which is perfect peace, but also the continued sincere effort invested, even when the goal is not completely attained. With this in mind, we should happily claim success and progress and be edified even when the result or outcome appears to be a failure or setback. That is why Saint Paul, although he had a thorn in his flesh that got in the way of his ministry, did not regard that anomaly as a failure even after he wished and prayed to God to help him get rid of it, which he did not. Saint Paul did not count it as failure because he did his best under the circumstances, and he accepted his plight as part of what he had to deal with for the sake of God. The satisfaction, or sense of fulfillment, we feel under such circumstances comes from the fact that God is with us in the process and that his supplied power is sufficient and better than ours alone. It also comes from the belief, just like in the case of Saint Paul, that when we are weak, vulnerable, frail, and face trials that overwhelm us, we can be strong; for even in those dire situations, God's power works in us, through us, and for us (2 Corinthians 12:1-10). With that belief in mind, our prayer should not just be to ask God to remove our pain or the cause of it but also to pray that what we go through may strengthen and inspire us as we aspire for higher goals and ideals. If we can exercise the same humility, wisdom, and patience that Saint Paul showed, we will undergo a personal and spiritual transformation that makes us realize we can accomplish all things though the power of God that strengthens us (Philippians 4:13), but according to God's plan and time. All we can do is to try and give our best in our search for peace, and because this counts as some success, the joy and peace we feel—even though imperfect—can propel us to hold firm and continue to work toward perfecting the peace we can and should know with the help of God.

As complicated as finding peace may sound and as elusive as feeling it may be sometimes, we can know and feel it in such a simple and natural way. After thanking the Christ the King family on my last weekend with the members, I sang the song "Don't Worry, Be Happy" by Bobby McFerrin. I also stood up for the first time in public, to show how their prayers, love, and support had helped me recover. Little did I know that those gestures and the Mass made such a difference in the life of at least one of my little friends. Sam wrote me this letter eight months after the bishop sent me to Jonesboro to serve the nuns:

11-9-10
Dear Father Udo,

Thank you for being at my school. You are a very good priest. You are a very amazing priest. At your last Mass, when you sang the song about being happy, that made me be not afraid. And when you stood, it made me feel like I could do anything I wanted to do. Please write back. I wish you were still at Christ the King. I really miss you.

From Sam Ray, 3B

We all have pleasant and difficult moments in our lives, and all those experiences, even the tragic ones, should lead us to find God's peace especially if we heed the advice of Saint Paul:

> Brother and sisters: Have no anxiety at all, but in everything, by prayer and petition, with thanksgiving, make your requests known to God. Then the peace of God that surpasses all understanding will guard your hearts and mind in Christ Jesus. Finally, brothers and sisters, whatever is true, whatever is honorable, whatever is just, whatever is pure, whatever is lovely, whatever is gracious, if there is any excellence and if there is anything worthy of praise, think about these things . . . . Then the God of peace will be with you. (Philippians 4:6-9)

This personal enduring peace, when found, becomes part of a necessary fundamental framework for societal and global peace, which we desperately need in our world today.

EPILOGUE

My rite of passage took place thirty-six years ago, and I still remember all that I witnessed and learned on that very day. I was seven years old at the time, and we lived in Umuahia City. My dad regularly visited the village, mostly alone, but on that day he asked me to accompany him. Though my pants and shirt were wrinkled a little bit and needed ironing, I felt like a king wearing them. Nothing could be more exciting than going on a trip with my dad even if I had to wear rags. I believed my dad felt the same way too, and he may have been too excited to notice my slightly rumpled clothes. It could also be that he had an appointment and did not want to be late, so ironing my clothes was the last thing on his mind. My mom, who could have helped, had gone to run errands. I was somewhat surprised my dad let me wear those wrinkled clothes because it was unlike him since he liked his pants and shirt ironed with military-style precision and always recommended the same for me.

As we walked through the street, he saw a photography shop and said, "Ogbuo"—meaning "buddy," which was what he called me—"let us have your picture taken. We haven't done that since you were born."

"Dad, why didn't we have my picture made?" I asked.

To which he replied with a joke and smile, "You weren't exactly the cutest kid when you were born! Your mom and I almost gave you away. Now I am glad we didn't."

At that point, he was laughing. He was funny, so I laughed with him, but I was still curious to know if there was some truth hidden in his humor. "Dad, was I ugly when I was born?"

Holding my hand, looking into my eyes and smiling, he said, "You were as handsome as Dee Joe!"

Dee Joe means "Big Brother Joe," an endearing name my mom called him. My dad called her Lucy. I heard those names so often that, when I was a little boy, my aunts and uncles asked me my dad's and mom's names, I sang while I jumped up and down, "Papa mu Dee Joe, Mama mu Lucy" (My dad is Big Brother Joe, my mom is Lucy). I am still being made fun of today, and my aunts and uncles make it a point to retell the story and sing me my favorite song.

When we arrived in the village, Dee Joe took me to the house where his father and my grandfather had lived. We went to the home where his mom, my grandma, grew up and also visited some of his close friends among other villagers. We had a midsized packed bag that had gifts in them. Dee Joe gave out those gifts as we visited family and friends. That visit, which I dubbed my rite of passage, paved the way to the birth of my consciousness as a person. As far as I can recall, that was the first time I saw myself as an individual person with roots. I no longer lived in a small world that encapsulated my parents, siblings, and me. I became more aware of my relatives, friends, and other people in the world. I saw how kindness and caring was able to transform lives and lift people up. I witnessed how Dee Joe suffered so much before he died at a very young age but never complained. He was always courageous, complimentary, and peaceful, and he smiled a lot.

Many of my friends, medical care team, and others have always wondered why, after my automobile accident and loss, I smile instead of cry, am consistently optimistic and faithful instead of fearful and doubtful, and thankful instead of complaining. God made it possible in so many ways, and one of them is the people he brought into my life who have never ceased to inspire me. My rite of passage led me to discover that I am human, and knowing that I am human led me to realize my dependency on God and those I am fortunate to have in my life. When I sit back and look at my life's journey, I see how God, family, and friends have played *Fri-fri Nta* (little bee), challenging me and cheering me on to sweat and share love in order to know the peace of God, not just as my name but indeed.

So, for me, the search for peace will continue! That is because seeking peace in spite of it being sometimes illusive and bitter-sweet, can be beautiful and truly rewarding. My prayer and hope for you is that the much fruit you reap in cultivating peace, may be part of the fuel that helps to sustain you in the relentless hunt for peace—until the day peace is perfected!

When little we dream about the moon, when youthful we play under the moonlight and when older we marvel at the one who made the moon.

—Father Udo Ogbuji

Biblical Quotes were taken From:

1. The Jerusalem Bible. Garden City, New York: Doubleday, 1966 by Darton, Longman, and Todd, Ltd., and Doubleday and Company, Inc.
2. The New American Bible, Saint Joseph Edition. New York: Catholic Book Publishing Corp., copyright 1992 by Catholic Book Publishing Corp., New York.

INDEX

Edwards Brothers Malloy
Thorofare, NJ USA
June 28, 2013